SPIES AND LIES

HOW CHINA'S GREATEST COVERT OPERATIONS FOOLED THE WORLD

ALEX JOSKE

Hardie Grant

BOOKS

Published in 2022 by Hardie Grant Books,
an imprint of Hardie Grant Publishing

Hardie Grant Books (Melbourne)
Wurundjeri Country
Building 1, 658 Church Street
Richmond, Victoria 3121

Hardie Grant Books (London)
5th & 6th Floors
52–54 Southwark Street
London SE1 1UN

hardiegrantbooks.com

Hardie Grant acknowledges the Traditional Owners of the country on which
we work, the Wurundjeri people of the Kulin nation and the Gadigal people
of the Eora nation, and recognises their continuing connection to the land,
waters and culture. We pay our respects to their Elders past and present.

 A catalogue record for this
book is available from the
NATIONAL
LIBRARY National Library of Australia
OF AUSTRALIA

Spies and Lies
ISBN 9781 74379 799 0

10 9 8 7 6 5 4 3 2 1

Typeset in Adobe Caslon Pro by Cannon Typesetting
Cover design by Josh Durham, Design by Committee
Printed and bound in Great Britain by Clays Ltd, Elcograf S.p.A.

CONTENTS

LIST OF ACRONYMS

CASS	Chinese Academy of Social Sciences
CIA	Central Intelligence Agency (US)
CICEC	China International Culture Exchange Center
CICIR	China Institutes of Contemporary International Relations
CID	Central Investigation Department
CIIDS	China Institute for Innovation and Development Strategy
CISM	China Institute of Strategy and Management
CCP	Chinese Communist Party
ESRI	Economic System Reform Institute
FBI	Federal Bureau of Investigation (US)
MSS	Ministry of State Security
NSA	National Security Agency (US)
PLA	People's Liberation Army
PRC	People's Republic of China
SSSB	Shanghai State Security Bureau
UFWD	United Front Work Department
USCPF	US–China Policy Foundation

INTRODUCTION

O NE APRIL DAY in 2001, Lin Di sat before an exclusive audience
in Washington, DC. His host, the former US government China
expert Chas Freeman, gave only a brief introduction to the talk. Lin
was well known to Freeman and the many foreign policy luminaries
gathered at the National Press Club. As secretary-general of a key
Chinese cultural exchange organisation, Lin had established contacts
across America's policymaking circles and Chinese communities. In
Beijing, he'd warmly welcomed dozens of American officials, China
scholars, congressional staffers and retired diplomats.[1]

A slightly built man with his face fixed in a disarming smile, Lin
began his address in a shaky voice. 'I'm a little bit embarrassed to speak
in front of a camera, and in English,' he admitted. He had studied the
United States extensively, including at the China campus of Johns
Hopkins University, but politely professed that he was no America
specialist. Instead, he'd come to talk about China.

Lin's optimism surprised the audience. China, he declared, 'is deepening her reform to build a more open, prosperous, democratic and
modernised nation'. Despite political disagreements between China
and the United States, he said that China wished to focus on the over-
whelming positives in the relationship. 'It is my sincere hope that in
this new century our two great countries will work together to build a
healthy and steady relationship for the lofty cause of world peace and

progress of human civilisation,' he said. People-to-people exchanges through his organisation would provide a crucial foundation for this endeavour. Closing off his speech, he described an idyllic future in which his children would look back and have no memory of a time when there was anything but friendship between America and China.

It was all a lie. In reality, Lin was chief of the Social Investigation Bureau of China's premier intelligence agency, the Ministry of State Security (MSS). He was a spy. At the time, his bureau was the primary US operations unit within the MSS, and he personally oversaw an extensive network of clandestine assets across the country. In between these public engagements he'd rendezvous with agents, like one woman the Federal Bureau of Investigation mistakenly viewed as their star source on China.

Yet handling double agents and spies wasn't the most impressive part of Lin's job. Far more impactful was the influence and leverage MSS spies carefully developed over elites around the world, and especially in the United States. This involved schmoozing, making friends and opening doors, and much less of cloak and dagger. It's exactly what Lin did that day in Washington, DC. With their high-level connections inside the Chinese Communist Party (CCP), Lin and other undercover MSS officers claimed to have insider knowledge of China's direction and could offer meetings with Party leaders to a chosen few.

Over decades, the MSS has deployed these techniques to mislead world leaders about the CCP's ambitions, lulling them into the comfortable belief that China would rise peacefully – maybe even democratically – and slot itself into the existing international order. Its targets have included former presidents and prime ministers, multinational corporations, business leaders, Buddhist monks, influential think tanks and respected China scholars. It's an influence operation that continues to this very day.

This is the first book to reveal the MSS's influence operations: this most potent part of the CCP's intelligence work has been the most overlooked, misunderstood and ignored. The few books on the Party's intelligence apparatus glide over the issue of influence operations. Dedicated studies of China's influence operations have only speculated about MSS involvement.[2] Even within counterintelligence agencies that try to interrupt the plans of China's spies, the significance of these activities has long been downplayed, and little has been done to impede them. This knowledge gap exists in part because the covert nature of MSS work means that its influence operations are often mistaken for those of more visible Party organs, such as the United Front Work Department (UFWD). On the contrary, this book suggests that most of the CCP's high-level influence operations are orchestrated by intelligence officers.

Instead, it's the more conventional parts of the MSS that attract the most scrutiny and have contributed to the perception of the MSS as an aggressive but unsophisticated intelligence agency. A recent deluge of court cases, leaks and media exposés has revealed the MSS's appetite for trade secrets, sensitive technology, and intelligence on foreign politics and dissident communities. Often these operations were exposed because the MSS officers involved in them made basic mistakes, like using unsecured phone lines to communicate with agents. Since the 2000s, greater numbers of MSS officers have been expelled or quietly barred from countries including the United States, Sweden and Germany. Starting in late 2017, governments started to publicly accuse the MSS of far-reaching cyber espionage campaigns against companies, individuals and government agencies.[3]

The immensity of the CCP's intelligence community is another distraction from its influence operations. Alongside the MSS, the People's Liberation Army (PLA) has three main intelligence agencies, roughly responsible for eavesdropping and hacking, human intelligence operations and analysis, and political warfare.[4] China's Ministry of Public Security, nominally a police agency, also has a long history of foreign intelligence operations, including an unsuccessful attempt to influence the Trump administration in 2017.[5]

Even within the MSS there are subordinate units in every region and major city of China that often take the lead on foreign operations. Put together, these local counterparts likely have well over 100,000 employees – perhaps ten times more than the MSS's headquarters.

Sitting around these core agencies, additional Party-state organs, private and state-owned companies and lone actors appear to feed into the Party's intelligence system. Chinese companies have been caught encouraging employees to bring back proprietary research from foreign rivals. A Chinese official might opportunistically glean sensitive information from a friend or relative in America. From the outside, it looks like an incoherent mess of overlapping responsibilities and unprofessional intelligence operations. And sometimes it is.

If you're looking for Chinese state intelligence activity, there's plenty of it – enough to keep you busy without having to step back and worry about influence operations.

What this shows is that the CCP supervises an extensive array of professional intelligence agencies and calls on hundreds of thousands of intelligence officers to do its bidding. Though coordinating this web of agencies and spies is a nearly impossible task, intelligence operations are a fundamental source of power and influence for the Party. Their activities are deliberately hidden, making them easy to forget and overlook, but their significance is difficult to understate. Peter Mattis, an expert on China's intelligence services, argues that delving into these organisations does much more than help catch spies. Properly analysed, MSS activities offer unrivalled insights into the Party's inner workings and ambitions. Understanding the operation of the Party's intelligence apparatus is essential to understanding China's past, present and future.[6]

The prevailing view until recently was instead that the Party used a 'thousand grains of sand' approach to gathering intelligence. This theory has since been thoroughly debunked, and its flaws help in understanding why the MSS and its influence operations have received so little scrutiny.[7] The 'grains of sand' analogy explains that if Russia needed to gather a thousand grains of sand from a beach (that is, a thousand pieces of intelligence), it would send a submarine to deploy a highly trained team of clandestine agents to shovel up sand in the dead of night. In contrast, China would send a stream of tourists to the beach in broad daylight, each picking up a single grain. Back in Beijing, each grain of sand is then analysed and aggregated to form a brilliant picture. The central claim of this theory is that China relies on ad-hoc masses of ethnic Chinese amateurs to steal huge amounts of low-grade information, with relatively little involvement by professional spies and intelligence agencies.

It's a catchy narrative with amusing imagery, but that's about all it offers. Instead of looking for the structure, mission and intelligence officers behind the CCP's influence efforts, the 'grains of sand' theory makes it easier to assume they're largely autonomous and driven by ethnic Chinese patriots. Peter Mattis criticised the theory for wrongly framing the threat in racial terms, when China's intelligence agencies have comfortably recruited people without Chinese heritage.[8] When Western governments also treated harassment and surveillance of ethnic Chinese communities as a minor concern, this helped the MSS face little resistance as it built up extensive foreign intelligence networks.[9]

My research into the CCP began from a similar position of ignorance about its intelligence apparatus. My entrée was the UFWD, a Party agency that had long been neglected by China scholars.[10] The department plays a leading role in efforts to co-opt important groups and individuals in China. Internationally, it seeks to manipulate and claim the right to speak on behalf of ethnic Chinese communities, which includes managing Chinese student organisations.

In 2016, I was a university student in Canberra studying China and working on my Chinese-language skills. After living in China as a teenager, I was surprised to discover CCP influence on campus. The previous year, the president of a Chinese government–backed student association threatened the university pharmacy until it stopped stocking copies of a dissident Chinese newspaper. Media reports claimed that similar groups were used by the Chinese government as informant networks to collect intelligence on students, fearful that they might bring Western ideas or verboten religious beliefs back to China.[11] After I published articles in the university newspaper about these findings, members of the same student association responded by aggressively following me around at an event, including into the bathroom, and accusing me of racism.[12]

It was terrifying and exciting to me, and I later had the opportunity to focus on this issue when I helped Clive Hamilton research his 2018 book *Silent Invasion: China's influence in Australia*.[13] Examining recent cases of what looked like CCP efforts to covertly influence Australian politics, media and society, we quickly found that the UFWD was connected to many of them. Billionaire property developers, self-appointed community leaders and numerous political candidates who had a history of alignment with the CCP's interests were almost invariably members of organisations controlled by the UFWD.

At the same time, a handful of scholars around the world were documenting the CCP's footprint in their own regions. From Europe to New Zealand and the United States, we saw similar patterns of UFWD influence on politics, media and academia.[14] One politician in New Zealand had worked for Chinese military intelligence earlier in his life, and it later emerged that he'd obscured that from the New Zealand government.[15] Media investigations into the activities of one UFWD-linked billionaire ended the political career of an up-and-coming Australian senator, who'd been swayed by political donations into siding with China's position on the South China Sea.[16]

It looked as if the UFWD were controlling the strings of Party influence abroad, but something didn't add up. The department has far less expertise in foreign politics than other wings of the Party. Its officials didn't appear to have the sort of leverage or resourcing you'd expect for targeted operations against political elites, even if they do give orders to sympathisers abroad. On top of this, some key agents of influence didn't have significant links to the UFWD and instead had friends in the military, police or propaganda apparatus.[17]

One missing piece stood out: the Party's intelligence apparatus. Far more powerful and resourceful than the UFWD, intelligence agencies like the MSS combine unchecked coercive powers with a penchant for clandestine operations. China's intelligence agencies are now the world's largest and dedicate themselves to protecting the Party's interests while projecting its power abroad. If I had only rarely seen the fingerprints of these organisations in CCP influence operations, was I simply not looking hard enough?

Investigating clandestine activities is intrinsically hard. I began to hoard information on the MSS, starting with historical sources like memoirs, old court cases and retired intelligence officers who would agree to interviews. These pointed to a long tradition of hiding intelligence operations through united front work. Party leader Zhou Enlai, the father of China's intelligence community, advocated 'nestling intelligence in the united front' in 1939, when the Party formed a tactical coalition with the Kuomintang against the Japanese invasion.[18] Then, as the CCP conquered China in 1949, some of its intelligence agencies outwardly called themselves UFWDs to obscure their secret operations.[19] Through the 1980s, Chinese intelligence agencies continued to embed spies into united front groups, media organisations, trade agencies and cultural exchange bodies, exploiting their networks for influence and espionage.[20] This is not 'united front work' but professional intelligence work masquerading as something else.

These footholds from history led to the discovery that, today, the MSS's symbiosis with united front networks, business empires, public diplomacy and universities is as strong as ever. Only one in a hundred clues led me to meaningful discoveries, but a few strong anchors were enough to begin identifying covert operations currently active across the globe. Recognising a handful of key individuals as undercover MSS officers and then tracing them from front group to front group eventually unravelled decades of covert influence operations, more sophisticated with each iteration. These operations are widespread, targeted and handled with direct involvement from Party leaders. More than anything else, this is what China's intelligence agencies excel at.

The greatest of these covert operations was the MSS effort to convince influential foreigners that China would rise peacefully and gradually liberalise. It was stunningly successful. Stepping back, it's clear that the MSS has woven itself into the very fabric of China's relationship with the world. It is the invisible thread that bound the United States to ideologies of engagement and mythologies of China's liberalisation. In these pages you will meet the plain-clothes MSS intelligence officers and agents who continue to broker access to information about China and its leaders. You will also meet the who's who of American and international politics, business and academia who they courted and fooled while Western intelligence agencies failed to understand and disrupt these influence operations.

'All governments are run by liars', to quote the journalist I. F. Stone – himself a target of failed KGB cultivation – but few lies and attempts at manipulation have shaped our world as much as those spun by the MSS.[21] This book tells the story of those lies.

CHAPTER 1

GEORGE SOROS, THE CHINA FUND AND THE MSS

L IANG HENG PUT on his navy-blue Mao jacket and threw a Chinese 'Serve the People' satchel over his shoulder as he walked onto the streets of New York. It was 1984, and ever since the publication of his memoir he'd been run off his feet giving talks and interviews while trying to finish graduate studies at Columbia University.[1]

Liang's *Son of the Revolution* was a bestselling personal account of a China that had only just reopened to the West. It revealed how his family suffered in the Anti-Rightist Movement of the late 1950s, shortly before the country was plunged into famine by the Great Leap Forward. Liang was forced to forage for edible weeds in a local park. At twelve, he was swept up in the Cultural Revolution as one of millions of Red Guards and journeyed to Beijing to witness Chairman Mao Zedong in the flesh.[2] Entering university after Mao's death, Liang fell in love with a visiting American language teacher, following her back to the United States where they co-authored his memoir.[3]

Most importantly, *Son of the Revolution* brought Liang to the attention of George Soros, the billionaire investor. With their shared vision of a more liberal and open China, the pair boldly worked with reformists inside the Party to shape the nation's future, only to meet a catastrophic end courtesy of the MSS. It was the first in a long series of efforts by the intelligence agency to manipulate foreign elites, turning their hopes for China into tools for influencing and infiltrating the West.

George Soros read Liang's memoir and reached out to the publisher. He wanted to meet the author himself. 'A businessman? I'm flat-out every day. Why should I see this businessman?' Liang thought. He hadn't heard of Soros before but agreed to the meeting anyway. Now he was on his way.[4]

They met for lunch at an upmarket French restaurant where Soros was a regular and had his own private booth. After nearly two hours of discussion about Liang's life, Soros began explaining his own philosophy and political work. His attention was increasingly focused on supporting liberal and progressive political causes in communist countries. Just that year he'd established his first 'open society foundation' in his country of birth, Hungary. The foundation partnered with the Hungarian Academy of Sciences and pushed boundaries behind the iron curtain, funding projects on issues as diverse as Western economic thinking to the plight of the Roma Gypsies. 'I got hooked on what I like to call "political philanthropy",' Soros later explained.[5]

Over cheeses and fruit, Soros finally got to the point. 'Does the China of today have opportunities for you to do something for it?' he asked Liang.

Liang believed they were at a key juncture in Chinese history, one that he wanted to take part in. He wanted to turn what he'd learnt through years of hardship during the Great Leap Forward and Cultural Revolution into something positive. At the time, he was preparing to set up a magazine for overseas Chinese intellectuals, but much more could be done. 'Liang,' said Soros, 'I support what you want to do. I also feel that China is undergoing great changes, and these changes will influence the whole world.'

Then and there, Liang agreed to work as Soros's advisor, helping him explore opportunities in China to replicate his efforts in Hungary by also setting up a foundation there.[6]

Soros needed partners in China he could trust. Out of all the officials and organs of the Chinese government (for no entirely independent institutions existed at the time), he needed Liang to find the right ones to back, those who both believed in his vision and had the political power to see it realised.

It was no easy task that Soros had given Liang. Neither fully understood the monumental political struggles they were about to find themselves in the middle of.

The China Fund

The kind of funding and opportunities Soros promised were almost unheard of in China, and it wasn't long before Liang secured introductions to reformist circles. Respected and politically connected economists like He Weiling and Zhu Jiaming (a friend of future vice president Wang Qishan) were eager to take part in the project.[7] With Soros's backing, Liang also met with a senior Party official to explain Soros's work and his idea of establishing a foundation to promote 'reform and opening'.

The key was to find a local Chinese partner institution, a requirement of operating in China, and Liang quickly made the right connections. Scholars from the Economic System Reform Institute (ESRI), a hub of progressive thinking backed by segments of the Party leadership, convinced their bosses to team up with Soros.[8] Soon, what became known as the Fund for the Reform and Opening of China, or the China Fund, was born. Its very name was a nod to the Party's official policy of reform and opening. As Soros's biographer Michael T. Kaufman wrote, '[Soros] sensed that within the extraordinary turbulence of Chinese society, he had luckily found the right people.'[9]

Soros's excitement was shared by the economists of the ESRI. A trip to Hungary, funded by Soros, electrified these young thinkers as they attempted to carve a new path for China in the wake of the Cultural Revolution. Many were travelling abroad for the first time. Their conversations with Hungarian economists, who were wrangling with similar puzzles of taxation, market competition and private enterprise, were 'like a chemical reaction – so inspiring', said one participant. The visit helped drive the confidence and creativity of Chinese reformists, spurring forward their advocacy of economic reforms, he said. 'Maybe too fast.'[10]

In October 1986, Soros travelled to China for the first time to formally open the China Fund in a signing ceremony at Beijing's Diaoyutai State Guesthouse.[11] His bold vision to kickstart true people-to-people exchanges between China and the West that would promote civil society, liberalism and economic reform was filled with optimism from his successes in Hungary. Liang Heng began spending most of his time in Beijing as Soros's representative, setting up a small office for the China Fund. Entrusting an enormous budget by Chinese standards to the ESRI, the fund 'was an institution unlike any other in China. On paper, it had complete autonomy,' Soros recalled.[12] The ESRI was close to the reformist premier Zhao Ziyang, who became the Party's general secretary the next year, and Zhao's personal secretary, Bao Tong, cut through red tape to champion the joint venture.

The China Fund's achievements were impressive. Soros afforded Liang and his staff in Beijing a great deal of autonomy as they worked through the growing mass of funding applications that arrived in the cramped courtyard house they used as an office. Within a year of its establishment, the foundation had set up an artists' club in Beijing and an academic salon at the prestigious Nankai University in Tianjin, supported the study of folk art in the Yellow River basin, and backed research on Thailand's efforts to attract foreign investment and on Boston's high-tech industry.[13] In its first two years it awarded more than 200 grants and received thousands of applications, making genuine contributions to the preservation and study of Chinese culture.[14] As in Hungary, it pushed boundaries by funding research on sensitive topics such as the Cultural Revolution – still carefully censored to this day – including a project to collect oral histories of people's experiences through the turmoil.[15] Influential journalist Dai Qing compiled *Yangtze! Yangtze!*, her tour de force of opposition to the ecological and social wrecking ball that the Three Gorges Dam would be, with support from Soros.[16] The China Fund's financer was particularly excited to support a conference on the philosophy of Karl Popper, his old doctoral supervisor whose writings on open society were the inspiration for his philanthropy.[17]

The end of optimism

Almost as soon as it emerged, the China Fund ran into a challenge that proved fatal. General Secretary Zhao Ziyang's aide had made a dangerous political gamble by backing the venture. 'Bao Tong was hated by many,' said one former Chinese government economist.[18] According to Soros, 'opponents of radical reforms, who were numerous, banded together to attack [Bao Tong]'. Bao and the ESRI had stuck their neck out too far. Hardline sceptics of economic liberalism and exchange with the West saw their chance to strike. And Zhao's influence as general secretary, nominally the Party's most senior leader, wasn't enough to insulate Soros's venture from the growing resistance of conservative Party elders. Liang rushed back from New York to Beijing, only to find that their Chinese partners had already decided on the next steps.[19]

In the face of complaints from Party elders about the China Fund, Zhao Ziyang ceded its control to new management. It wasn't a fight he wanted to pick, nor one he could dare to. Zhao agreed to sever ties between the ESRI and the China Fund, bringing in the China International Culture Exchange Center (CICEC), a group under the Ministry of Culture, as its new partner institution.[20] Things weren't all bad, or so it seemed. CICEC had the backing of senior Party leaders, including Xi Jinping's father, and served as one of the only official channels for cultural exchanges with the outside world. Its strong ties to officialdom could insulate Zhao and the China Fund from those who wished to see it destroyed.[21]

By the time this decision had been made, neither Soros or Liang had even met with representatives of CICEC. The ESRI's director quickly arranged a meeting between Liang and the head of CICEC, Vice Minister Yu Enguang. Yu quickly convinced him of the merits of this new arrangement and told him he believed in the importance of friends like Soros who could support China's modernisation. 'Once I heard about this plan, I understood that at the time there was no other choice,' Liang reflected. They had to agree to work with CICEC if they were to survive.[22]

Soros took these changes in his stride, accepting some degree of political interference as a necessary compromise when operating in China. In February 1988 he travelled to Beijing to reconfirm his commitment to bankroll the foundation and sign a revised agreement with Yu Enguang, his new Chinese co-chair. As Xinhua News Agency reported at the time, 'academic research on reform and opening, and funding activities by non-governmental organisations' remained priorities for the China Fund. The article described Soros as a 'friendly American figure', perhaps a rung below the coveted title of 'old friend of the Chinese people', a term used by the Party to recognise foreigners who've made major contributions to its efforts.[23]

Soros was initially pleased with the China Fund's new management from CICEC. He got along well with Yu Enguang at a personal level. This impeccably well-connected interlocutor helped Soros secure a rare meeting with a Party leader in Beijing's Zhongnanhai leadership compound.[24]

But cracks quickly emerged. 'I was taken to visit one of our projects, a mobile library unit operated by the Young Pioneers, and was appalled,' Soros recalled. 'It was a formal affair, the children in uniform, the instructors making stiff, meaningless speeches, the children forming a *tableau vivant* to demonstrate the use of the library. Worst of all, the secretary of the foundation was so pleased that she had tears in her eyes.'[25]

Liang was disappointed too. His friends in Beijing mentioned that fewer and fewer people were applying for China Fund grants. Under CICEC, the China Fund continued supporting cultural activities, but none were true civil society initiatives. Instead, CICEC used Soros's money to fund its own officially sanctioned exchanges with foreign organisations.[26] It made a complete 180-degree turn from the project's original goal of promoting open society. CICEC's 1988 yearbook inadvertently offered the most apt summary of the situation when it promoted its new partnership with the man it called 'George Sorrows'.[27]

The Soros incident

The year 1989 brought the death of Hu Yaobang, Zhao Ziyang's predecessor as the Party's general secretary and an inspirational reformist, a figure still widely respected by the Chinese public despite being purged in 1987. Hu's passing in April catalysed gatherings that grew into the Tiananmen Square protests of 1989 and ended with the massacre on 4 June.

In early 1988, Chinese intellectuals had already begun to be scared off by political interference in the China Fund.[28] The next year, Soros received a letter from the journalist Dai Qing, one of the grant recipients, alerting him to how the program had been infiltrated by security operatives.[29] China's security agencies had in fact been scrutinising Soros's activities from the beginning.

Amid the chaos of the Tiananmen massacre, the Party's security operatives attacked decisively. The China Fund and Soros's hopes of influencing China collapsed as General Secretary Zhao Ziyang was stripped of power and placed under house arrest. As Soros told the audience at the Davos World Economic Forum in 2019, '[Party conservatives] claimed that I was a CIA agent and asked the internal security agency to investigate.' The China Fund's Beijing-based manager, Liang Congjie, was arrested and interrogated after the massacre. At least fourteen researchers from the ESRI, the fund's original partner organisation, were detained too. Chinese reformists feared their rivals were seeking to use the allegation that China Fund was a CIA front to brand them counterrevolutionary traitors and help justify the brutal crackdown.[30]

Soros, pessimistic about the direction of Chinese politics, wrote to Yu Enguang to swiftly shut down the China Fund just before the Tiananmen massacre, to Liang's frustration and disappointment.[31] 'You're using an investing mentality to go about politics,' Liang complained. 'You have no political loyalty – you should know how many of our Chinese friends will pay the price and be placed in danger because of you entering and then pulling out of China.' They didn't see each other for another three years.[32]

Chen Yizi, the original Chinese chair of the fund and president of the ESRI, went into hiding and was smuggled out of the country a few days after 4 June because of his close association with Zhao Ziyang. Months later, from his refuge in Paris, he shared what he knew of the inside story: 'In July 1987 the then Minister of Public Security Wang Fang wrote a report to Zhao Ziyang, saying Soros is a stead-fast anti-communist and supported the 1956 Hungarian Uprising.

He instigates unrest in socialist countries and his fund's people have ties to reactionaries.'[33]

In November, Minister Wang followed up with another report. This time, he doubled down on his accusations, specifically pointing fingers at Chen Yizi and other allies of Zhao Ziyang.[34]

It was these pointed accusations, more than mere grumbling from conservatives, that had really forced Zhao to hand the China Fund to CICEC back in 1987.[35] Though Zhao Ziyang was nominally the party's highest leader, Minister Wang had backers in high places.

Black hands

But that's only a side of the truth, one that leaves the most secret and mysterious arms of Party power unexposed. Even for a defector like Chen, some things are still best left unsaid.[36] As one former Party official explained, the Soros incident remains a taboo topic even now.[37]

Investigating Yu Enguang, the China Fund's co-chair from CICEC, reveals exactly why it's such a sensitive story.[38] Yu was a member of China's National People's Congress, serving on its foreign and legal affairs committees. He also worked in London and Washington, DC, for China's Xinhua News Agency, becoming fluent in English.[39] Yet for someone who held such senior positions, there's remarkably little information about him available.

Soros and Liang thought Yu and CICEC could help protect them from the Party's conservatives. Other evidence indicates Yu was deeply distrustful of the capitalist world and spoke out against the threat democratic countries posed to China. In 2000, for example, he warned China's congress that 'Internal and foreign hostile forces are taking advantage of the internet to engage in reactionary and damaging activities, taking advantage of the internet to spread the West's so-called democracy and human rights.'[40]

Yu clearly did not share Soros's vision for China, so why did he stick his neck out to lead the China Fund? One clue comes from the Paradise Papers, a trove of more than 13 million financial records leaked to the media in 2017.[41] Among the leaked documents is one from the early 2000s that names none other than Yu Enguang as the director of a company registered to the Caribbean territory of Bermuda.[42] It records

Yu's personal address as an apartment in '100 Xiyuan' in Beijing's Haidian District.[43] The Xiyuan or West Garden compound occupies an entire block just east of the Summer Palace, an opulent imperial resort that was looted by foreign armies during the Boxer Rebellion. Street imagery from Chinese internet giant Baidu shows its guarded entrance decorated for the Spring Festival and large golden letters giving another name for the compound: *Yidongyuan*, the East Summer Palace Garden. Few tourists wandering past its modest walls would know that it houses the headquarters of the MSS, China's peak espionage agency.

According to George Soros, Yu Enguang, co-chair of his China Fund, was in fact an undercover 'high-ranking official in the external security police' – the MSS.[44] The fund's partner organisation, CICEC, had never really been part of the Ministry of Culture. It was MSS, through and through.[45] Under the pretence of protecting their China Fund, Yu had persuaded Soros and Liang to hand over control of the venture to this intelligence agency. And Yu's mission wasn't just to protect China from external threats but to lay the groundwork for influence operations that shaped the world.

CHAPTER 2

SPYMASTER: YU ENGUANG

Yu enguang's story has never previously been told. Before his death in 2013, he rose into the highest ranks of China's intelligence community. He was instrumental in creating the organisations, practices and culture that make influence operations by today's Ministry of State Security so successful. The MSS continues to emulate the boldness Yu showed as he engaged directly with an international power player, turning Soros's dream of an open society in China into a source of funds, legitimacy and cover for influence operations.

The China International Culture Exchange Center that Yu led was an MSS-run front organisation, custom-built for engaging with foreigners like Soros. Nearly forty years later, it's still in active operational use.

To foreigners who met him, Yu seemed like a man deeply interested in and acquainted with the capitalist world, not some paranoid Stalinist. He was a witty and memorable character, skilled at interacting with targets and adept at English – something that stands out in all accounts. While posted to America undercover as a Xinhua journalist, he charmed a *Washington Post* reporter with his commentary on the Cantonese meal they were sharing.[1] He'd been trained well – the ability to introduce

Chinese cuisine to foreigners was specifically drilled into Chinese spies during their English-language courses.[2]

Yu made a mark on Soros representative Liang Heng too, who was persuaded to accept MSS control over the China Fund: 'The impression Yu gave me was quite good. He was about fifty, tall, with strong eyebrows, big eyes and a sophisticated manner and he talked pragmatically … he'd been to many countries, seen and experienced much, and spoke fluent English.'[3] Soros likewise bonded with him, despite some apprehension about his special background. Both of them had lived in London and Soros liked the British accent of Yu's English.[4]

Yu was not just any MSS officer. At the time he was a vice minister of the agency and among the Communist Party's top foreign intelligence officers. Few within the agency could rival the depth of his overseas experience. Most of all, his operations in hostile capitalist nations taught him that loyalty to the Party came before all else. Only a politically secure officer would feel comfortable 'dropping cover' by revealing his MSS affiliation to Liang and Soros. This is also reflected in the fact that he was trusted to represent the MSS abroad, where he built partnerships with foreign intelligence agencies such as in Afghanistan.[5]

But who was he, really? The first two decades of his spy career were spent embedded in the state-owned Xinhua News Agency, giving him rare opportunities to travel the world. In the 1970s he worked in Xinhua's London bureau for eight years.[6] One Thai woman living in London who met him at a Chinese embassy function noted that 'he often worked at home late at night writing dispatches'.[7] Clearly, he had more on his plate than journalism.

From London he was reassigned to the United States, which had only recently opened diplomatic relations with the People's Republic of China (PRC). During the Carter and Reagan years he headed the newly established Xinhua bureau in Washington, DC, overseeing coverage of the White House.[8] 'While I tirelessly reported on the activities and speeches of Carter, Mondale, Reagan and Bush and other key White House figures, I also observed many phenomena and gathered many materials,' he reflected years later in a compilation of his US reportage, which doesn't reveal his MSS affiliation. Hinting at his dual life as a spy and a journalist, he wrote that it was a job where most achievements were 'fragile goods, and hard to attach to my name'.[9] By 1985, while he was officially deputy director of the Xinhua department responsible for foreign correspondents, he was in fact probably leading an entire bureau of MSS officers.[10]

Dual identities

Yet 'Yu Enguang' may not have existed at all. MSS officers use pseudonyms throughout their careers, even as vice ministers. These aliases often read like puns on their true names, with characters dissected and jumbled into new ones, or surnames replaced with homophones.

Yu is no exception. Though one writer on Chinese espionage assumed they were different people, little-known MSS vice minister Yu Fang looks identical to Yu Enguang.[11] In the only published photo of Yu Fang, taken after his retirement, he stands with the same slouch, wears the same belt and dons the same pair of shaded glasses as Yu Enguang. Both reportedly studied at Renmin University and grew up in Liaoning province in China's northeast.[12] Yu Enguang was just a pseudonym for Yu Fang.

Among his comrades in the MSS, Yu Fang was just as respected as 'Yu Enguang' was by the targets he cultivated. At some point in his career he headed the agency's important central administrative office, and in the early nineties helped secure the passage of China's first National Security Law, which expanded and codified MSS powers.[13] The authors of several MSS publications, marked for internal distribution only, thank him for advising on and improving their drafts.[14] He also oversaw MSS production and censorship of histories, TV dramas and movies about spies, which were designed to build public awareness and support for the MSS's mission.[15]

Ironically for a man who helped bring Chinese intelligence history into the public sphere, Yu's true legacy is an official secret. Official references to his achievements are brief and elliptical. The authoritative *People's Daily* eulogised him in 2013, an honour only a handful of intelligence officers receive: 'In his sixty years of life in the revolution, Comrade Yu Fang was loyal to the Party, scrupulously carried out his duties and selflessly offered himself to the Party's endeavours, making important contributions to the Party's state security endeavour.'

The article also noted that he'd been a member of the National People's Congress, China's national legislature, but lists of delegates include only his pseudonym.[16]

The MSS seizure of the China Fund was an impressive display of the agency's confidence in engaging with one of America's best-connected and wealthiest men. What it learnt could be applied to future operations as the agency grew more aggressive and internationally focused over the following decade. But it was far from a flawless effort: exposing Yu Enguang and CICEC as arms of the MSS leads to a string of covert operations against the United States, continuing right to the present day.

Soros had at first accepted the management change at his China Fund as a necessary cost of operating in China. Liang Heng claims he told Soros the truth about Yu's identity in 1988.[17] The MSS and Ministry of Public Security 'were co-equal and they couldn't interfere in each other's affairs', Soros argued in 2019, but partnering with the MSS offered quite the opposite of protection in the end.[18] He may have thought he could handle the situation, that his ties to Party leaders could override the conservative proclivities of their spies. After all, his political philanthropy was thriving in Hungary and the Soviet Union despite their security agencies having been formed in the same ideological mould as the MSS.

It's easy to see why Yu Enguang – or Fang – succeeded in convincing Liang and Soros to accept an MSS takeover of the China Fund, even if it wasn't an offer the billionaire could easily refuse. But barbs lay behind his charm. Internal MSS reports show what the agency really thought of its American 'guest'. Its claims about the Soros China Fund, perhaps compiled by Yu, reflected the paranoia and confirmation bias behind the Party's decision to unleash military force on the people of Beijing in the Tiananmen Square massacre, just a year after Yu Enguang took control of the China Fund.

The Tiananmen Papers, a leaked trove of internal Party reports related to the massacre, reveals much. Updates by the MSS on the student protests form a large chunk of the cache, including one from three days before the massacre that was sent up to the Politburo. In it, the MSS repeated the line that Soros's China Fund was a CIA front, painting a picture of an enormous conspiracy by hostile foreign forces to control reformists within the Party's ranks and use the student protests to spark subversion. 'Our investigations have revealed that Liang Heng, the personal representative of the [China Fund] chairman George Soros, was a suspected US spy. Moreover, four American members of the foundation's advisory committee had CIA connections,' it claimed.[19]

According to the MSS's narrative, Soros showed his 'true colours' by asking Yu to close the fund in May 1989 once he realised that supporters of reform were being purged. Writing to Deng Xiaoping three months after the massacre, Soros denied any CIA involvement in his activities in a letter that was republished in the Party's 'internal reports' circular, sent out to all senior officials. All the China Fund's projects were open and accountable, and effectively sanctioned by both the Chinese government and the MSS. Still hopeful, he made an offer to Deng:

If the Chinese Government indicates its desire to pursue a policy of economic reform and openness, and makes it clear that those associated with the China Fund will not suffer any adverse consequences for their association, I would like to begin again to provide support for the activities of the Fund. Nothing would please me more than to be able to resume a friendly and productive association with your government.[20]

But the MSS and its leaders in the Party had already made up their minds. That the winds of power were blowing against political reform was obvious. The ministry's 1 June report to the Politburo, which purported to cover the various forms and means of Western infiltration into China, was unforgiving:

Many facts demonstrate that the international monopoly capitalists and hostile, reactionary foreign forces have not abandoned for a moment their intent to destroy us. It is now clear that murderous intent has always lurked behind their protestations of peace and friendship. When the opportunity arises they will remove the facade and reveal their true colors. They have only one goal: to annihilate socialism.[21]

Chen Yizi, the ESRI director who was booted out and replaced by Yu Enguang as the chair of Soros's China Fund, drew a direct link between the charges of espionage laid against Soros and the factional battles that erupted into the Tiananmen massacre. It was an early ambush laid by the conservatives, who 'were clearly trying to topple reformist forces within the Party', Chen believed. 'After they toppled [reformist general secretary] Hu Yaobang, they again sharpened their swords and prepared to take down Zhao Ziyang', Hu's successor, whose staff were working with and supporting Soros.[22]

As Chen went into hiding and was smuggled out of China after the massacre, one of his institute's researchers, Cheng Xiaonong, was in Germany. While news of the crackdown spread, Cheng received a call from a colleague in Beijing, cryptically warning him not to come back. He later learned security officers detained a dozen of the institute's staff and others associated with Soros's China Fund. 'Their goal was to get them to say that Zhao Ziyang had been conspiring with foreign states,' Cheng said.[23]

Cheng suspected the MSS had been planting informants in the ESRI well before the Tiananmen protests began in order to monitor reformists and the institute's foreign contacts. In fact, the ESRI's representative in Japan at the time, officially *China Economic Daily*'s Tokyo correspondent, was probably an undercover MSS officer.[24] According to Cheng, 'After June 4, [conservative Party leaders] wanted to take out Zhao Ziyang, so they desperately needed an excuse for doing so.' The combination of MSS surveillance of Soros's activities and his links to Zhao created the perfect recipe for made-up charges. The Party's spies settled on the line that Zhao's aide was in frequent contact with the institute, which had in turn partnered with George Soros, who they alleged was a CIA spy. As Cheng puts it, 'The conclusion is that Zhao Ziyang was a spy, a US CIA spy.'[25] Treason, in other words.

Yet the MSS may not have wanted to pursue the question further. The truth that it had been secretly running Soros's China Fund inconveniently implicated its own officers in America's supposed 'counterrevolutionary strategy' to turn China into a liberal democracy. Soros knew this and could have exposed the MSS's hand if it harmed the China Fund's associates. Likewise, the political and social consequences of accusing a crestfallen Party leader of capital crimes may have proven as unpredictable as the Tiananmen protests, and to do so was not the MSS's prerogative in any case. This was a matter of the highest levels of elite politics. In the end, it seems that none were punished for their involvement in the Soros China Fund.[26]

Ultimately, the MSS didn't need to formally reach a verdict either. Party crimes were to be sorted out by the Party elders themselves and the MSS was only there to justify the ruling it made: that the Tiananmen massacre had been a necessary struggle against anti-Party extremists and foreign agitators, and that Zhao Ziyang must be purged and indefinitely placed under house arrest.

CHAPTER 3

NESTLING SPIES IN THE UNITED FRONT

IN 1990, GEORGE SOROS looked back on the failure of his China Fund. 'China was not ready for it because there were no independent or dissident intelligentsia,' he wrote. 'The foundation could not become an institution of civil society ... because no such society existed.'[1] Whether partnered with the ESRI or CICEC, he could not extricate his venture from the Party and the MSS.

The full story behind CICEC shows just how far the MSS's connections reach across Chinese society. It was the first in what is now a long line of covertly controlled vehicles for the MSS, showcasing the agency's united front traditions as well as its unique emphasis on building social networks and executing influence operations. CICEC and its MSS officers used these advantages to embed themselves into key channels for engagement with China, and from there manipulate and infiltrate the outside world.

The assets

At its establishment in 1984, CICEC was nearly unrivalled for the representation it had across Chinese high society.[2] At first glance, the newly created cultural organisation's ties to intelligence were far from obvious. Representing the Party leadership at CICEC's founding was Xi Zhongxun, considered a relatively open-minded and reformist official. Xi's leading role in the united front and intelligence communities was not widely understood by foreign observers even though he had also attended the MSS's founding the year prior.[3]

Famous Chinese with strong international contacts filled CICEC's list of 139 members. They ranged from future Party leader Hu Jintao to calligraphers, poets, a Manchu prince, ballet dancers, scientists and the leader of the state-approved Protestant church.[4] Many had been victims of the Cultural Revolution, but their return to prominence reflected how the Chinese Communist Party wanted to present 'New China' to the world: open, reforming, culturally rich and increasingly cosmopolitan. Their international standing and roles as *de facto* cultural ambassadors were magnetic to foreigners interested in China.

Many, if not most, of these people had something in common beside their CICEC membership. They were people the MSS could rely upon to help its officers make international contacts among the diverse social circles and professions they represented. With their influence and connections to the outside world, they were masks China's spies could wear to monitor, influence or even recruit outsiders. These people were intelligence assets.

A close look shows that several of CICEC's earliest members had backgrounds in intelligence work. Ying Ruocheng, the famous Chinese actor who became vice minister of culture in the late 1980s, was both an intelligence asset and a CICEC member. His wife, in fact an employee of the MSS, was officially the secretary of another CICEC member, the playwright Cao Yu. Towards the end of his life, Ying's work as an informant over more than thirty years, reporting on his interactions with foreign friends such as Arthur Miller, began to trouble him deeply and only became known with the posthumous publication of his memoirs in 2009. Even approaching death he refused to tell the full story. Perhaps demonstrating his mixed feelings about intelligence work, Ying's invitation to CICEC's 1985 council meeting recently appeared for sale online for ¥35 (A$7).[5] Ying's biographer had to piece together a more complete picture of his affiliation with intelligence agencies through interviews with his son.[6]

A more willing friend of the MSS was Peng Chong, the senior politician chosen as CICEC's founding chairman. As a vice chairman of
China's congress, Peng was involved in supervising security agencies
but was most notable in his career for having never stuck his neck out.[7]
Likewise, CICEC's first secretary-general had for decades been an asset
to China's spies, helping orchestrate the defection of a high-ranking
Kuomintang general to Beijing.[8] If these people were the MSS's assets
then who was really in charge?

Social investigations: The 12th Bureau

CICEC was not meant for routine intelligence work; it is the MSS's
custom-made organ for meeting, covertly influencing and recruiting elites from around the world. Its spies have handled the kinds of
operations that the MSS's many provincial branches might not be trusted
to carry out, from schmoozing with China scholars to penetrating US
intelligence agencies. Politically sensitive missions like engaging directly
with George Soros or posing as liberals within the Party in order to gain
the trust of foreigners are home turf for these officers.

To this day, CICEC's secretariat is home to a cadre of serving MSS
officers. Biographical information on them is often scant and vague, but
every now and then it's possible to find a clear link to the MSS. Initially,
several MSS deputy bureau chiefs were mixed in among the group's
members, as well as many more junior officers.[9] These deeply embedded
officers often stayed with CICEC for more than a decade, allowing
them to build deep relationships with the Chinese luminaries among its
members, and with the many foreigners CICEC engaged with. As MSS
Vice Minister Yu Fang advised in a piece of calligraphy he dedicated to
the organisation, they were 'using culture to make friends'.[10] But rather
than being the objective of this group, building China's cultural influence was only a convenient and disarming way to place agents beside
foreign targets, and give spies chances to travel abroad.

Another clue to CICEC's behind-the-scenes MSS officers comes
from its membership lists, some of which have been doctored in what
looks like an attempt to scrub references to spies.[11] Lists published on
CICEC's website appear to be mostly complete. A second set of lists
from a CICEC promotional video has erased fourteen names. Many of

those censored names can be linked to MSS officers, including two vice ministers specialising in foreign intelligence and the agency's cyberespionage chief.[12] What can be found on the other officers shows backgrounds in foreign languages, arts and culture that make them uniquely suited to carrying out intelligence work through CICEC.

Take Jiang Xue, a member of CICEC's council until 2013 and one of those whose names were redacted. He's an accomplished poet and calligrapher.[13] In 2014, his lyrics 'River of Love' formed the theme song for a Chinese movie, where he's credited as a former Ministry of Public Security employee, a commonly used cover by MSS officers.[14] He's also lectured at two MSS academies: the University of International Relations and the secretive Jiangnan Social University, a mid-career training institution with what looks like a shooting range on its campus.[15] He's an MSS officer.

CICEC's links to spies converge in the Ministry's Social Investigation Bureau, also known as the 12th Bureau. Mao Guohua, head of the bureau in the 1990s, concurrently served as a secretary-general of CICEC.[16] CICEC member and undercover MSS Vice Minister Yu Fang was the MSS leader who supervised the 12th Bureau.

The bureau's most senior officers can still be spotted at CICEC events and among its staff. In July 2020, Sun Qingye emerged as the deputy director of the PRC's new national security office in Hong Kong. He's an MSS officer, just not under that name.[17] As Sun Wenqing, he is a vice president of CICEC and a delegate to the Chinese People's Political Consultative Conference, and probably ran the 12th Bureau until he was sent to Hong Kong.[18] Earlier in his career he studied in Japan before working undercover as *China Youth Daily*'s Tokyo correspondent.[19]

No one seems to agree about this bureau's true mission but every intelligence officer who's studied it is intrigued and has their own theory. Taiwan's Ministry of Justice Investigation Bureau – a counter-intelligence agency at the coalface of MSS infiltration – described the bureau as responsible for 'managing relations with social organisations'.[20] Experts on Chinese intelligence Peter Mattis and Matthew Brazil believe it's in charge of 'MSS contributions to CCP's united front work system'.[21] A former US intelligence officer called it the 'mini MSS' because of the breadth of its activities, which included spying on US intelligence agencies, monitoring dissidents and political influence operations.[22] Others have proposed that it might be the MSS headquarters' own foreign operations bureau. Normally, local branches of the MSS in cities like Shanghai and Guangzhou carry out the bulk of foreign operations based on instructions from Beijing.[23] Despite the bureau's central role in MSS foreign operations, few Western spy catchers working on China would be familiar with it.[24] It was only around the early 2000s that it began to attract greater, if still minimal, scrutiny.[25]

The bureau's structure says much about how it operates: it has directly set up and managed more front organisations than any other unit of the MSS, many of which look similar to the various community associations run by the UFWD. Here, some helpful context comes from an internal MSS textbook used for training officers, which implies that the ministry controls several social groups, underwriting their budget and inserting 'personnel responsible for state security work' among their ranks.[26] The bureau alone has controlled or been associated with four publishing houses, a Japanese magazine, a well-known think tank, an arts troupe, an international travel agency, a university alumni association, a film production company, a California bookstore, Hong Kong's *Sing Tao Daily*, the China Writers Association, a public relations professionals association, a medical centre, an international calligraphy competition, a record company and countless international conferences. That's only those that can be identified through open-source investigations. Most of these fronts remain active today.[27]

United front traditions

From its very earliest days, CICEC's activities exemplified the Leninist united front strategy of forming alliances of convenience with outside groups, only to discard or marginalise them when they are no longer needed.[28] Its very first operation, an effort to scrounge for funds, shows how the MSS Social Investigation Bureau draws on the best intentions of unwitting foreigners to strengthen its covert activities.

The MSS of the 1980s only had a meagre budget, and China as whole was cash-strapped after the devastation of the Cultural Revolution. Foreign investment was just as important to the country's economy as it was to its intelligence agencies, which by the 1990s were running some of China's largest business empires.

China's intelligence community found its opportunity to harvest foreign cash in a Hong Kong charity group. In 1981, while the MSS's establishment had only just been proposed, the Jian Hua Foundation (literally the 'Build China Foundation') was set up by four evangelical Protestant businessmen. They wanted to show how Christians could contribute to China's 'four modernisations'. These four goals of modernising industry, agriculture, national defence and technology were Deng's signature policy for reform and opening.[29]

Huang Zhen, the Party's head of foreign cultural exchanges and the Propaganda Department's number-two man, helped steer the Jian Hua Foundation's philanthropy.[30] Huang allowed the foundation to become one of the first non-governmental organisations operating in China since the Cultural Revolution, but it had to work on the Party's terms.

The foundation's first commitment to the Party was that it would fund the construction of what became CICEC's headquarters. The building, in Beijing's inner east, symbolised China's triumphant reopening to the world. Designed to look like a musical reed pipe with eighteen storeys, it was one of the tallest and largest buildings being planned for Beijing at the time.[31] According to one of the foundation's founders, interviewed by China scholar Miwa Hirono, 'The idea for the [CICEC] started when Deng Xiaoping wanted to develop people's diplomacy. [Deng suggested that the] relationship should start with friendship between people; not so much [between] officials at the conference table.' The Party envisioned the CICEC building with state-of-the-art amenities, including a modern theatre that could serve as a conference venue and a performance hall.[32]

The Jian Hua Foundation, thinking it was being given privileged access to China and its elite, was used to fund a brand-new intelligence front. CICEC was the PRC's first body of its kind during the reform and opening period. It was set up 'under the attentiveness and care of the central leadership', its members selected by the Central Political-Legal Affairs Commission and approved by Xi Zhongxun.[33] This leading MSS front group even describes itself as carrying out overseas united front work, although this is just a pretence for intelligence work.[34]

The Bank of Credit and Commerce International, registered in Luxembourg but backed by the Sheikh of Abu Dhabi and Saudi intelligence, also contributed to the project through loans and a gift of US$2 million.[35] Separately, the bank's branches in Shenzhen and Hong Kong were being used by the Party's investment companies and arms exporters to access international markets, and by senior officials to siphon off their own gains.[36] China International Trust Investment Corporation or CITIC, a gargantuan state-owned corporation with MSS links, was a client of the bank until it collapsed in 1991 under the weight of corruption, reckless lending practices and US law-enforcement actions.[37]

It's no coincidence that the MSS draws on the Party's united front tradition. When the MSS was established in 1983, cops and spies made up the bulk of its workforce, but less known is that two other organisations contributed personnel to the newly formed organisation.[38] One was the Commission of Science, Technology and Industry for National Defence, a military organisation active in technology theft efforts. More intriguing are the officials transferred from the United Front Work Department (UFWD). The department, long overlooked, has seen a resurgence of attention from both the Party leadership and foreign observers in recent years. It focuses its work on strengthening the 'united front' of groups within and outside China working towards the Party's goals. The basic principle is to target or manufacture representatives of important interest groups and use them as platforms for influence work and infiltration.[39]

More powerful than the UFWD alone, the grouping known as the united front system – covering the dozens of agencies and front groups that are tasked with such activities – is surging in prominence under Xi Jinping.[40] Implementing the ideas he once advocated for as a lowly municipal Party secretary, Xi personally convened the first-ever central conference on united front work in 2015 and re-established the high-level coordinating body for united front work his father, Xi Zhongxun, chaired in the 1980s.[41] The UFWD itself has undergone its largest reforms and expansions in decades, subsuming three smaller agencies and receiving official blessing to manage China's ethnic, religious and diaspora affairs.[42]

Xi Jinping is simply reading from an old playbook. Party leaders since Mao Zedong have referred to the united front as one of their three 'magic weapons'.[43] Together with armed struggle and efforts to strengthen Party organisation, the two other magic weapons, the CCP credits the united front work with major contributions to its victory in 1949, China's modernisation and subsequent economic development.[44]

United front work is the subtle and but no less effective cousin of armed struggle. It aims to expand the Party's control beyond its membership, building a network of friendly contacts in China, and increasingly around the world, who can align their actions with Beijing's wishes. It focuses on individuals in positions of influence or those who claim to represent key segments of society – ethnic community leaders, business magnates, religious figureheads and so on. This same strategy underlies the forced assimilation of Xinjiang (a policy area overseen by the united front system) and the extinguishing of freedoms in Hong Kong, where Beijing has successfully co-opted key elites.

Abroad, the Party replicates these methods of cultivating elites and community leaders. As recent cases from around the world have shown, the Party seeks to insert itself into segments of diaspora communities and then mobilise them as political influence. Co-optees can be used to suppress dissidents, make political donations, mentor political candidates and staffers, and otherwise apply pressure in support of Beijing's interests. In Australia, businesspeople with strong ties to the UFWD have channelled millions of dollars into political parties, attempted to change foreign policy, and placed their associates in politicians' offices and even in parliament.[45] For a time, the secretive nature of some of the UFWD's activities led the FBI to mistakenly label some UFWD officials, operating as diplomats in the United States as they built clandestine networks in Tibetan diaspora communities, as MSS officers.[46]

On its own, united front work is bad enough. It serves as a way for the Party to push its influence beyond its own ranks, including abroad. But the biggest problem with united front work is not with those activities themselves but how they enhance the work of professional spies with grander ambitions than the UFWD.

United front networks are a golden opportunity for the Party's spies because they represent groups of Party-aligned individuals who are relatively receptive to clandestine recruitment. The ways intelligence agencies ride atop these networks is the most concerning yet least understood aspect of CCP influence, but one that goes back to the earliest days of the Party. For example, in 1939, Party leader Zhou Enlai advocated 'nestling intelligence within the united front' and 'using the united front to push forth intelligence.'[47] The state of affairs is unchanged today: the united front system provides networks, cover and institutions that intelligence agencies use for their own purposes. The same methods of political influence and infiltration that led to the Party's 1949 victory were later trialled in the US before being used by the MSS Social Investigation Bureau and People's Liberation Army for their influence operations across the globe.

History provides another angle on the Social Investigation Bureau's work. Its name harks back to the Social Affairs Department, the Party's primary intelligence agency during the last decade of the Chinese Civil War.[48] Like the MSS, which counts the Social Affairs Department as one of its predecessors, espionage, analysis, counterintelligence and protection work were integrated under it.[49] And like today's Social Investigation Bureau, the Social Affairs Department heavily used united front networks to meet and recruit agents.[50]

Key to understanding the Social Affairs Department's legacy is its massive expansion of efforts to understand the Party's foes, 'friendly parties', social groups and other societies. 'Our understanding is still rough, patchy and cartoonish, and lacks a thorough understanding of the system. The ways of subjectivism and bureaucratism still haven't been entirely eradicated,' the Party Central Committee complained in 1941.[51] In order to remedy this, the whole Party was urged to contribute to 'investigation and research' under the coordination of the Central Social Department.[52] The targets of this information-gathering exercise were varied and broad: 'a village, a district, a county, a city, a village, an army, a division, a factory, a store, a school, a problem.' The key was understanding the classes of a society and the relationships within it, and on that basis recognising contradictions or cracks that could be exploited. As a young Mao Zedong wrote in 1925, 'Who are our enemies? Who are our friends? This is the revolution's foremost question.'[53]

Leading scholars, journalists, religious figures, bandit chiefs, overseas activists and even famous prostitutes were subjects of this effort. Dossiers reaching up to thousands of words were to be compiled on each person, recounting their lives, histories, ambitions, interests and weaknesses in order to determine the appropriate way to recruit, influence or marginalise them.[54] An official Chinese intelligence history describes how the Party carried out these 'social investigations' during the Chinese Civil War to identify targets for recruitment behind enemy lines who could help the invading communist army take and then occupy key municipalities.[55]

The MSS's Social Investigation Bureau's dozens of front organisations used to mediate and exploit China's interactions with the outside world are the legacy of those Civil War tactics. These facades have given the MSS a front seat in China's opening to the rest of the world. Foreigners hoping to visit China could be directed to MSS travel agents. International writers, self-aggrandising politicians and business leaders shopping around manuscripts of their memoirs, novels or poetry could have them translated and published by the MSS. They could mingle with peers in MSS-run associations and set up long-lasting friendships and exchanges. Wealthy and well-connected foreign philanthropists could find a conduit for their generosity in one of several MSS-controlled charities. When Australia's Edith Cowan University explored partnerships with Chinese universities, undercover Social Investigation Bureau officers were there to help build bridges.[56] Front organisations such as CICEC have held international conferences on technologies such as microelectronics, space propulsion and semiconductors – tailor-made settings for economic espionage.[57]

The MSS's commitment to running these groups like genuine cultural associations sometimes led to comical results. Richard Clayderman, the popular French pianist, found his largest audience in China with help from the MSS. Known to millions of Chinese fans as the 'Prince of Romantic Piano', Clayderman's initial tours in China were organised by the Social Investigation Bureau's arts company.[58] Clayderman was certainly clueless to the MSS's hand, but the agency probably found the relationship helpful for giving its front groups some status in France and providing officers excuses to travel there. The MSS front group also brought Spanish pop star Julio Iglesias to China, where he became the first Western entertainer to perform live on Chinese state television.[59] Years earlier, the Guangdong International Culture Exchange Center, a branch of CICEC run by the Guangdong State Security Department, hosted Wham! frontman George Michael on the band's 1985 tour of China. A photo of the banquet held for Wham! shows Michael sitting beside the MSS's Wang Shuren, a senior spy who worked in the Chinese embassy in Cambodia before building a specialisation in smuggling agents into Hong Kong.[60]

The thousands of employees and members of these front organisations would also serve as a recruiting ground for both future officers and assets. Young, intelligent and linguistically gifted university students might have enjoyed MSS-run magazines about the foreign world and decided to work for them after graduating, not knowing who was paying the bills. Front groups with members from the business world make convenient channels for arranging covers or new identities for MSS officers as businesspeople. The MSS also forges symbiotic relationships with business leaders who receive political protection in exchange for enriching its officers and serving as high-level intermediaries in their operations.[61] To give one example, in 2016 *The Wall Street Journal* revealed that a Chinese intelligence officer was suspected of masterminding a plot to have a Macanese billionaire bribe United Nations officials.[62] In another case, a since-deleted Chinese state media article reported that a wealthy tai chi master (also an active member of CICEC) was claiming to be affiliated with the MSS 12th Bureau and showed off photos of himself with Party leaders.[63]

The overseas activities of these fronts help MSS officers travel abroad and identify recruitment targets. For example, officers could be embedded inside a film crew going to France to interview actors, join a conference delegation, or act as escorts to a troupe of dancers going abroad. Once overseas, they might disappear, perhaps to meet an agent or collect stolen documents.

MSS politics

For all the Party's emphasis on the rich traditions of the united front, the limitations placed on the early MSS are a defining part of the Social

Investigation Bureau story. Counterintuitively, it's these constraints that helped craft MSS influence operations into the powerful weapon they are today.

In 1985, Deng Xiaoping forced MSS officers out of China's embassies, favouring his friends in military intelligence.[64] With few exceptions, the MSS was prohibited from using Chinese diplomatic missions to manage clandestine agents abroad.[65] Before then, intelligence gathering was such a feature of Chinese diplomatic life that one insider recalled how Deng's direction sparked uproar from China's embassy in India, but they had to comply.[66] Around the same time, the MSS also lost much of its access to plum journalistic posts in Xinhua and the *People's Daily*, which forced it in turn to rely on more unofficial forms of cover and find other Chinese newspapers willing to let the MSS run its foreign correspondents.[67]

Without the freedom to work from diplomatic missions until perhaps the late 1990s, the MSS developed a unique methodology for its operations. Officers posted overseas, often as journalists with newspapers such as the *Guangming Daily*, *China Youth Daily*, *China Economic Daily* and Shanghai's *Wenhui Bao*, were famously cautious in Western countries during this early period. Rarely were they caught doing anything untoward for a journalist, which still gave them broad latitude to gather political intelligence as they met and 'interviewed' sources. Apart from not wanting to stick their necks out, they did so because the hard business of recruiting agents was often done within China – especially by the Social Investigation Bureau. The bureau was the best-placed unit in MSS headquarters to recruit agents and influence outsiders because of its unrivalled ability to plug itself into existing united front networks and an array of front organisations through which it invited foreigners to China and dispatched spies abroad.

Why did the MSS face these unusual restrictions? The story goes back to the political struggles behind the MSS's founding, and a scandal shortly after.

In 1985, Ling Yun, the first minister of state security, was fired after just two years in the job and denied the appellations normally awarded to someone of his status.[68] His second in command responsible for foreign intelligence left soon after, reappearing as the secretary-general of China's peak united front forum, the Chinese People's Political Consultative Conference.[69] They'd taken the fall for one of China's greatest intelligence blunders: the defection of MSS officer Yu Qiangsheng earlier that year.

The CIA recruited Yu, the son of a high-ranking revolutionary, before the MSS was even established. Many spies had their cover blown as Yu shared his knowledge of Chinese espionage networks. In the process, the CIA uncovered two key overseas agents of the MSS, reflecting the ministry's main predecessors: the Central Investigation Department and the Ministry of Public Security.[70]

French diplomat Bernard Boursicot, arrested in 1983, was the first to fall because of information shared by Yu.[71] Starting in 1964, the Central Investigation Department, then the Party's premier foreign intelligence organisation, hatched a sensational scheme to recruit him. At a diplomatic function, the naïve and young Boursicot was befriended by Shi Peipu, a Peking opera actor who specialised in female roles. Incredibly, Shi convinced Boursicot that he was actually a woman. Boursicot fell in love and was so credulous and sexually inexperienced that he believed he had fathered a son with Shi – actually an adopted Uyghur boy. By 1970 Shi introduced Boursicot to his handlers from the Central Investigation Department, and he began providing them classified information. The case was as tantalising as it was tragic: Boursicot tried to kill himself after learning during his trial that Shi was in fact a man.

Then, as the US government prepared to smuggle Yu out of China, it acted against one of its own, arresting retired CIA analyst and translator Larry Wu-tai Chin, who was mostly handled by the Ministry of Public Security. Often simply characterised as China's police force, the public security agency has a long history of clandestine foreign operations.[72] Chin, who'd secretly worked for the Party for forty years, was found suffocated in a plastic bag as he awaited his court sentencing in 1986.

With its creation, the MSS subsumed these two intelligence organisations, incorporating the entire Central Investigation Department and significant chunks of the Ministry of Public Security's intelligence units.[73] At face value, this looked like a reasonable renovation of

China's intelligence apparatus. By combining the law enforcement and counterintelligence powers of the Ministry of Public Security with the Central Investigation Department's foreign expertise, the result would be a potent and comprehensive agency with responsibilities similar to the Soviet Union's KGB. This is more or less the official story – that Deng Xiaoping and the Party's 'deep analysis' of risks posed by China's opening to the world resulted in a remodelling of the intelligence apparatus.[74] And, as a symbol of reformist trends, the MSS reports to China's government – the State Council – and not the Party itself.

In reality, animal spirits and elite politics defined the MSS's creation even more than rational explanations. Moulding the MSS was in part a process of reckoning with the unresolved legacy of the Cultural Revolution, which had ended with Chairman Mao's death in 1976, and establishing Deng Xiaoping's primacy.

Both the Central Investigation Department and Ministry of Public Security had been wrecked by the Cultural Revolution.[75] Most of their leaders were locked up in Beijing's notorious Qincheng Prison, where prisoners were beaten and administered experimental drugs.[76] The remnants of both agencies were also enlisted to help investigate and purge fallen Party leaders.[77] Years after the Cultural Revolution, workstreams still needed to be rebuilt and internal rifts continued to cripple morale.

The Central Investigation Department's head, Luo Qingchang, was particularly divisive.[78] Wronged veterans of the department pointed the finger at him for their imprisonment during the Cultural Revolution.[79] Party historian Gao Wenqian points out that it was unusual that Luo was never purged during the Cultural Revolution.[80]

Luo and Deng Xiaoping developed a deep loathing for each other. Luo's attitude was common among the older generation of intelligence officers, who didn't see Deng, a Red Army man, as one of their own.[81] Deng, for his part, sought to rein in Luo's powers. Two former officers of the Central Investigation Department revealed that Deng first ordered the department to pull its people out of Chinese embassies in 1978, but Luo told his officers to ignore the directive.[82] Luo responded the next year by writing publicly about his close relationship with the late premier Zhou Enlai, framing himself as an inheritor of Zhou's legacy when Deng was also viewed as Zhou's successor.[83]

Deng's ultimate solution was to disband the Central Investigation Department, forcing Luo into retirement. As early as 1981, Party officials began exploring the idea of a new intelligence agency to replace the embattled agency.[84] Xi Zhongxun, the father of Xi Jinping, and two senior foreign affairs officials were successively sent in to assess the situation in the department. Meeting with its leadership in 1982, Xi Zhongxun stressed the importance of passing knowledge down to younger generations and sorting out issues left over from the Cultural Revolution. Some would have to gather the courage to self-criticise, he told them.[85] It was a sign of the end to come.

The result was the MSS, a compromise between Deng and Party elders who were themselves of the intelligence world. Combining the Ministry of Public Security's law enforcement powers with the Central Investigation Department's intelligence work amounted to a substantial expansion of its abilities when Deng could have simply abolished the Central Investigation Department and swept its remnants into his favoured military intelligence system. Likewise, Deng succeeded in pushing Luo into retirement and approved of the new agency's chief, but Luo's protégé stayed on as a deputy head of the MSS.[86]

The role played by Party leader Chen Yun may have proved decisive. He'd been head of the Party's first intelligence agency fifty years earlier, stood atop a different faction of Chinese politics to Deng and was among those consulted about the MSS's creation.[87] Chen was a creature of the civilian intelligence system. This was his bastion. These were his people. He had a history of throwing his weight behind the intelligence community.[88]

The compromise between these two wings of Chinese politics has given the appearance that the MSS was meant to be apolitical.[89] On the contrary, its political significance meant that neither side could allow the other to gain too much influence over it. It's no coincidence that it has since been involved in several elite corruption scandals, both as accomplice and investigator.[90] The corruption case that Party rivals used to bring down Beijing mayor Chen Xitong in 1995, then China's largest financial scandal, centred on a company that was in fact a front for the MSS's Beijing bureau.[91] In 2012, an MSS vice minister personally flew to the southwestern city of Chengdu to apprehend a close associate of Xi Jinping's main rival, who attempted to defect to the American consulate.[92]

Whichever side of Party politics MSS leaders may lean towards, loyalty to the Party has always been treated as the most important foundation for state security work. The message from the MSS's crest is clear: the Party's hammer and sickle sit above the five stars of the country's flag. Its creation was negotiated and approved by Party leaders many months before it passed through the country's powerless legislature.[93] While officially subordinate to the State Council, the MSS has been run by the Party through its Central Political-Legal Affairs Commission, which provides leadership over security, law enforcement and justice agencies.[94] The ministry's training materials hardly mention loyalty to the people, and its officers are rigorously selected for their own political purity as well as the backgrounds of their family members. Many are the descendants of revolutionaries or intelligence officers such as Peng Zhen and Marshall Zhu De.[95]

As Vice Minister Yu Fang once said about the process of selecting intelligence officers, 'We first look at their political qualities, meaning their beliefs and their belief in communism. What that means now is their loyalty to the Fatherland. This aspect is paramount – their ideological character must be good.'[96] Having served undercover in the UK and America as 'Yu Enguang' for over a decade, he was well positioned to comment on the matter. Similarly, an internal manual for MSS officers repeatedly stresses three core traits: 'absolute loyalty to the Party', a willingness to become a 'nameless hero', and, like the lotus of Buddhism, the ability to 'rise through mud unsoiled'.[97] These are the Party's spies, a vanguard within a vanguard. Politics, domestic or foreign, is their bread and butter.

CHAPTER 4

A BLOODBATH MARKS A NEW ERA

A FTER THE TIANANMEN massacre of 4 June, the MSS's leader-ship reflected that '1989 had been an unusual year'. International capitalists, they claimed in an annual review, had been using China's growing openness to catalyse a transition towards liberal democracy. However, 'in the trial by blood and fire on the verge of spring and summer last year, state security personnel showed the elevated aware-ness and excellent quality of their absolute loyalty to the Chinese Communist Party and the state'.[1] By the MSS's own account, it had protected the Party by catching supposed Taiwanese spies and expelling American journalist John Pomfret, who was rewarded for his reports on the protests with the charge of stealing state secrets.[2] The messy Soros incident and the tide of defections in the massacre's aftermath was left out of this official narrative.

The massacre marked a new era for China and the MSS. The Party establishment had laid out its position with the blood of protestors: it wasn't going to accept 'peaceful evolution' of China into a liberal democracy. Those in the Party leadership who'd sympathised with the protests or were too close to ousted leader Zhao Ziyang had their careers cut short. In the years since, the Party has closely studied the disintegra-tion of the Soviet Union, which has only strengthened its conviction to never tread that path.[3] Amid these political currents, the Social Investigation Bureau led MSS efforts to aggressively build networks abroad, placing its officers and assets close to the centre of foreign powers and intelligence agencies. From humble beginnings, these MSS operations did much more than protect the Party from threats; they slowly but surely worked their way into the heart of American policymaking and the world's understanding of China.

This low point in the Party's morality and international standing was also a chance to start afresh and rebuild China's relations with the rest of the world. The Party and the MSS in particular sought to use the massacre as the pretext for a feigned reinvention.

Blood had been shed, but the Party was regretful. It needed time, tolerance, understanding and support from the West to liberalise and integrate into the international rules-based order. Or so the line goes. In the eyes of George Soros, whose early effort to promote open society in China met its end in 1989, the massacre helped create an 'independent intelligentsia' in China and spelled the beginning of the end for the Party's hardliners.[4]

The picture inside the Party was very different. Reformists were weaker than ever, and the security state went into overdrive. Six months after the massacre, outstanding intelligence officers were personally awarded by Qiao Shi, chief of the Party's justice and security system, for their contributions over the six years of the infant ministry's existence.[5] Rather than prompting solemn reflection, the massacre meant loyal Party members in the MSS were praised for their conviction. The message was that the MSS should be steeled by 1989's atrocities. It was a bloody baptism from which the agency would emerge more powerful, adventurous and confident.

Little is known about how officers of the MSS really reacted to the military crackdown. China's intelligence agencies are bastions of ideological conservatism eager to see the black hand of foreign enemies behind such domestic unrest. Although the Party's public rhetoric has become modern and inclusive of capitalists, a confidential history of Chinese military political warfare published a decade after the massacre revealed that intelligence agencies were still guided by concepts, such as class struggle, that had long been cut out of official language.[6]

To the doyens of the intelligence community, the year's events deepened their fears about the West and thereby their belief in steeling the Party for future struggle. In 1990, Chen Yun, one of the Party's highest leaders and a former spymaster, asked his fellow elders to study imperialism, warning that it was still a force to be reckoned with. Citing Chen's advice, Luo Qingchang, the last head of the MSS's predecessor agency, declared to a gathering of retired spies that 'US relations with China can't return to how they were ten years ago. The United States is an imperialist country, and as long as we're socialist it won't be at ease and will put pressure on us.'[7]

On the other hand, some intelligence officers were deeply unsettled by the events of June 1989. The aftermath of the massacre saw several officers defect to the West. Intelligence officers had suffered horrendously in various internal purges since the 1930s, their ties to the enemy turned into evidence of 'counterrevolutionary activities'. They had good reason to be sceptical of the Party's more extreme actions.[8] Some of them had only been rehabilitated years earlier. The awards issued to MSS officers in December 1989 were an effort to reaffirm the agency's integrity and reputation, both to its officer cadre and to the Party's leadership, most of whom no longer had personal experience as underground revolutionaries and spies. Some of those awarded were long-retired spies whose achievements dated to the 1940s.[9]

The old guard: Mao Guohua

One of the MSS's old guard, Mao Guohua, took charge of the Social Investigation Bureau around this time and helped set in place networks that were so powerfully used for influence operations in later years. A pencil-thin and bespectacled intelligence veteran, Mao was a leading force in MSS operations against the United States. He was born in 1933 in Xikou, the same home town as Kuomintang leader Chiang Kai-shek. The two were distantly related, and Chiang's first wife shared Mao Guohua's surname.[10]

Mao's national service began in December 1950. Just seventeen years old, he signed up to a 'Resist America and Support Korea' military academy when Chinese forces intervened in the Korean War. Expecting to be sent into battle, he was instead chosen to join an elite group of students destined to serve on the covert front.[11] The 495 students, handpicked from high schools across the country, were enrolled in Beijing's Foreign Languages School, which employed the same secretive and closed recruitment system as military research institutes at the time.[12] There he was taught English by Isabel Crook, a Chinese-born Canadian communist whose husband once spied on George Orwell for Stalin's NKVD.[13]

Over the following years, Mao built up what might be the most extensive list of covers used by a Chinese intelligence officer. He exemplified the traditions of united front work and 'social investigations' that are central to the Party's influence operations. On a 1980 trip to Australia, Mao appeared as a journalist. Later he donned the hats of a book publisher, cultural official, university alumni association representative and medical association official.[14]

After being sent to one of the country's notorious labour reform camps during the Cultural Revolution – his ties to the Chiang family meant he was accused of being a rightist and traitor – he was brought back into the Party's fold to help manage Nixon's historic visit to China in 1972.[15] He was assigned as a minder for members of the nearly hundred-strong American press corps covering Nixon's visit.[16] The need for fluent English speakers with experience handling foreigners – nearly all of whom would have run into trouble during the Cultural Revolution – outweighed questions about Mao's politics.

The American journalists, with few exceptions, were clueless about China. The first impressions they formed with Mao's help would shape American public sentiment and coverage. As one participant later said, 'I knew nothing about China. Nobody had any idea what it looked like. It really was like going on the moon.'[17] Mao Guohua was chosen to accompany one of the only journalists with experience in China, Theodore White, *Time* magazine's China bureau chief during World War Two.[18]

In the end, it was a success. The press corps were frustrated by their minders, who accompanied them day and night and stuck like glue to the Party line. Nonetheless, China, which had been almost inaccessible to Americans since 1949, entranced them. Suddenly, a rich and expansive country had opened before their eyes in a way that defied any Cold War caricatures. China was still communist, but its animosity towards the Soviet Union and relationship with Vietnam could also be helpful to the United States.

For its part, the Chinese government managed to win subtle concessions from the United States in its negotiations with national security advisor Henry Kissinger. The joint communiqué they produced stated that 'all Chinese on either side of the Taiwan Strait maintain there is but one China and that Taiwan is a part of China', a controversial and now increasingly inaccurate claim. No mention was made of the mutual defence treaty between the US and the Republic of China in Taiwan.[19]

But to American television viewers, 'China had suddenly come alive, and all the rest is commentary', one reporter who covered the trip reflected.[20] It was perhaps the most important US presidential trip in history. The unabashed optimism it embodied would come to define much of the next forty years of US–China relations.

Mao Guohua was one of dozens, if not hundreds, of minders employed for Nixon's 1972 visit to China. But by the late eighties he would lead the MSS's Social Investigation Bureau and personally handle one of its most notorious US spies, Katrina Leung.

Triple cross: Katrina Leung
Katrina Leung was the FBI's star source on China for eighteen years.

An active member of the Los Angeles Chinese community, she had an uncanny ability to gather information not just on activities in California but also within China. Her first serious mission sent her into a Chinese prison. In 1983, the FBI tasked her to visit Hanson Huang, an old friend who'd been convicted of espionage in China. Although he was a US citizen, diplomats were having trouble arranging consular access to him.[21] He'd been a person of interest in an ongoing investigation into PRC espionage against the US nuclear weapons program but had somehow gotten on the bad side of the MSS. Now the FBI thought there was a chance he could be flipped – turned into an asset for US intelligence. Somehow, Leung pulled off the prison meeting, even if the information she gleaned from it was of little value.[22]

J. J. Smith, the FBI counterintelligence officer who recruited Leung, played a dangerous game from the beginning. She'd come across the FBI's radar well before Smith approached her and came from murky origins. As the US government report on her later concluded, 'Leung's family background is unclear.' She arrived in the United States in 1970, aged around sixteen, alongside a woman who claimed to be her mother but was probably her aunt. Her passport was Taiwanese but stated that she was born in China's Guangdong province.[23]

Soon after she arrived in America, Leung attracted the FBI's attention. As a college student she joined the pro-China Diaoyu Islands movement, which advocated for China's sovereignty over what Japan calls the Senkaku Islands. China, which didn't yet have an embassy in the United States, made contact with Leung and the student movement through a Chinese official whom the FBI believed was an intelligence officer.[24] During this period she also became active in the National Association of Chinese-Americans, a pro-Beijing advocacy group with branches across the country that included leading scientists among its members.[25] An entry on the association from the 1992 *China United Front Dictionary* described it as America's largest 'Chinese political organisation', active in promoting ethnic Chinese political candidates.[26] Its inaugural president, theoretical physicist Yang Chen-Ning, was a Nobel laureate who was among the first American visitors to China during the Cultural Revolution, where he was chaperoned by intelligence officers.[27] He would eventually renounce his US citizenship and move to China.

Katrina Leung's husband told journalist David Wise that her activism as a university student 'was the beginning of her trouble', bringing her into the orbit of China's intelligence networks. Things got a lot more concerning after she moved to Los Angeles in 1980, where she worked for a trading company that was under active FBI investigation for economic espionage.[28] Even her residence was suspect. The FBI described her apartment building as a 'nest of spies' because many of its inhabitants were connected to Chinese intelligence.[29] It wasn't long before Leung herself came under investigation, but the case languished under an FBI agent who was disinterested in counterintelligence work.

'The FBI knew little about China's quest for technology,' a later US government assessment stated.[30]

A year after the bureau's investigation into Leung petered out, J.J. Smith had recruited her as a paid informant, codenamed Parlor Maid. It's typical of intelligence agencies to try to recruit agents of foreign powers. The same Chinese intelligence links that brought her under scrutiny could also be advantageous if carefully managed, helping the US government gain greater insight into covert CCP operations. Smith had run background checks on her, and she spun a convincing tale about how she'd woken up to the reality of China under communist rule and distanced herself from the Diaoyu Islands activists, but her long-running links to the CCP and its united front work weren't fully appreciated. She leant into American overconfidence and hubris towards China to great effect. Born a communist, 'she's now a rock-ribbed Republican', Smith reportedly told his colleagues.[31] The year after he recruited her, Smith, a married man, took her on as his mistress. She would later initiate an affair with a second FBI counterintelligence officer.

Smith wanted to turn her into more than a low-level source of information on the LA Chinese community. She was asked to tout her connections to the FBI and build up her reputation as a Chinese community leader, then pay a visit to the MSS at its Xiyuan headquarters in Beijing. She was now a double agent for the FBI, actively building a relationship with Chinese intelligence at America's behest. As a star source of information on CCP politics and intelligence agencies, she was handsomely rewarded. In total, she raked in US$1.7 million for services and expenses from the bureau on top of millions from business activities made possible by her friendships with Chinese officials.[32] Leung's successes were Smith's too. In 1989 he won the HUMINT (Human Intelligence) Collector of the Year Award from the CIA, perhaps for Leung's reporting from within China on elite politics after the Tiananmen massacre.[33]

Before long, the close professional and romantic relationship between Smith and Leung crossed another line. Smith treated her 'as though she was a member of his squad', investigators later concluded. The treasured information Leung was feeding him placed Smith beyond reproach – his supervisor was later criticised for treating him deferentially – and he exploited this to check classified documents out from the office and into his briefcase as he went to visit Leung at her home.[34]

It wasn't long before evidence pointing to Leung's deception began piling up. In 1987, surveillance found that she'd asked a Chinese diplomat to call her from a payphone, implying she knew the consulate was bugged and didn't want the FBI to listen in on the conversation. The bureau's investigation into the matter was eagerly closed up after they realised Leung was Smith's asset.[35] No one followed up on it.

In 1990, the FBI learnt that Leung told the Chinese consulate it had been bugged.[36] Somehow, she also disclosed a 'highly classified FBI counterintelligence program' that Smith himself wasn't privy to. Again, the bureau's response to the incident went nowhere. Smith and Parlor Maid were beyond reproach. Too much had been invested in the pair for the hundreds of reports they'd produced to all be brought into doubt.[37]

Later that year, FBI agent William Cleveland, who'd begun an affair with Leung the year prior, bumped into a man Cleveland's colleague called 'the subject of the single most important investigation of [Cleveland's] career'. Even more puzzling, this random encounter happened in the most improbable of places – China, with its billion inhabitants. Cleveland had joined a State Department group to assess the security of its diplomatic facilities in China and was wandering around a hotel in northeastern China when he stumbled upon Gwo-Bao Min. A former US government nuclear weapons scientist suspected of passing secrets to China, Min shared a mutual friend with Leung: Hanson Huang, the man Leung had been sent to visit in a Beijing prison back in 1983.[38]

What should have been the final red flag came in 1991. The US National Security Agency (NSA), responsible for signals intelligence and eavesdropping, recorded a phone call between none other than Mao Guohua of the MSS Social Investigation Bureau and a woman who introduced herself as Luo. She then proceeded to describe active, secret FBI investigations. The intercept made its way to William Cleveland, who recognised the voice of the woman he'd been having an affair with. It was Katrina Leung. To the FBI she was Parlor Maid; to China, she was 'Luo Zhongshan', a double or even triple agent. This side of Leung's relationship with the MSS was all news to the FBI.

Cleveland hurriedly phoned his colleague from the China trip: 'They knew we were coming even before we left.'[39] He thought his encounter with Gwo-Bao Min was connected to Leung and probably a ploy to put the FBI officers off kilter. He also passed on the bad news to J.J. Smith.

Visibly upset, Smith confronted her. She had never told him about the codename or the phone call, but somehow managed to calm Smith down. Incredibly, Leung remained a paid FBI asset for years afterwards, and Smith was promoted to head the Los Angeles China Squad. The pair's relationship continued, and Leung kept scanning documents from Smith's briefcase when they met. The full implications of the intercepted phone call were buried. Smith assured his superiors the slip-up was under control. He told himself he'd regained her loyalty.[40]

What Smith didn't understand, or perhaps didn't want to understand, was that it looked like Leung had been working for China all along. From her very first mission – the trip into a Chinese prison – and later a visit to the MSS's headquarters from which she brought back footage of the compound, her ability to tread the narrow path of a double agent had been too good to be true. A more complete account of her betrayal would only surface, by pure chance, many years later.

Robert Swan Mueller III was sworn in as FBI director in August 2001. The September 11 attacks came weeks later, kicking off a massive expansion in counterterrorism work within intelligence communities around the world, expenditures that often came at the cost of counter-intelligence capabilities. Around the same time, US contractors delivered a custom-fitted jet to Beijing for China's president, Jiang Zemin. Almost immediately after it landed, the Boeing 767 was dismantled, stripped and forensically analysed on a military airfield. Somehow, the Chinese military's signals intelligence officers knew that American spies had riddled it with advanced satellite-activated listening devices.[41] The ensuing FBI investigation into a possible leak brought Katrina Leung under surveillance.

Mueller went 'ballistic' when the investigation uncovered Leung's relationship with Smith and hinted that the bureau had been infiltrated by China, according to journalist David Wise.[42] To make things worse, Leung was still being paid by the FBI as a source. The pair were arrested, but the judge dismissed the case against Leung due to prosecutorial misconduct arising from a technicality.[43] Smith negotiated a plea bargain and avoided jail time.[44] The two eventually married.

The bookseller: Xie Shanxiao

The story of Katrina Leung should have ended there. But in 2018 a retired Chinese public servant using the name 'Morning Bird's Song' began posting anecdotes, poetry and personal photographs onto WeChat, China's most popular social media platform. He'd worn many hats over the course of his fascinating life – student, metallurgist, book publisher, to name a few. He'd travelled the world, secretly met a future Taiwanese president, been among the first Chinese students sent to study in America after the Cultural Revolution and talked business with Murdoch's media empire.[45] And he'd met Katrina Leung in Los Angeles. He was Xie Shanxiao, a member of the MSS Social Investigation Bureau and one of Leung's handlers.

The stream of WeChat posts reveals new details about the Parlor Maid disaster, and the MSS's deep integration with united front networks and dedication to influence operations. Xie's official title was general manager of China International Culture Publishing Company, an MSS front company with Social Investigation Bureau chief Mao Guohua as its executive chairman.[46] Acting as a book publisher enabled Xie to befriend intellectuals in Taiwan, Hong Kong, Singapore, Japan and Los Angeles. It was a form of cover that allowed him to travel with ease into enemy territory. A testament to the MSS's focus on influence operations, its numerous publishing houses also served as vanity publishers to elites. In 1987, for example, the bureau was involved in publishing a poetry collection by Bangladesh's military dictator.[47]

Unlike Mao Guohua, Xie set foot in the United States several times, and even studied metallurgy at Ohio State University before returning to China as a technical intelligence analyst.[48] 'The moment I walked through Beijing Airport's security checkpoint, I realised I was about to tread upon a dark continent that hadn't been touched by the sunshine of socialism … A solemn feeling came over me and my heart suddenly grew nervous and terrified,' he wrote of his first trip to the United States.[49]

Xie's earliest liaisons in the United States brought him into the realm of influence operations targeting scientists. In January 1980, a Chinese physicist living in California published the first edition of *Science and Technology Review*. The hefty Chinese-language magazine featured interviews with and articles by Nobel laureates, and congratulatory letters from both Chinese and American leaders. According to Xie, distinguished Chinese American scientists who, like Leung, had been active members of the Diaoyu Islands movement, filled the periodical's editorial board.[50] 'I and many others ... feel that we should try to help China acquire more modern scientific knowledge,' Nobel laureate and *Science and Technology Review* co-founder Yang Chen-ning later said.[51] The FBI believed Qian Ning, the magazine's founder, had been sent to the United States by Chinese intelligence.[52]

Interviewed by journalist David Wise in 2009, Qian denied working for the MSS, maintaining she set up the magazine to 'help China understand the market economy' so as to promote reform even though conservatives were in power.[53] But by 1984 she was in touch with Xie Shanxiao. *Science and Technology Review* was penniless and had ceased publication. If Qian were indeed a Chinese spy, her likely backer no longer existed. The Central Investigation Department had been dissolved into the MSS the year before, and some of the department's overseas operatives were sometimes expected to scrounge for funds on their own. One complained that the agency 'had never been willing to spend money' on him and only gave him and his wife about US$200 when they were infiltrated into Hong Kong.[54] The details are unclear, but Xie, then working as an aviation technology intelligence analyst in China's military-industrial complex, became the magazine's China manager and restarted the publication, this time from Beijing.[55] Qian's ties to America's scientific elite had officially been handed over to China. Many of the magazine's affiliated academics eventually moved to China and were instrumental in setting up research ties between the countries.

Influence and espionage are inextricable in the Chinese Communist Party's intelligence operations. Gwo-Bao Min, the US nuclear weapons scientist suspected of spying for China, moonlighted as *Science and Technology Review*'s advertising manager. Qian, the magazine's publisher, once helped arrange for Min to visit China.[56]

Katrina Leung embodied this integration of influence and infiltration too. Though the sexiness of Leung's affair and betrayal of the FBI far eclipsed it, and the FBI's failure to appreciate it doomed its handling of Parlor Maid, the truth is that Leung was as much an agent of influence as a spy. She was a united front leader, what the Party calls an 'overseas Chinese leader' or *qiaoling*.[57] In fact, Chinese-language media reported that, a month after her arrest, Beijing's peak united front group for diaspora leaders accidentally published its new list of advisors with Leung included.[58]

The Party viewed Leung and her friends from the Diaoyu Islands movement as a bulwark from which it could supplant Taiwan's influence over American Chinese communities and build influence over US politics. Known as 'Little Taipei', Monterey Park is a city in Los Angeles County that's been a focus of those activities. When Xie led a Chinese publishing industry delegation to LA in 1988, representatives from a Chinese city were also in town to open a Chinese garden. Visiting the Monterey government office, they were shocked to see a stone memorial celebrating Monterey's sister city agreement with Taipei. The two sides were at an impasse – neither Monterey Park nor the Chinese representatives were willing to compromise on the matter of the memorial. So, in the dead of night, Xie and Peter Chow, who ran a Chinese bookstore with Katrina Leung, stole the stone tablet, loaded it into a van and dumped it in a vacant lot. After that, the ceremony went ahead.[59]

When Chow asked for Xie's help a year later, he wasn't let down. It was a month after the Tiananmen massacre. Chow and LA united front leader David Fon Lee were in Beijing to meet the president of China, Yang Shangkun, a former intelligence chief better known as a pivotal supporter of the bloody crackdown.[60] After the reception, Xie sat down with them. Chow and Leung's Monterey Books and Stationers was nearly bankrupt. They wanted the Chinese government to help. With President Yang's backing, Xie's publishing house invested in the store to become its majority owner, Lee its chairman, Xie its CEO and

Katrina Leung one of several directors. Three staff members provided by the MSS publishing corporation were sent to LA to run the newly reorganised business.[61]

President Yang was a patron of Parlor Maid too. Xie wrote of a book launch in Beijing where President Yang Shangkun 'made a beeline to Leung, who had received him on his trip to the United States'.[62] US government investigations found that Yang also arranged for US$100,000 to be wired to Leung because he 'liked her'.[63]

The bookstore was a minor errand compared to the mission Leung received from the MSS in 1990. Early one spring morning, Party General Secretary Jiang Zemin held an audience with Leung and the Social Investigation Bureau's Mao Guohua. The makeup of the group was almost as alarming as its topic: influencing US politics. Jiang wanted to know how next year's presidential election would turn out and encouraged Leung to involve herself in politics. Leung wrongly predicted that George H. W. Bush would keep office. 'We will give you the support you need,' he said. That evening, Mao and Leung retreated to her hotel, where they discussed the details of influencing the Republican Party. Mao's tasking was broad but the guidance clear: donate, mingle with politicians, and make friends for China.[64] A decade after her arrest, Leung wrote, 'I was generous with my donations, and used my generosity to get politicians to do things for me … in fact when those governors and mayors attended Chinese events it was because I'd "bought" their attendance.'[65] Ultimately, this meant FBI funds, Leung's wealth from doing business in China and Hong Kong, and a small amount of cash from Beijing were being mixed together and plugged into politics at the MSS's behest. Already, in 1990, the MSS was trying its hand at political influence operations in the United States. A decade later, it perfected this playbook.

A cesspool of corrupted cases
Leung's political activities alone may not have had a significant effect on politicians and their parties, but Xie's journals also point towards a more disturbing conclusion. Leung was one among a score of CCP-aligned Chinese 'community leaders' in the United States who were approached by the MSS in the eighties and nineties. On top of that, Xie reveals how the MSS began working its way into international media organisations.

As one former intelligence officer explained, there were at least fifteen or twenty other 'Parlor Maids' along the west coast – people who were both MSS assets and US intelligence sources. He described it as a 'cesspool of corrupted cases'.[66] For example, local restaurateur, travel agency owner and united front leader David Fon Lee was another FBI contact who was also in contact with Xie.[67] He was one of the only community leaders to publicly back Leung through her trial, and Leung in turn eulogised him as 'the person who had the greatest influence' on her after her father and grandfather. Lee described her as like a niece to him.[68]

US intelligence agencies were clearly out of their depth in a culture and language that the FBI in particular had little understanding of. The FBI failed to grasp the significance of the MSS's entanglement with united front work and the challenge it posed to its intelligence collection efforts by undermining the reliability of their assets in the local community. They were not alone. Until as late as 2016, counterintelligence agencies around the world paid scant attention to united front work, viewing it as trivial or incidental to their core work of catching people who tried to steal classified information. But the enmeshing of open influence peddling and clandestine operations – Chinese intelligence's integration of 'black' and 'white' activities – is slowly seeing broader recognition.

In contrast, operating in diaspora communities has always been a core modus operandi of Chinese intelligence agencies that predates the PRC's founding. They excel at it. Since the CCP's inception, its united front efforts have sought to organise and rally sympathetic ethnic Chinese communities to its cause. In fact, all major Chinese revolutionary movements in modern history did the same. Expatriate Chinese communities helped provide the funding, refuge and radical ideas that catalysed the Chinese revolution of 1911, ending imperial rule over China, and the communist takeover after that.

It was also the inadequacies of Chinese intelligence agencies that pushed them towards recruiting people who spoke their language and came from their culture, if not from mainland China itself. A string of recent espionage cases in the United States and Europe show that the MSS is now more than willing and able to recruit foreigners, including foreign intelligence officials, but one intelligence veteran told me that his Chinese counterparts 'always sucked at languages'.[69] Russian aside, genuine foreign-language experts were relatively rare in China before the 1980s. Mao Guohua himself had atrocious English.[70] Even today, the MSS continues to treat personal and familial political loyalty, not linguistic or analytical ability, as the most important criterion when recruiting officers who will engage with outsiders. In a recent and unusually brazen approach, Canadian scholar Charles Burton was ambushed in Shanghai by MSS Canada Desk officers who had a 'sophisticated grasp of the minutiae of Canada-China relations' but no fluency in the English language.[71] University recruitment notices issued by the MSS often clarify that Party members, Communist Youth League members and student representative cadres are preferred.[72] Those with significant overseas experience or family connections to the outside world are likely to be weeded out in the early stages of vetting.

It should therefore come as no surprise that one of the MSS's first uses for its premier front group, CICEC, was to hold a gathering of diaspora Chinese in late 1984, including many from the US west coast. Celebrating the thirty-fifth anniversary of the PRC's founding, CICEC's event attracted over fifty foreign attendees who went on to become leading promoters of the Party abroad. 'China is their original home, and revitalising China is the duty of all descendants of the Yellow Emperor,' the *People's Daily* wrote in coverage of the event.[73] Many of their individuals have well-documented united front links, but the fact that they were also courted by the MSS shows how the two spheres intersect.

Peng Chong, the trusted Party elder who was CICEC's original figurehead, addressed the group. The *People's Daily* summarised his speech: 'The compatriots and friends here today are all experts, scholars and notable figures with social influence and academic prestige ... who have played important roles and worked hard for friendship and cooperation between our country and other countries.'[74]

Some of those present may have innocently answered Peng's call through their promotion of Chinese art and culture. Wan-go Weng, described by the Museum of Fine Arts Boston in 2018 as 'one of the most respected collectors and connoisseurs of Chinese painting in the world', was among those who attended the event.[75]

Another guest, San Francisco Chinese newspaper publisher Huang Yunji, was at least a degree removed from espionage.[76] One of his newspaper editors, Russell Lowe, went on to spend twenty years working in the Californian office of Senator Dianne Feinstein before being exposed as an MSS asset in 2018, probably working for the Social Investigation Bureau.[77] One other newspaper staff member later became a city councillor.[78] Also at the CICEC reception was journalist Weng Shao-chiu, who ran united front groups such as the San Francisco Council for the Promotion of the Peaceful Reunification of China that advocated for Beijing's overseas interests.[79]

Similarly, Xie Shanxiao's contacts through the publishing business went far beyond Katrina Leung. Liu Bing, CEO of another Chinese bookstore in Monterey, was one of International Culture Publishing Corporation's overseas advisors.[80] So was Sally Aw, then publisher of one of Hong Kong's largest newspapers, *Sing Tao Daily*. In 1992, Aw agreed to establish a magazine with the MSS publishing company after running into financial troubles, the first such joint venture publication in China. It was a massive win for the Party as it prepared for the 1997 Hong Kong handover. Aw had been 'pro-Taiwan and anti-CCP' at first, Xie writes, but was later appointed to the Party's top united front forum, the Chinese People's Political Consultative Conference.[81] *Sing Tao*, which has editions in Canada, Europe, Australia and the United States, described its political position in 1988 as 'neutral but leaning towards supporting the government of the Republic of China', but the 1990s saw it fall under greater self-censorship and a pro-CCP editorial line.[82] Since then, the newspaper's ownership has changed hands, bringing it closer to the CCP. Today the outlet is officially designated by the US government as a foreign agent involved in political influence efforts.[83]

At one stage, Xie claimed International Culture Publishing Corporation was negotiating a partnership with Rupert Murdoch's News Corporation before it was called off when the media giant published two books that 'hurt US–China friendly relations, attracting the fury of the central leadership'.[84]

CHAPTER 5

CHINAGATE: THE PLOT TO BUY THE WHITE HOUSE

IN THE YEARS before Katrina Leung's arrest in 2003, China's intelligence agencies prepared for a far more ambitious gambit: an attempt to buy influence in the White House.

California was a treasured staging ground for political influence operations and economic espionage. Its extensive united front networks, clusters of advanced technology and undeniable electoral heft make it prime territory for MSS officers. Today, the state holds the honour of having an MSS unit dedicated to influence and intelligence work in it.[1]

But Washington, DC, the nation's capital, is where operations ultimately come to fruition. These efforts successfully converted MSS cunning into new friendships for the Party and an international environment permissive of China's rise. By patiently working on national leaders, Congress, diplomats, think tanks and business leaders, the MSS convinced key decision-makers that China would gradually liberalise while averting their gaze from the Party's ambitions and authoritarianism. This was the Party's effort to lull the rest of the world into complacency as it built up its strength and never forgot its revolutionary core.

A newly uncovered document reveals the framework behind these covert influence operations. Buried on page 1433 of the second volume of a collection of theses by mid-career officials studying at the Central Party School in 1997, it's no surprise it never attracted outside attention until now. Almost casual in tone, the paper offers 'A few thoughts on strengthening work on the US Congress' from the Ministry of State Security 2nd Bureau's freshly appointed chief, Gao Yichen.[2] Emphasising using legal means to cultivate opinion leaders and build influence across American society, business and politics, Gao's writings help unravel the MSS's deliberate effort to influence and manipulate US perceptions of China.

When he laid out his thoughts on influence operations, Gao had just returned to Beijing after five years as 'Gao Fengyi', a journalist for the *Guangming Daily* in Washington, DC. Appointed head of what's known as the MSS's 'open-line' operations bureau, he now managed the agency's network of spies posing as diplomats, journalists, and trade and tourism representatives. These individuals all have some degree of overt government affiliation and an 'open line' to Chinese diplomatic missions and officials.[3] Political intelligence is a core part of their work. The distinction is an important one in MSS tradecraft, contrasting with 'illegals' operating under deep cover, for example as private business-people. Under his pseudonym, Gao was also a vice president of CICEC. After a few years in charge of the open-line bureau, he was promoted to vice minister of the MSS.[4]

Gao, like his fellow undercover journalist and MSS US expert Yu Fang, was a tall native of China's northeast. He claimed to be fluent in Russian and French in addition to English and had also worked undercover in Moscow.[5] This career spy hardly held up his pretence of being a foreign correspondent. He enjoyed the mystique of the intelligence world and wore mirror-lens aviator sunglasses indoors. 'He had this sleazy look about him,' said a US official who met him several times. 'He should have had MSS tattooed on his forehead.'[6] Despite this, the insights he gained into American politics have left their mark on today's MSS influence operations.

It was an exciting time to live and work in the heart of American power. 'When I arrived in Washington, my first impression was its atmosphere of peace and tranquillity that's hard to come by in capital cities,' Gao later wrote.[7] Scandal and uncertainty lay below the city's clean architecture and broad avenues. Gao knew DC was 'erupting with incidents' – and espionage. The Cold War had ended but left in its wake a whole new set of security challenges for Washington. Russia, the former Eastern Bloc, China and the Middle East were at the top of the pile.

The Chinagate scandal

Gao's recent experience with bungled influence operations in DC undoubtedly inspired his paper on influencing Congress. He watched and might have participated in poorly coordinated and immature efforts to influence the 1996 presidential election, dubbed 'Chinagate' by the US media. The story of the incident, or rather incidents, is as politicised as it is convoluted because it involved a messy web of alleged Party agents making illegal donations to Clinton's presidential campaign.

The operations implicated multinational corporations, the owner of a small faxing business, a restaurateur, a Buddhist temple, a Thai government lobbyist, and the head of Chinese military intelligence in attempts to cosy up to both sides of US politics. Little seemed to connect this unlikely cast but their often murky ties to the Chinese Communist Party.[8] One after another, they popped up as donors to the Democratic National Committee, inside the White House, or at a function with Republican Speaker of the House Newt Gingrich. It was an 'intercontinental connect-the-dots puzzle in which there are plenty of dots but few firm connections', reported *The Washington Post.*[9]

Johnny Chung was at the heart of the controversy. An Asia expert at the White House's National Security Council described Chung best in an internal memo, calling him a 'hustler'. Born in Taiwan, Chung rapidly transformed himself from a struggling businessman into a frequent visitor to the White House with enough spare cash to give generously to the Democratic Party. In 1994, his Automated Intelligence Systems – not a clandestine organisation but a 'blastfax' business that could push out thousands of faxes on command – made less than US$20,000.[10] After making a meagre donation to the Democrats that year, he was invited to join, at his own cost, a Department of Commerce trip to China.

Chung's biggest kickbacks from the visit were the photos he snapped with US officials that could help promote his business ventures. But it was on this trip that he first entered the Chinagate story.

After landing in Beijing, a senior US Commerce official introduced Chung to Charlie Trie, a fellow political donor and American citizen. Trie and Chinese property developer Ng Lap Seng tried to convince Chung to let them buy the Chinese marketing rights to his blastfax business, but Chung claimed he turned down the offer.[11] After a stint as an international fugitive, Trie would later plead guilty to illegally laundering donations from Ng, who secured ten meetings in the White House with Trie's help.[12] Like a score of other billionaires wrapped up in China's influence operations, Ng landed a seat on the country's peak united front forum shortly after Chinagate.[13]

Ng was never prosecuted for his donations to the Clinton campaign, but two decades later a New York court convicted him of bribing two UN ambassadors as part of a scheme to gain support for a conference centre in Macau that would have expanded China's presence in UN affairs.[14] 'He comes here principally to bribe people,' a US attorney told the judge.[15] But the law enforcement operation's white whale, who might have unlocked secrets about the Party's elite influence operations, got away. The billionaire Ng treated Qin Fei, an obscure Chinese businessman, with deference, and was seen carting around his bags. The FBI suspected Qin of being an intelligence operative, linking him to a smuggling operation by Chinese military officers in New York.[16]

Johnny Chung had none of Ng's wealth, yet his steady stream of donations meant he 'hustled' to cash in fifty visits to the White House and photo opportunities with Republican heavyweight Newt Gingrich, Senate leader Bob Dole and President Clinton as business deals in China.[17] He eventually ran into a business partner unlike all others: Lieutenant Colonel Liu Chaoying, a fashionable Hong Kong–based arms broker, daughter of navy chief and Politburo Standing Committee member General Liu, and a pathway to Chinese military intelligence.[18]

With an introduction from Liu, Major General Ji Shengde of the Military Intelligence Department greeted Chung at a Hong Kong abalone restaurant three months before the 1996 election. Ji directed him to deepen his stake in US politics, and President Bill Clinton in particular. 'We hope to see him re-elected. I will give you 300,000 US dollars. You can give it to the president and the Democratic Party,' General Ji told him over the meal.[19] This was an elite influence operation, both in its perpetrators and targets. It was also reflective of the deep corruption that infused the Party's military. Ji's unusual (at least to Western intelligence agencies) personal involvement may have been motivated in part by a need to keep his black budgets under intimate supervision. Ultimately, Chung used most of the cash for his own needs, and Ji was later imprisoned in one of China's most spectacular corruption scandals.

It was a mutually beneficial scam. Chung profited from hyping up his ability to gain political influence in the White House when all he had to show for it were photo opportunities. General Ji might be able to claim to Party leaders that real ground had been gained through his operations.

Hints of the MSS

Chinese military intelligence's role in Chung's donations is undeniable, but the intelligence links of other key players in Chinagate were never specified. James Riady, the Chinese–Indonesian head of the Lippo Group property and banking conglomerate, would in 2002 plead guilty to his role in illegal donations.[20] Journalist Bob Woodward revealed that the US government's classified investigations indicated Riady and his father 'had a long-term relationship with a Chinese intelligence agency' revolving around their business interests.[21] US intelligence agencies also identified Ted Sioeng, another Indonesian with investments in China whose businesses and family donated to both sides of politics, as an agent of influence for the Chinese government.[22] Sioeng had joined Vice President Al Gore at a fundraiser held by a Buddhist temple in California, where Gore received eleven US$5000 cheques from nuns who had ostensibly taken vows of poverty.[23]

Traces of the MSS pockmarked the scandal, even though it was primarily a military intelligence operation. When Sioeng came under scrutiny, none other than Katrina Leung stepped up to defend him: 'If there is one criticism I can make of him, it is that he got himself in the limelight for so long that he attracted rumours and speculation.'[24]

Both were active in Los Angeles, where Sioeng owned a pro-CCP Chinese newspaper.

Likewise, Thai billionaire Dhanin Chearavanont surfaces again and again at the edges of Chinagate, and of US politics for years thereafter, without ever attracting serious controversy. With help from a lobbyist who later pleaded guilty to delivering hundreds of thousands in illegal donations to set up such meetings, Chearavanont met Clinton for a 'coffee meeting'.[25] Two weeks earlier, Chearavanont had also wired US$100,000 to Charlie Trie.[26] China–US relations dominated the discussion for good reason: the entrepreneur was all over Asian markets for agricultural products, telecommunications services and motorbikes, but China was where his entanglements went deepest.

Chearavanont is in his eighties but is still the head of one of Asia's richest clans, with a family worth upwards of US$30 billion. They trace their roots to Chaozhou, a region of southern China with rich mercantile traditions. The family business, CP Group, returned to China after the Cultural Revolution and still benefits from the blessing of Shenzhen's first-ever foreign investor certificate – numbered 0001. Chearavanont was soon elevated into the upper ranks of the united front and now receives the seat of honour at state banquets for united front figures.[27]

Like many other united front figures, Chearavanont also intersects with the MSS. The year of Clinton's election, 1992, CP Group had partnered with CICEC's audio-visual publishing business to set up a record company in China, Chia Tai Ice Music Production.[28] Though a mediocre operation by CP Group's standards, a joint venture with a covert subsidiary of the MSS Social Investigation Bureau should raise eyebrows given Chearavanont's inroads into the highest levels of the United States government.

Chearavanont's political generosity has been bipartisan. As he secured his coffee meeting with Clinton, he'd also developed a close friendship with the Bush family. CP Group hired former president George H. W. Bush to promote its business in Asia after he left the White House, taking him on a glitzy tour of China and Thailand. Neil Bush, the younger brother of George W. and Jeb, who runs a US–China relations foundation under the family name, was a CP Group business partner. In 1996, CP Group signed up Brent Scrowcroft, formerly

Bush Sr's national security advisor, to run a new institution promoting US–China relations.[29] The project fell through, but in 2016 it funded the US$10 million Initiative for US-China Dialogue on Global Issues at Washington's Georgetown University. Congressman Mike Gallagher attacked the partnership because of the involvement of several former US government officials. Dennis Wilder, who was a top CIA official under Obama, was selected to lead the program, alongside several other administration foreign policy experts from the Obama days. Though the initiative maintains its independence, Gallagher's concern, almost identical to those of Congress during the Chinagate scandal, was that the 'CCP may be using proxies to weaponize the "revolving door" between the public and private sector'.[30]

Looking back, it seems incredible that monitoring and responding to the Party's influence operations and united front work didn't become a focus of the world's intelligence communities until a whole twenty years after Chinagate. At least three figures from Chinagate – Ng Lap Seng, Dhanin Chearavanont and Lieutenant Colonel Liu Chaoying – continued peddling influence and resurfaced in similar controversies over the next two decades. Reflecting how the problem was overlooked, former CIA China analyst Chris Johnson dismissively referred to the threat of 'so-called influence operations' and 'the idea that somehow China is trying to subvert the rules-based global order' as 'chasing ghosts' in a 2018 interview. 'I'm really surprised by how much Washington has become focused on this issue of influence operations and so on. You know, when I was working in the government, we didn't care that much about the activities of the United Front Work Department, and I think there's still a reason why we really shouldn't care that much', said Johnson, who worked in the intelligence community from the time of Chinagate until 2012.[31]

Years after General Ji Shengde broke campaign finance laws to funnel cash to the Clinton campaign, Johnson brushed off alarming indications of CCP-backed interference in Australia as a product of its large Chinese community and relaxed donations laws, which allowed foreigners to contribute to political parties until they were amended in 2018. 'We don't have these things in the United States,' he claimed.

'I do not see, for example, the Chinese diplomatic presence here or even some of their think tanks and so on doing anything like what they were doing [in Australia].'[32]

Lessons that were staring everyone in the face – that the Party's intelligence agencies ride atop united front networks to carry out relationship-focused influence campaigns through a multitude of proxies – were not lost; they were simply never learnt.[33] 'Nobody took it particularly seriously,' a former intelligence official reflected.[34] Tantalising leads, nodes in an international web of intelligence-linked united front figures, sat in Langley safes seldom perused by even those with the privilege to access them. The Party's ability to allegedly co-opt and mobilise some of the richest men in Asia for influence should have made the prospect of future operations under a wealthier, more savvy and more aggressive China, targeting many more countries, a top concern.

The US intelligence community saw Chinagate as laughable because of how unprofessional it had been. 'People have been looking for a magic link that shows how the Chinese money affected policy,' James Mulvenon, an experienced observer of China's military and intelligence agencies, said at the time. 'All I see are a bunch of coincidences standing around the same room trying to introduce themselves.'[35] No real political influence had been gained, and the Party showed it hardly understood how DC worked. 'They were so fricking ignorant about how things were done in Washington,' said one former US intelligence official.[36] The extent of known illegal donations – perhaps a few million – was small enough that the Democrats were willing to cut their losses and return the money.

These operations backfired on China without achieving any immediate wins. The People's Republic was left with a self-inflicted black eye and nothing to show for it. But the presidency stepped in to protect the US–China relationship, with the White House claiming it had no evidence showing the Chinese government had sought to influence elections (others who'd received the same briefings disagreed). The establishment strategy reigned dominant. 'We believe there's no basis for any change in our policy toward China, which is one of engagement,' the White House press secretary maintained.[37]

Beyond the P-factor

Digging deeper, one finds the failure wasn't entirely fruitless. Chinagate provided a model that could be improved on and replicated in countries less willing and able to intervene in corruption and interference from the CCP.

The scandal foreshadowed a similar effort by business figures to buy their way into Australian politics that was only unwound in 2018. Notably, Australian media revealed in 2017 that political donor Helen Liu was a friend and business partner of Liu Chaoying, the blue-blood colonel who helped pass on military intelligence cash to Johnny Chung. During the 2000s, Helen Liu became a close friend and backer of then defence minister Joel Fitzgibbon, even renting a property to him, and befriended several other senior politicians.[38] When Australian media first raised the alarm about Liu's activities in 2009, Australia's counter-intelligence agency responded that it had 'no information relating to Ms Helen Liu which would have given rise to any security concern regarding her activities or associations', eschewing its long-standing practice of not commenting on operational matters. Australian defence officials then used the statement to reassure their US counterparts that there was nothing to worry about.[39] The ignorance had come back full circle. Since then, the same patterns of CCP influence have once more surfaced in countries from the United Kingdom and Canada to El Salvador and the Czech Republic.[40]

In Chinagate, the Party had sought a quick and easy route to influencing American politics. Key players from military intelligence carelessly chipped in, presumably looking more to impress their leaders than achieve long-term results. They found eager participants in businessmen looking to raise their status in China and make a quick buck. Johnny Chung, the 'hustler', exposed China's core mistake in an interview with the *Los Angeles Times*. 'The White House is like a subway: You have to put in coins to open the gates,' he said.[41]

This reflected China's misplaced emphasis on what's known as the 'P-factor'. In his book *The China Fantasy*, journalist James Mann explained how he learnt of the term. It was 1992, an election year. The incumbent President Bush Sr was on the verge of selling F-16 fighter jets to Taiwan. Throughout his presidential campaign, Bill Clinton criticised Bush's closeness to China, accusing him of coddling dictators. Instead, Clinton pledged to make China's continued access to favourable trade terms dependent on its human rights situation. Without an improvement in its treatment of religious groups, political dissidents and ethnic populations, Chinese trade would suffer. One analyst predicted a downward trend in the US–China relationship regardless of who controlled the White House.[42] Reviewing these prospects, a Chinese diplomat complained to Mann, 'What's happened to the P-factor?'[43]

The P-factor was China's discovery that 'whenever it had difficulties with the lower levels of the US government, it could rely on an American president or his highest aides to intervene with a decision in China's favor'. The presidency will often 'sweep aside the complexities' (human rights, technology theft, unfair trade practices, political interference operations and so on) to settle on an outcome in line with their strategic priorities.[44] When the strategic priority was to support China's emergence as a responsible world player, to invest in its economic development, eventually watch it liberalise, and later to cooperate on counterterrorism and climate change, this consistently worked out in China's favour.

MSS officer Gao Yichen acknowledged the power of this force in the very opening of his paper, seeing the personal relationship between Chinese leader Jiang Zemin and Bill Clinton as 'actively correcting' the Clinton administration's China policy and contributing to 'rare upward momentum in recent years'. The P-factor was working its magic.[45]

Chinagate had reaffirmed the helpfulness of the presidency and the unwillingness of White House policymakers to digest evidence that challenged their strategy, but also drew Gao's attention to serious shortcomings in these influence operations. 'We should see with clear eyes that voices unfriendly to China within the US Congress still continue,' he warned, and had been undoing the 'warm atmosphere' achieved by President Jiang's 1997 tour of America. Focusing on strong relations with the White House had been right, Gao believed, but the presidency was still contradicted by Congress on China. 'Just as dialectical materialism tells us, seizing the core contradiction of a matter does not mean neglecting, and certainly not totally ignoring, the non-core contradiction,' he wrote.[46]

The plan to influence the United States

The next time around, things had to be done differently. Gao advised, 'We must recognise that in strengthening work on US Congress we can't hope to see results immediately. Rome wasn't built in a day. We can't fantasise about coming across a miracle one morning. Rather, we should sufficiently prepare ourselves for its long-term nature, difficulty and complexity.'[47]

Inside the MSS, the Chinagate catastrophe was driving home the need for a broader, more patient and more deliberate campaign. They had to do more than manipulate the presidency. China's spies needed to shape and cultivate the entire DC Beltway foreign policy establishment. Plenty of scholars, bureaucrats and congresspeople were arguing for maintaining China's access to trade privileges, glossing over human rights concerns and weakening America's alliance with Taiwan, while arguing against any policy of competition with China. They just needed a push in the right direction.

At the same time, the Party's influence operations needed to be better at dodging the attention of law enforcement and media. Gao pointed out the obvious: 'American political and media circles getting worked up over the so-called "Chinese involvement in political donations" incident should give us many important revelations.' In the future, 'We must ensure that all activities are carried out within the allowed boundaries of the law, not leaving behind anything that can be used against us,' he wrote. A remarkable statement for an intelligence officer to make, and a difficult one to believe.

Broad US laws prohibit some of the most basic tasks of foreign intelligence officers, although they are rarely used for prosecutions. In September 2018, an electrical engineer and army reservist was arrested in the United States. Ji Chaoqun's charge: acting as an illegal agent of the government of China.[48] Apple iCloud files seized by the FBI allegedly show how he was recruited years prior by the Jiangsu State Security Department, one of the MSS's provincial outfits. While Ji's case is ongoing, prosecutors haven't accused him of theft or any attempt to gain classified information. Instead, criminal allegations focus on State Security directing Ji to purchase open-source background checks on US defence contractors.[49] In other words, assigning even the most rudimentary of tasks to intelligence assets can place them on the wrong side of the law. And while Deng Xiaoping had ordered intelligence officers out of China's embassies in 1985, DC's importance made it an exception where some spies were allowed to stay in place.[50] The nature of their work meant they inevitably crossed criminal lines at some point.

Gao's recommendation also contained a grain of truth, crucial to understanding why so many of the MSS's influence operations have gone largely uninterrupted. The ministry's greatest actions haven't relied on clandestine activity, which can backfire dangerously. 'If you look at the way influence [operations] are run, it's about working the relationship,' one former intelligence official said. 'There's a lot less of formal payments.' In other words, less of what might normally ping on counterintelligence radars as activity that needed to and could be stopped.[51] The MSS even has a specific term, *xin zhao bu xuan* (literally 'hearts shine without showing'), to refer to this kind of tacit recruitment, where people become de facto agents without their handlers ever forcing them to recognise this fact.[52] Clandestinely gathered information including hacked databases, or analytical reports purchased from retired officials as 'consulting services', help steer and refine influence operations. Yet dozens of mainly legal channels for building influence lay at the MSS's disposal. The meat of these operations comes from the integration of overt and covert work so prized by China's intelligence agencies. Covert proxies and co-optees such as prominent PRC academics or retired statesmen working with the MSS are key to their success. They might have benefited from espionage and fancy tradecraft, but they didn't depend on it.

Gao's paper reflects this more sophisticated understanding of influence work, dancing along the boundaries of the law and drawing on China's strengths as well as the best practices of other countries. In overly simplistic terms, influence operations could be described as seeking to cause a change in behaviours, beliefs or actions. But China's activities often reaffirm, expand and encourage views already held by sympathetic individuals. These efforts can take place through carefully curated trips to China, interactions with Chinese officials or relationships with united front figures.

Having armed their targets with a greater confidence in their views about China, the Party then helps them gain influence within their political system. For politicians this can mean donations; research funding and privileged fieldwork opportunities for scholars; or business opportunities for entrepreneurs. Danish scholar Jonas Parello-Plesner wrote about how undercover officers of the Zhejiang State Security Department, an MSS branch known for its focus on Europe, attempted to recruit him through the career networking website LinkedIn and then in person. Working with them would help avoid conflict between the United States and China, they promised, and 'You could have access to any top Chinese official'.[53] Years after Parello-Plesner turned down the pitch, German authorities revealed that it had been just one node of an MSS campaign to reach out to over 10,000 targets through social media.[54]

The MSS's ability to broker access to Party leaders and senior officials, coveted by those foreign commentators who trade off even the briefest of meetings for credibility and consulting jobs, can be a particularly powerful tool. As China expert Peter Mattis observes, this is essentially what Katrina Leung did: work with the MSS to gain access to Party leaders and mediate the US intelligence community's insights into elite politics.[55] Party leaders themselves are important actors in these operations by making their guests think the lies they're being peddled are instead privileged insights into what the Party *really* thinks. Many, such as former president Hu Jintao and vice premier Liu He, China's top trade negotiator with the US during the Trump years, have relationships with the MSS Social Investigation Bureau. Both were vice presidents of its CICEC front group. Another former CICEC member, Li Yuanchao, was touted as a progressive in the Party leadership. His promotion to vice presidency under Xi was misread by some observers as a signal of impending liberal reforms.[56]

Familiar with these tactics, Gao used his paper to highlight six mechanisms for influencing Congress that would help China construct a 'beneficial international environment'.[57] Many are familiar or obvious, but this MSS document reveals new details about their scale and intent, and provides further proof of the role of Chinese intelligence agencies in these activities, paraphrased here:

1. Invite congresspeople to China, arranging for English-speaking and politically experienced experts and scholars in international affairs to accompany them and 'subtly influence' them.

2. Expand engagement with congresspeople on the ground. While China already has diplomats tasked with engaging Congress, visiting delegations of scholars can be incredibly valuable for influencing congresspeople. 'Reflecting the high status and prestige of scholars and experts in American society, we can send out delegations of well-known professors and scholars … specifically visiting America to engage with congresspeople.' Scholars can seem 'less official', allowing them to build long-term relationships and 'produce excellent results from their interactions with congresspeople'.

3. Lobby congresspeople through various channels such as reputable public relations firms, law firms, and organisations established by 'patriotic overseas Chinese' but funded and guided by the Chinese government. These entities, 'in addition to directly lobbying Congress as our legally registered agents, can also provide us with internal information on Congress and provide advice on improving our congressional work'. The Chinese government should also set up a 'Sino–US relations research centre' that can focus on influencing the foreign policy community with congresspeople and their staffers as the focus. (Since 2005, the Chinese embassy has engaged one of DC's leading lobbying firms, Squire Patton Boggs, paying it a US$55,000 monthly retainer in 2021.)[58]

4. Work on political and business elites and interest groups in congressional districts. Members of Congress 'absolutely cannot do without the support of their district's political and business elites'. According to Gao, these influence efforts can take the form of inviting local politicians to visit China, deepening business relationships with those areas to 'advance work on members of Congress', and establishing sister-city or sister-state relationships. 'Those congresspeople who aren't too friendly towards China should be a focus of these activities.'

5. 'Borrow the strength of major American enterprises to carry out work on members of Congress.' The business sector's aspirations

for the China market mean that 'Without letting it be known, we can "use economics to advance politics".' Gao recommended deepening commercial ties to companies while also 'prompting them to carry out work on congresspersons according to our plans'.

6. Finally, united front work on Chinese communities. 'Even though Taiwanese authorities currently have greater control and influence over American Chinese communities than we ... a gradual transformation is possible,' and it will be possible for numerous Chinese communities to become 'an important force we can draw on to carry out work on Congress'.

This influence campaign would rely on more than the MSS. The importance of overt and covert influence, not just clandestine operations, meant counterparts could be called into action. The full weight of China's bureaucracy was being drawn into this fight. Gao believed influencing Congress required the active participation of China's Ministry of Foreign Affairs, the Ministry of Commerce, the Overseas Chinese Affairs Office (now part of the United Front Work Department), the Propaganda Department and China's National People's Congress (as the US Congress's counterpart). The Chinese government also needed to carry out extensive background research to understand Congress and its members. Over the following years, the Chinese embassy's congressional affairs team grew to become a highly effective and well-resourced section.[59]

Many of Gao's recommendations are simple and predictable. They're the kinds of things any major power would hope to carry out. Much of what he had in mind were mere extensions and elaborations of ongoing efforts to influence the United States, but China was starting from a low base. The Cultural Revolution was still recent history, Deng Xiaoping had only just passed away, and China still had a lot of time left to 'hide its capabilities and bide its time' – Deng's strategic guidance to the Party.

It's important to also recognise what Gao hinted at but left out: the covert side of China's influence. His paper, buried though technically public, doesn't mention the role of his own ministry. The visible slice of

MSS networks in California up to the 2000s, of which Katrina Leung was only one node, shows how deeply united front work and covert MSS activities intertwine, to the point of being inextricable. In the years since, the CCP has well and truly succeeded in displacing Taiwan's presence in most Chinese communities through united front work. The global Chinese-language media environment is dominated by Party-aligned outlets, driven again by united front work and the dominance of China's WeChat social media app. With little to stop them until recently, MSS influence operations have 'grown in scale and scope and sophistication over time', said one former US intelligence officer who worked on China.[60]

Intelligence activity is the missing piece in our understanding of China's rise. With the benefit of hindsight, the MSS's systematic manipulation of the West's understanding of China shows it was already preparing the ground for confrontation, years before the Party made undeniable its intention to challenge the United States and witness what General Secretary Xi Jinping predicts as the 'eventual demise of capitalism and the ultimate victory of socialism'.[61] At the time of the Clinton donations scandal, China had years to go before glimpsing its economic potential and finding confidence in aggressive displays of power under Xi Jinping. It needed to buy time so that it could challenge the rest of the world on its own terms, at its time of choosing. This was the MSS's chance to shine and prove it had outgrown the public failures of its early years. Luckily, it had just the man for the job.

CHAPTER 6

PLAYING THE LONG GAME

L IN DI BECAME head of the MSS Social Investigation Bureau around the turn of the millennium. With Lin at the helm, the bureau's experience with the outside world and elite networks saw it become the MSS's 'de-facto US operations bureau', in the words of one former intelligence official.[1] Through an array of front groups like CICEC, this bureau has been the hidden force behind many of the CCP's most impressive operations in the United States. As we will see, it has excelled at influencing elites and manipulating key American interlocutors with China.

Lin represented the new breed, the first generation of officers to be raised and trained by the MSS itself. They were young, fluent in English, interested in America and dead loyal to the Party. Many, like Lin, came from 'red' families with long histories in the Party. One of Lin's uncles was a senior Chinese diplomat, and another was a colonel in the military.[2] His ancestor Lin Zexu became a national hero for his opposition to the opium trade in the mid-nineteenth century.

Most importantly, Lin was the son of a martyred spy. His father, best known by his alias Li Liang, worked for the Tianjin Public Security Bureau in the 1950s, where he was responsible for catching 'imperialist' spies.[3] Li's years of underground revolutionary work, fluency in English and experience working for Western news services propelled him into important assignments.[4] Despite his intellectual air and 'high status in the old society', Li's former boss recalled him as humble, devoted to the Party and dedicated to work.[5]

The Tianjin bureau was mostly tasked with counterintelligence, but Li was chosen for two overseas missions. Only the most trusted and capable officers were given such tasks. At best, they risked exposure by foreign agencies; at worst, they might defect. Nothing is known about these missions, but other spies sent abroad by the same agencies handled double agents in the CIA and Taiwanese intelligence.[6] Today's Tianjin State Security Bureau focuses on Korea and Japan and is a proving ground for foreign intelligence officers, at least two of whom have gone on to become senior MSS leaders.[7]

Li's second overseas assignment proved his last. The Cultural Revolution was in full swing by the time he returned to China in 1967.[8] Even though his mission had been approved by the Ministry of Public Security's headquarters, his overseas connections and bourgeois family background made him an ideal target for the Red Guards. The next year, he was locked up and accused of harbouring 'secret ties to foreign countries'. Eleven months later he was dead, denounced as a 'counter-revolutionary race traitor, western slave and foreign conspirator'.[9] Starvation was the most likely cause.[10]

Separated from his family, Lin Di spent the rest of the Cultural Revolution toiling in labour communes where he was criticised and teased on account of his father. The family's political troubles ruled out any chance of him entering university, at least while the Cultural Revolution was still underway, and Lin's mother encouraged him to self-study. Coaching himself in English became a way to mourn his father. 'The English books left behind by Dad became my inseparable friend,' Lin recounted.[11]

Finally, in October 1977, the year after Mao's death, the end of the Cultural Revolution and coup that ousted the Gang of Four meant 'our dreams turned into reality', Lin wrote. The Central Organisation Department, which oversaw rehabilitation of Cultural Revolution victims, and the Ministry of Public Security set up a team to investigate the case and recover Li's ashes. He was quickly exonerated; the family's appeals had been heard after ten painful years.[12] Among the worshippers of Li's legacy was Ling Yun, soon to become the first head of the MSS.[13]

Lin Di's entry to the intelligence world probably predates the MSS's 1983 founding. In 1977, by then around twenty-three years old, he was accepted into a teachers' college.[14] But by the end of that year, indications are that he was working in the Tianjin Public Security Bureau.[15]

By 1980, Lin was working undercover at the Chinese Academy of Social Sciences (CASS).[16] The state-run institute advises Party leaders, collaborates with scholars around the world, hosts thousands of international visitors each year and also dispatches delegations overseas through its foreign affairs bureau where MSS officers like Lin worked.[17] The academy's close relationship with the MSS remains in place; many CASS scholars sit on the councils of intelligence front organisations. Its Institute of Taiwan Studies is the public face of the MSS's Taiwan affairs bureau, staffed by the agency's analysts.[18]

Lin's undercover work meant putting his English skills to use, charming foreign visitors and anyone he encountered overseas. If suitable, these individuals would also be targeted for recruitment, drawing on ideology, blackmail or venality. Such attempts haven't always gone to plan. One Chinese delegation's 'interpreter' was arrested by Russian authorities in 2010 after trying to purchase information on surface-to-air missile technology for the MSS.[19] Good recruitment opportunities are rare and can be risky. Working in the open to shape foreigners' perception of China, misleading them about the Party's intentions and direction, building friendships with influential individuals or those who might rise into prominence can be just as worthwhile as stealing missile technology. Why do you need missiles if you can convince your enemies to point their weapons elsewhere, or, even better, at your enemies?

Lin's political reliability, demonstrated primarily through his family background, made him one of the few MSS officers trusted to take frequent trips abroad and mingle closely with foreigners. By 1984, Lin had travelled to Australia as an interpreter to a CASS delegation.[20] He later entered the first class of master's students at the Johns Hopkins University School of Advanced International Studies in Nanjing.

The program put American and Chinese students side by side on a dedicated campus. American students would learn about China, and Chinese students about America by, for example, studying the autobiography of Chrysler CEO Lee Iacocca. Both groups would study international relations, politics and history, preparing them to spearhead engagement between their two countries.[21]

Lin was one of many intelligence officers embedded in the unique program, preparing for future operations against the United States.[22] We know this in part because the year after Lin graduated from the program, a PLA intelligence officer studying at the Hopkins–Nanjing Center fell in love with her American professor, who she'd been tasked to monitor, and eventually moved to the United States after the Tiananmen massacre to tell all in an autobiography.[23] Again testifying to the unusual trust he had earned, Lin was allowed to lead a scholarly delegation to Japan just a month after the massacre.[24] A few years later, he even managed what was then the largest-ever CASS delegation to Taipei. To the MSS, this would have been a journey into the heart of enemy territory.[25] The next step would be operations in the United States.

Fellow travellers: The US–China Policy Foundation

Lin and his colleagues – the same network of Social Investigation Bureau officers that handled Katrina Leung – found their entrée to US politics in 1995. Lin now worked through CICEC, the Social Investigation Bureau's leading front group, and began cultivating networks for influence operations.

While the FBI slept on evidence of Leung's betrayal, Lin sealed a partnership with a group of American China experts. At that time, the US–China Policy Foundation (USCPF) had connections to the heart of US policymaking on China. When I visited the group in 2018, it had gerontified out of its former influence, occupying a cramped office in Washington, DC. Wang Chi, the group's octogenarian president, seemed on the verge of being swallowed by his suit as he shared his thoughts on US–China relations and recalled his personal experience as an intermediary between the two powers. With National Security Advisor Henry Kissinger's permission, he secretly travelled to China in 1972 to set up exchanges with libraries there. Later he served as China head at the Library of Congress, and a professor at Georgetown University.

Wang's memoir details just about every interaction he's had with Chinese leaders and senior cadres, including military intelligence officers like the future General Ji Shengde. Yet his dances with the MSS, which appeared time and time again in my research, were absent.

Back in 1995, Wang led the USCPF together with Chas Freeman, who had recently retired from the Pentagon as assistant secretary for international security affairs.[26] Freeman accompanied President Nixon as the interpreter for his groundbreaking 1972 trip to China, the beginning of a long career in diplomacy.[27] Their foundation had a weekly TV program, held monthly roundtables with China experts and government officials, and published a journal on China for policy wonks.

Leading China scholars and policymakers like David Lampton and Kenneth Lieberthal sat on the foundation's board. Dianne Feinstein, Max Baucus (later ambassador to China under Obama) and Chuck Hagel (a future secretary of defence under Obama) – all influential senators who believed in closer relations with China – were honorary advisors.[28] Feinstein, unaware until many years later that one of her staff had been recruited by the MSS, wrote that the USCPF could 'play a key role in exposing U.S. policymakers to the people, perspectives and information necessary to make informed choices on important issues in U.S.-China relations'.[29] Maurice Greenberg, then chief of the insurance company AIG, was the foundation's honorary chairman.[30] Greenberg was a leading donor to American foreign policy think tanks and once threatened to pull funding from the Heritage Foundation after one of its analysts wrote a paper calling for tougher policies on China.[31]

General Alexander Haig – a central figure in the opening of US–PRC relations, and secretary of state under President Reagan – was an honorary advisor to the US–China Policy Foundation. After leaving his government career behind, Haig turned to consulting for arms manufacturers that wanted to expand their international clientele, carving out a niche with his ability to open doors in China. He also served as the advisor to a PRC guide on American business and industry produced by the MSS Social Investigation Bureau. One of Katrina Leung's handlers' names appears alongside his in the credits.[32]

'He doesn't register as a foreign lobbyist, but he's effectively a voice for a foreign government,' a former Hill staffer complained after watching Haig's persistent efforts to shut down bills that were tough on China.[33]

A few months after the foundation's inception in 1995, and before it had become a rallying point for advocates of softer policies towards China, Wang Chi flew to Beijing to meet with Party leaders. Lin Di and MSS Vice Minister Yu Fang, undercover as members of CICEC, were there to accompany him.[34] The next year he returned again with Freeman and other USCPF board members, where they were welcomed by CICEC at the Great Hall of the People.[35] Wang was later honoured as one of eight foreign advisors to CICEC, together with former Clinton White House official Ernest J. Wilson III, Jillian Sackler of the Sackler pharmaceuticals family, a former Malaysian politician and others.[36]

CICEC was Wang's gateway to China, and the US–China Policy Foundation was the MSS's ticket to Washington, DC. While most of CICEC's US interlocutors were sincere and interested in navigating the challenges of US–China relations, the MSS could only have viewed the relationship as a golden opportunity for influence operations. The two groups quickly became important partners in what was thought to be a mutually beneficial arrangement.

The result looked very much like what Gao Yichen, who was promoted to MSS vice minister shortly after returning from DC, recommended in his paper on influencing the US Congress. CICEC worked with the US foundation to bring delegations of congressional staffers and other policymakers to Beijing for study tours. In return, the MSS sent its officers and assets to the United States to study the country, meet with agents, network with elites and spread the Party's influence.

MSS officers must have marvelled at the doors that opened to them, with no apparent resistance from American authorities. With the US–China Policy Foundation's help, Vice Minister Yu Fang now returned to DC as an honoured guest at a National Press Club event, though still using his alias, Yu Enguang.[37] Through his open role as a member of the National People's Congress Foreign Affairs Committee, Yu became a staple in the opening of parliamentary exchanges with the United States, taking part in the Chinese congress's first delegation to America.[38]

Lin, presenting himself as the secretary-general of CICEC, was afforded significant privileges and access. At a National Press Club talk in 2001, the USCPF's Chas Freeman introduced his friend to DC's elite. 'It is a great pleasure to welcome Mr Lin Di ... who has been very helpful to the United States [China] Policy Foundation on numerous occasions when we have arranged educational travel for congressional staff and others to China ... I think Mr Lin is actually known to many of you,' Freeman said. Surely none of them realised they were look-ing straight at one of the most important officers in the MSS's history, and a chief architect of its efforts to undermine and influence the United States.

After Freeman's introduction, Lin expressed his gratitude towards those who'd helped him build bridges with America. 'I am pleased to report to you that in recent years my organisation has worked with foreign counterparts such as US–China Policy Foundation [and] accomplished many fruitful achievements in this regard,' he said.[39]

Without a hint of irony in his voice, the undeclared intelligence officer advised his audience, 'To conduct the effective dialogue, both sides should keep the dialogue channel open and try to build up mutual confidence through consultations on an equal footing ... Each side should respect and trust the other side and the Cold War mentality should be completely abandoned.' The kinds of 'cultural exchanges' carried out by CICEC, he proclaimed, were key. 'To promote the devel-opment of China–US relations, China needs to know the US better and vice versa. What is the best angle to learn a foreign country? I think it is her culture.'

Lin was clearly playing to America's ill-informed hopes about his country. 'China,' he proclaimed, 'is deepening her reform to build a more open, prosperous, democratic and modernised nation.' These were no off-the-cuff comments by a pro-democracy rebel within the Party. Lin was nervously reading from a script that must have passed through several layers of bureaucracy in China. It was a script for influence operations that the MSS would deepen and elaborate on to tremendous effect over the following years.

The event was a succinct demonstration of the core narrative CCP influence operations try to promote to this day, as well as the stark imbalances that too often come to define engagement with China. On the one hand was a civil society group that wanted to better understand China, on the other was an intelligence front run by experts in influence operations and agent handling. Rather than educating US policymakers and scholars on the Party's true intentions, Lin and many other MSS officers acted like mirrors reflecting the West's misplaced confidence that China would democratise, liberalise and become a 'responsible stakeholder' on the world stage.

Implicitly, Lin was also dissuading his audience from waking up to those lies. The flipside of Lin's advocacy of lofty causes like world peace, friendship, culture and cooperation was his admonishment of those who might impede the Party's progress. While internally the Party leadership, and the MSS especially, views the United States as its greatest threat, Lin warned that 'the Cold War mentality of demonising the other side as a threatening enemy could easily incite suspicions, panic, resentment, hostility and, finally, confrontation'. Questioning PRC sovereignty over Taiwan, a country with a separate history, culture and identity to CCP-controlled China, was another line that Lin said should never be crossed.[40]

In particular, Lin attacked the belief in facts that the Party itself has begun to prove through its aggression, rampant interference efforts, disturbing human rights abuses and violation of international agreements. 'Now in the US there is a kind of opinion that is shared by some senior government officials and social celebrities. That is China cannot be a partner of the US. China will be competing with the US on the international stage. Some people even go further to identify China as a potential enemy and a threat to the security of the United States and the world. I'm afraid that we cannot agree with this at all.'[41]

Through years of engagement with the United States, Lin built up an unrivalled list of contacts and acquaintances as he climbed the hierarchy of the MSS, becoming the Social Investigation Bureau's chief around the time of his National Press Club talk.[42] Accompanying renowned Chinese economist Fan Gang (a member of several MSS front groups), Lin spoke at a 1997 Harvard University conference alongside Jeffrey Sachs, the eminent American economist and UN advisor whose growing support for the Chinese government has recently pushed him towards denying the existence of genocide in Xinjiang and into an advisory role at a Chinese military intelligence–linked think tank accused of bribery at the UN.[43] Under Lin, CICEC worked with the Sackler pharmaceuticals family's foundation to hold calligraphy competitions around the world.[44]

Congress and local governments were top priorities for Lin and his bureau. The US–China Policy Foundation placed at least three delegations of congressional staffers in CICEC's hands for tours of China, with approval from the US State Department.[45] CICEC's cultural exchanges with the state of Kentucky led to its powerless figureheads, Peng Chong and Cheng Siyuan, being honoured as Kentucky Colonels, joining the ranks of estimable ambassadors of the Kentucky Commonwealth alongside Kentucky Fried Chicken's Colonel Sanders.[46]

Donning an array of masks, Lin and his MSS colleagues also embedded their intelligence work into the Party's united front courtship of sympathetic diaspora leaders. In 2001, Lin appeared at the annual meeting of the Committee of 100, a highly influential Chinese community body of which Wang Chi remains a member.[47] Through another front group called the Chinese Association for the Promotion of Cultural Exchange and Cooperation, Lin held annual welcoming parties for the most faithful united front members from around the world: those handpicked as delegates to the Chinese People's Political Consultative Conference. The group's Chinese-language name hints at its role as a counterpart to CICEC more focused on Taiwanese and Chinese diaspora targets.[48] Unlike CICEC, its mission is not 'international' exchange. Its China is not that of *Zhongguo* – the common name for the People's Republic of China that means literally 'Middle Kingdom' – but *Zhonghua*, an ambiguous and expansive concept encompassing Chinese culture, heritage and ethnicity. Officially, the group reports to China's National Radio and Television Administration, but its addresses over the years lead first to the offices of an official MSS magazine at number 21 in central Beijing's Daxing Hutong, and then to CICEC's building in the city's east.[49]

The Chinese Association for the Promotion of Cultural Exchange and Cooperation continues to plug itself into united front networks, and for reasons unknown it has gained a focus on Central and Eastern

Europe. The association's current president is Huang Ping, head of the Taiwan, Hong Kong and Macau Research Center at the Chinese Academy of Social Sciences.[50] Until recently, Huang headed CASS's European Studies Institute and ran a think tank network under the banner of Beijing's '17+1 Initiative', a push to deepen China's influence in Central and Eastern Europe, which worked with the MSS to host and engage with European scholars.[51] Huang's successor as head of the think tank network is also affiliated with the MSS, having recently served as deputy head of the MSS bureau known as the China Institute of Contemporary International Relations.[52] The think tank network, proposed by Premier Li Keqiang, includes Hungarian, Polish, Hungarian, Serbian, Czech, Slovenian and Romanian scholars on its academic committee.[53] In 2021 the MSS group began exploring deeper cooperation with Huaqiao University, a leading Chinese university administered by the United Front Work Department that specialises in educating and researching Chinese diaspora communities.[54]

Friends in high places

The MSS plays a long game of cultivating relationships with China-friendly voices in order to understand and influence politics, and perhaps one day see its contacts rise into the upper echelons of government, academia and business. The fact that many of these targets may not have realised their Chinese friends like Lin Di were intelligence officers has hardly lessened the effectiveness of these operations.

This game nearly paid off when the US–China Policy Foundation's Chas Freeman was picked as the chair of Obama's National Intelligence Council. Dennis Blair, head of the US intelligence community and a former member of the US–China Policy Foundation's board, hand-picked Freeman for the ultra-sensitive role in 2009.[55] Freeman, in China when news first broke of the decision, quickly severed his various board roles and affiliations.[56] 'I understood [Blair] was "asking me to give up my freedom of speech, my leisure, the greater part of my income, subject myself to the mental colonoscopy of a polygraph, and resume a daily commute to a job with long working hours and a daily ration of political abuse,"' Freeman wrote, nonetheless eager to take up a job that would have been the pinnacle of his long career.[57] As chairman of the National Intelligence Council, Freeman would have served as the bridge between intelligence and policy, preparing top-level analysis of the most important security issues facing America and occasionally joining Blair on trips to the White House to deliver the president's daily intelligence briefing.[58]

News of Freeman's imminent appointment sparked an explosion in the media. Freeman's numerous interactions with undeclared Chinese intelligence officers like Lin Di, which extended to unknowingly helping them build networks in America's capital, didn't surface in the ensuing vivisection of the retired diplomat's beliefs and allegiances. Neither did the 'contrarian' realism of national interest of values that may have eased Freeman's entry into the MSS's orbit and provided the basis for Nixon's Sino-American rapprochement escape scrutiny. Freeman's thoughts on the Tiananmen massacre, shared to a private email group, were leaked to the press within days. In Freeman's view, which he points out is shared by many in China, 'the truly unforgivable mistake of the Chinese authorities was the failure to intervene on a timely basis to nip the demonstrations in the bud, rather than … to intervene with force when all other measures had failed to restore domestic tranquility to Beijing'.[59] Freeman's jarring realism is as strong as ever: in a 2020 interview he took a similar position on China's crackdowns in Hong Kong, and argued the United States should avoid conflict with China by winding down its military support for Taiwan, which he called a 'rump state created by the Chinese Civil War'. Freeman studied in Taiwan in the 1970s and appreciates it as 'the most admirable society that has ever existed on Chinese soil'. But the bottom line is that 'it is on Chinese soil'.[60] Never mind the views of those who inhabit it, over two-thirds of whom identify exclusively as Taiwanese.[61]

Dozens of commentators weighed in, many attacking Freeman's closeness to Saudi Arabia, where he'd served as ambassador, and critical take on America's relationship with Israel.[62] Many others stood up for Freeman – for his intelligence, experience and freethinking attitude most of all. 'You can't cow him and you can't find someone with a more relentlessly questioning worldview,' one said.[63] In the end, Freeman withdrew from his stillborn nomination, finding the Israel lobby responsible. 'I have never sought to be paid or accepted payment from any foreign government, including Saudi Arabia or China,' Freeman wrote in his withdrawal statement. 'I am my own man, no one else's.'[64]

Officers like Lin Di, with their extensive connections within and without China, air of inside knowledge and cover as promoters of cultural diplomacy, were well equipped to shape the opinions of those they met. But the big whales like Chas Freeman – members of Congress, retired ambassadors, business leaders and so on – are generally deeply loyal to the United States and often have a strong sense of independence. The MSS would be foolish to try a recruitment pitch on them, promising, for example, cash payments in exchange for information. In the high-stakes game of elite influence operations, a light touch is often the best approach. But that doesn't mean deals can't be sounded out.

CHAPTER 7

ZHENG BIJIAN AND CHINA REFORM FORUM

FAR FROM THE smog and concrete of Beijing, Hainan's Bo'ao Forum for Asia is the Party's platform of choice to present itself to foreign notables in painstakingly airbrushed technicolour. Each year, hundreds of world leaders gather at the beachside venue to talk foreign policy. They're surrounded by marble and red carpets, immaculately groomed topiaries and pedantically drilled staff, and probably a few thousand bugs and hidden cameras. Outside, palm trees sway in the Pacific breeze, and beyond them stretch the island's famous sand beaches.

In November 2003, Zheng Bijian stepped up to the podium at Bo'ao to deliver a speech that could not have been a greater triumph. His articulation of the idea that China can peacefully become a great power sparked excited discussion among China watchers and international relations scholars around the world. It quickly caught on as his 'theory of China's peaceful rise', which is explored more in the next chapter. Zheng argued that China's growth towards superpower status, feared by some, would in fact 'safeguard world peace' and 'boldly draw on the fruits of all human civilization'.[1]

Yet of all the false hopes China's spies covertly peddled, none landed quite like 'peaceful rise'. For all of Bo'ao's breeziness and pats on the back, the 'peaceful rise' slogan was a cynically crafted riposte against growing apprehension towards China's mounting power. The theory and its untold origin story lay bare how the Chinese Communist Party fooled the world about its ambitions.

The rise of Zheng Bijian

For decades, the Party theoretician had deftly navigated the vagaries of internal politics. Yet despite all Zheng's achievements and experience, and perhaps because of his years working with purged leader Hu Yaobang, he'd never actually been the top leader of a central agency. The Party's leaders shuffled him between important roles, but always as second in command. Likewise, he'd long been interested in international affairs but had never been at the heart of foreign policy. It must have been frustrating. He still had his old connections and now had help from China Reform Forum, the think tank he chaired, but his wits were doing the heavy lifting.

The story of Zheng's adventures goes back to the county of Fushun, a region of China's southwestern Sichuan province where he was born in 1932. Not long after the communist victory of 1949, Zheng found himself in Beijing, joining the Party as a student in Beijing Renmin University's Marxism–Leninism program, entering the Party's Propaganda Department a few years later.

In the ideologically charged aftermath of the Cultural Revolution, Party leaders manoeuvred to interpret Mao's legacy and, in turn, their place in China's future. Zheng's skill in rhetoric and apparently passable track record during the Cultural Revolution, when he spent time in a rural work commune, landed him a senior role in the Central Committee office editing Mao's collected works, which functioned as a sort of speechwriting and advisory body to the leadership. Perhaps as much by chance as cunning, he soon found himself on the winning side of Deng Xiaoping's quest to control the Party.

In 1980 he was handpicked to help compose the 'Resolution on certain questions in the history of our Party since the founding of the People's Republic of China', an attempt to synthesise Mao's disastrous mistakes with the reality that his legacy and reputation were wedded to that of the Party.[2] Damning criticism of Mao would undermine the Party's legitimacy, and any unorthodox re-examination of the past (known as 'historical nihilism' in today's Party-speak) could spark turmoil.

The text's uninspired title hides how the lengthy drafting process of nearly two years became a mechanism for rationalising the defenestration of Chairman Hua Guofeng, who had seized power after Mao's death. The whole affair was closely controlled by Deng Xiaoping, whose strawman of Hua remains the conventional appraisal of him to this day.[3]

By the time the Party's Central Committee approved the 'Historical resolution' in June 1981, Hua had been removed from positions of power, his faction already disintegrated. Deng replaced him with Hu Yaobang, an old comrade-in-arms who had followed Deng for much of his career.[4] The 'Historical resolution' served to legitimise the takeover – to outdate Hua's leadership. Who better to serve as Hu's secretary and aide than Zheng Bijian, whose diligence through the drafting process proved his willingness to serve the cynical machinations of elite infighting and helped land Hu in the leadership?

Thus, Zheng was elevated from ideological hitman to a Party leader's aide. He was good at it. One Party journalist was stunned by Zheng's familiarity with classic Marxist–Leninist literature. Once General Secretary Hu struggled to recall a Marx quote relevant to the topic at hand while delivering a speech to a gathering of Party officials. Zheng immediately scribbled down the line and passed it over to him.[5]

Zheng faced the most precarious moment of his career after Deng Xiaoping decisively toppled Hu Yaobang in 1987, wary of Hu's growing insistence on genuine reformist policies. Zheng's colleagues and associates were being purged left right and centre. Those whose controversial opinions were tolerated under Hu now faced a reckoning. Zheng had to sell himself to the conservatives: he must have convinced Party leaders that his loyalty to the Party trumped all else, and that his usefulness as a 'hired pen' was still relevant.

In 1988 he was appointed director of the CASS Institute of Marxism–Leninism–Mao Zedong Thought, and in 1992 became the senior deputy director of the Central Propaganda Department and a member of the Party's Central Committee. Five years later, the Central

Committee appointed him senior vice president of its Central Party School, the peak training academy for China's political elite.

By 2003, Zheng was officially retired and out of the Party bureaucracy, and his place in the new era of Chinese politics and foreign policy was by no means certain. His long-time superior at the Central Party School, Hu Jintao, was now the Party's leader – on paper. Even Hu's status was in dispute: his predecessor, Jiang Zemin, maintained immense influence and personally held onto the reins of the Chinese military for two more years. Yet, if Zheng were looking for a legacy, his 'peaceful rise' speech at the Bo'ao Forum that November could not have been a greater triumph.

Here was a Party insider with the ear of the nation's leaders proposing an experiment at a global scale that seemed to contradict the logic of history. It was tantamount to refuting a physical law. Was this the spirit of Hu Yaobang and the Party's undercurrent of liberalism and reform speaking? As Zheng argued in an earlier speech at Washington, DC's Center for Strategic and International Studies, China would not be like Germany in World War One or Japan in World War Two, which he thought were mistaken for attempting 'to overhaul the world political landscape by way of aggressive wars'.[6] Nor would China be like the Soviet Union, competing against the United States in an arms race and through its global sphere of influence. According to Zheng, 'China will have a totally different path of development from the path of rise of all major powers in the world since modern history.'

It *could not* be like them. 'China's only choice is to strive to rise and, more importantly, to strive for a peaceful rise,' Zheng said. The alternative path – that of confrontation and conflict with the United States – was 'doomed to failure'.[7] It sounded like the best of all possible worlds and a commitment to end great power competition.

China watchers, policymakers and intelligence analysts took note, some with scepticism, but many with optimism and hopefulness, describing Zheng's idea in adulatory tones.[8] Zheng was connected to chiefs of the Party; he had developed a reputation as a 'confidant' or trusted advisor to China's leadership. His height, tone and experience make him a strikingly statesmanlike figure. Though much taller than the average Chinese man, he has an uncanny resemblance to Yoda.

One person who met him was impressed by his 'gentleness' and professionalism.[9] Another noted his deep intellect and theoretical interests.[10] Henry Kissinger praised Zheng and called his peaceful rise narrative a 'quasi-official policy statement'.[11] Here was a roadmap to a peaceful and stable twenty-first century.

But the concept of peaceful rise was always a hollow one. The very vehicle Zheng hung his hat on and which enabled his promotion of the narrative, China Reform Forum, was simply an MSS-controlled front group that had selected him as its latest figurehead. He was not in control. Outwardly, Zheng is closest to the Party's propaganda system, the ideological apparatus that dictates history and seeks to frame the present and future, but it is to the MSS that he owes his international fame.

For his part, Su Shaozhi – an academic purged in 1987 who knew Zheng – thought of him as a modern-day Feng Dao, a medieval politician commonly regarded as 'an extreme case of a treacherous minister' for having served five different regimes.[12] Similarly, China journalist Jonathan Mirsky wrote after attending a speech by Zheng, 'If Zheng Bijian is the face of reformist "liberalism," I tremble for China.'[13] These warnings went unheeded in every way that mattered.

The operation of the decade: The MSS and China Reform Forum

China Reform Forum – to many scholars and policymakers the think tank brings to mind dreams of change and liberalism in China. To the handful of Western intelligence officers who were aware of its true nature, the name draws a mixture of admiration and frustration. Chinagate (see chapter 5) and other early MSS entanglements in the politics of Washington, DC were the full dress rehearsal for this global operation. Led by Zheng Bijian, the think tank touted unmatched access to China's leadership, superior pedigree through its affiliation with the Party's highest training academy, and a track record of policy influence. Its Beijing office was decorated with photos of visits by retired American policymakers and politicians – president George H. W. Bush, national security advisors Henry Kissinger and Brent Scowcroft, Bill Clinton's secretary of defence William J. Perry and so on.[14] It was cocaine for China watchers from Washington to Tokyo and Paris, manufactured in Beijing by the MSS.

Most of MSS's influence operations are difficult to track. Their secrecy and sheer volume create formidable barriers to working out what's really going on. A suspected MSS Social Investigation Bureau officer appears in Hong Kong, using it as a base to cultivate connections in the islands of Mauritius and Macau. His name might pop up in the Panama Papers, chained to a company with no public presence. The many aliases he undoubtedly uses are unknown. From there the scent dies out. One is left with pieces of a web, the sense of a network but not its mechanisms, its aims and its consequences. It's the kind of frustrating experience one has time and time again while digging into the MSS.

China Reform Forum is the exception to that rule for the same reason it's been stunningly successful. Its achievements haven't relied on spies operating in the shadows, high-tech gadgetry or daring thefts of classified documents. The brilliance of this scheme is its recognition that an open influence operation is sometimes the best influence operation. Despite the operation's breadth, few in the US intelligence community were familiar with it, and some of those who were simply viewed it as an MSS-connected think tank but not a major cause for concern.[15]

Somewhere in its Beijing headquarters, the MSS must have recognised how only some of its spies were running into law enforcement blockades. Counterintelligence agencies like the FBI have traditionally busied themselves with protecting state secrets, protected technology and government employees. They worry much less about think tanks and foreign policy conferences. Even though it took many years for the MSS's understanding of foreign political systems to mature, it quickly recognised the importance of these organisations on the verge of officialdom.

At the time, countering influence operations wasn't a focus for the FBI, and few understood just how much emphasis the CCP placed on such activities.[16] US prosecutions of Chinese espionage have been overwhelmingly focused on economic espionage, yet it is only one of many areas in which the MSS is active. Few other countries have ever taken China's spies to court. The more court cases and public exposures of China's economic espionage operations, the more it makes people think these often clumsy plots really do represent the bulk of MSS activity. Cautiously orchestrated operations that span several years are intrinsically much harder to bring to light.

It's simply more exciting and fruitful to track a foreign intelligence officer who's using skilled tradecraft and breaking well-tested laws than one who chats to foreign policy scholars without obviously recruiting any of them. A career-minded counterspy would have to be stupid to dedicate their efforts to chasing influence operations that almost never lead to prosecutions. When an engineer working for the Chinese government steals the results of a US defence contractor's jet engine research program, the cost can often be literally accounted for in the hundreds of millions of dollars. The effect of a long-term influence operation is only obvious once it's already too late. Frustrated Western intelligence officers who wanted to push back against China's influence operations gained little buy-in from their leadership, especially because their criminal aspects were harder to point to.[17]

There are other reasons to pay no mind to elite influence operations. By targeting and manipulating prominent political figures, the MSS forces uncomfortable political choices upon spy catchers who'd rather stay out of the media and parliamentary inquiries. According to one former US intelligence officer, executives in intelligence agencies 'hate dealing with political cases' because of the sensitivities they involve, and a fear of upsetting political parties.[18] The kinds of people targeted by the MSS usually don't react well to anyone telling them they've allowed themselves to be manipulated by a foreign power. And when these operations move with ease from country to country, within and beyond China's borders, they also exploit the unclear and contested bureaucratic lines between a country's counterintelligence and foreign intelligence agencies, which often aren't in perfect sync.

Humble beginnings

Quietly founded on 1 March 1994, China Reform Forum initially focused on exchanging ideas with international experts on economic policy.[19] It was affiliated with the China Economic System Reform Society, a group of economists and policymakers navigating the balance between capitalism and socialism with Chinese characteristics.[20] Wang Guiwu, a retired government economist, was selected as China

Reform Forum's first chairman. Wang could tout his connection to China's premier and chief economic policymaker Zhu Rongji, an old classmate of his, but he had little international name recognition and hadn't been particularly senior in his government career.[21]

Those behind the scenes of China Reform Forum are much more interesting. The first time the group appeared in national newspapers, in a January 1996 article about a Spring Festival celebration it held for international economists, 'Lin Rong' was described as its secretary-general.[22] About a decade later, he reappeared as deputy secretary-general of the MSS's CICEC front group.[23] According to a profile of him from a 2001 conference in Bangalore held by New York's Asia Society, 'Professor Lin' was a graduate of Beijing's Renmin University and France's National School of Administration, but there's almost no other information available about him.[24]

The address China Reform Forum uses in government registration records also provides another MSS link: 35 Baofang Hutong in Beijing's inner east (now numbered 69) is the same location once used by two magazines and two front groups controlled by the MSS Social Investigation Bureau.[25] Lin Di, the MSS Social Investigation Bureau chief who had cultivated DC elites through the agency's CICEC front group, was a vice president of China Reform Forum.[26]

From the beginning, this think tank was a staging ground for influence operations.

In China Reform Forum, the MSS was drawing on what by now had become one of its traditions going back to at least the 'Soros incident' of the 1980s. It wisely recognised that foreigners who invested in China's project of reform and opening, both in principle and with their wallets, would become China's greatest advocates. Their good intentions could be taken advantage of to manipulate foreign politics and perceptions of China.

To this end, a cohort of internationally recognised Chinese intellectuals and economists, including Fan Gang, Justin Yifu Lin and Hu Angang, joined the forum in its early days. Another member was Ding Xueliang, a scholar at the Australian National University who had been sponsored by the MSS-infiltrated Soros China Fund in the 1980s. Peng Puzhang, a Japan-based businessman who once worked alongside MSS officers in the Chinese Academy of Social Sciences Foreign Affairs Bureau, was also listed as a member.[27] Their presence would ensure foreign policymakers, investment bankers, economists and scholars could be drawn to this front. Their names undoubtedly helped the MSS build partnerships in Japan and attract guests from Europe, Australia, Singapore, Canada and the United Kingdom to its economic conferences.[28]

Despite its modest beginnings, the seeds of future growth were there. Economic reform proved a wise theme for the operation. American and European think tanks, like the influential RAND Corporation and the French Institute of International Relations, soon began holding regular conferences and exchanges with China Reform Forum. Within China, the forum's members may have benefited from the political shield MSS contacts offered them as they explored their respective fields and policy ideas. Any of their articles or ideas that proved politically fraught in China could perhaps be excused as attempts to influence foreign audiences in coordination with the MSS.

An expanded mission: Political influence operations

A few years after China Reform Forum's birth, something changed. The Party's leaders might have grown more demanding of the ministry, which was being outshone by its counterparts in military intelligence.[29] At the same time, Party leaders Jiang Zemin and Zhu Rongji were attempting to tackle the fabulous levels of corruption in the People's Liberation Army, and the MSS may have sensed an opportunity to show what it was capable of. Regardless of the true cause, the MSS stepped up its political influence game at the turn of the century, selecting China Reform Forum from among its fleet of fronts.

The MSS's mission for the forum had evolved and grown. Wang Guiwu and other boffins of his Economic System Reform Society were no longer suited to the task. China Reform Forum would continue leveraging hopes for reform and opening to observers of the Chinese economy, but this was now a secondary mission.

Its newfound value was in advanced political influence operations targeting the thinkers and institutions that shape foreign policy around the world. Better suited to this objective, the Central Party School became the group's new benefactor. Central Party School executive vice president Zheng Bijian was chosen as China Reform Forum's new chairman in February 2000.[30] As the top academy for senior cadres, the school both indoctrinates and acts as a brains trust for the Party, with extensive ties to its leaders.[31] A stark upgrade from China Reform Forum's previous affiliation, the Central Party School partnership may have reflected the Party leadership's growing trust and confidence in the MSS.

It was no big deal if some association for economists was exposed as working with the MSS, but the Central Party School is a far more sensitive matter. A senior Politburo member or leader-in-waiting is usually selected as the institution's figurehead while deputies actually run the school. Hu Jintao, two years out from becoming Party leader and China's president, was chancellor of the school when it became China Reform Forum's patron. In 2007, none other than Xi Jinping was placed in charge of it as he was being positioned to lead China. Now that Xi Jinping has risen to general secretary, his close friend Chen Xi heads the Central Party School.

China Reform Forum's connection to the Central Party School makes it a child of the Party's nerve centre. Most other Chinese think tanks are controlled by lesser agencies, like the China Institute for International Studies, which reports to the Ministry of Foreign Affairs. In contrast, 'China Reform Forum was always a kind of oddity', one American China scholar who was familiar with the group told me.[32] It had none of the age or established reputation of other official think tanks, but its star shone brightly. In large part it owed this to the Central Party School, which reaches across the upper ranks of the Party, training officials from all agencies, and was unique in having the general secretary-in-waiting as its chancellor. Most of all, Zheng's presence was magnetic. When China Reform Forum set up its website a month after Zheng became chair, the network server was so overloaded with visitors that it had to be rebuilt with greater capacity.[33]

To many observers, China Reform Forum offered the chance to foretell China's future and tap into the thoughts of its leaders. It was a crystal ball into the closed hallways of the Zhongnanhai leadership compound. It might even be used to influence China's direction and encourage reformist forces within the Party.

China Reform Forum broke the mould of stodgy Party bureaucrats in Mao suits who seized any opportunity to lecture their guests on the West's problems (although its staff sometimes did that). Its researchers didn't always follow the Party line. They could seem urbane, liberal and willing to share what they'd heard from the Party's inner sanctum. One of them even voiced support for 'inevitable' democratic reform in China and expressed sympathy for Zhao Ziyang, the Party's reformist general secretary who was dismissed and placed under house arrest after the Tiananmen massacre.[34]

Waves of foreign officials and scholars conversed with the group throughout the 2000s. Embassies turned to it for insight that would help them write classified cables and inform policymakers back home about China's direction. Foreign think tanks and academics leapt at the chance to engage and partner with this wormhole to Zhongnanhai. Some saw it as a chance to influence the Party and urge it towards democracy and reform. Few stopped to wonder why so many of the think tank's staff were ghosts with little verifiable past to speak of. Those that did have a public history often came from public-facing parts of the MSS – its China Institutes of Contemporary International Relations (CICIR) think tank or other front groups run by the Social Investigation Bureau. Even experienced intelligence officials seemed oblivious at first to the ambition of China's influence operations. Unwittingly yet recklessly, China Reform Forum's foreign interlocutors helped propagate MSS lies into capitals the world over.

Spymasters

The arrival in 1998 of a new chief of the MSS, Xu Yongyue, came just in time for him to help orchestrate China Reform Forum's success. Zheng's acquaintance with Xu proved to be one of the most consequential relationships he formed as a political secretary. Through the 1980s, Xu worked on the opposite peak of Chinese politics to Zheng, as secretary to conservative Party elder Chen Yun.[35] In China Reform Forum, they came together.

Xu surprised observers with his promotion to lead the MSS, an agency he'd never worked in. His appearance and manner certainly lent itself to this reading of him as an unassuming 'dark horse' candidate. China analysts in Taiwan's counterintelligence agency described the prevailing view at the time, writing that 'Xu Yongyue with his flat-top haircut looks just like a country bumpkin'. But their information indicated that 'in reality, he is a highly talented writer, smart and meticulous in his work'.[36]

Chen Yun, the old spymaster, drilled Marxist philosophy into Xu and probably imparted a deep appreciation of Party history and intelligence work upon him. But the reality of managing an agency of covert and clandestine operations was daunting. For five years before entering the MSS, Xu had been a Party leader in Hebei province where he oversaw the local security and law enforcement system. It was some experience, but not enough to know the ins and outs of a world that prides itself on secrecy and conspiracy.

What he lacked in experience, Xu made up for by being whip smart. Shortly before moving into the MSS, he gave an 'electrifying' speech on using sophisticated governance mechanisms to improve social order and reduce crime that was circulated nationally through the *People's Daily*.[37] Under his leadership, the MSS underwent organisational reforms and attempted to audit and divest its business fronts as they exploded in number and corruption.[38] Xu's fifteen years as Chen Yun's secretary also gave him broad connections among elites that few would have been able to compete with. These would have proven valuable for his own security but also for state security.

China's spies take social status and connections seriously when recruiting domestic informants and agents. Of course, coercion could be used instead, but a willing agent is usually far more useful and reliable. The higher the status of the recruiter, the greater the chance the asset would continue to cooperate. For the MSS to have recruited Zheng Bijian, a ministerial official, as the willing face of its most ambitious influence operations, Xu Yongyue must have been intimately involved in calling on his old colleague.

Even as intelligence officers now surrounded him, whatever Zheng Bijian knew of their activities was strictly on a need-to-know basis. The MSS often picks retired officials with international repute to head its

front groups. They're trusted but never enough to really run the organisations or the operations that exploit their reputation. Yet the MSS
found in Zheng an unusually deep and effective partnership.

Imbued with rhetorical talent, Zheng was undoubtedly one of the
best picks China could have made if it wanted to manipulate foreigners.
He was certainly better suited to the job than his predecessor at China
Reform Forum and had already begun playing a larger role in the group
before his appointment.[39] The flexible character to which he owed
his career also made him perfect for dancing between the Party line
and the West's dreams and expectations of China, finding convenient
but misleading ways to reconcile the two. His cynical familiarity with
the Party, its ideology and factions subtly yet always in flux, at times
erupting into purges, had prepared him well for this.

One experienced former intelligence officer who met Zheng
quipped that the secret to his long career in Beijing's centre of power
lay in his alignment with the 'wind faction'.[40] It's impossible to pin
him down as a member of any particular faction in the Party. Rather,
he goes where the winds of power blow, landing him important roles
under six Party leaders in three decades. For someone with his close ties
to the purged Hu Yaobang, there was surely no other way to survive.
Far from merely clinging on for life in the Party system, he thrived amid
a succession of power struggles.

CHAPTER 8

THE CONCOCTION OF CHINA'S PEACEFUL RISE

ZHENG BIJIAN'S ARTICULATION of the 'peaceful rise' concept marked the beginning of a phenomenally successful influence operation orchestrated by the MSS through China Reform Forum. The United States' dogmatic confidence in China's political liberalisation, coupled with the MSS's influence peddling, doomed Washington to failure in recognising and reacting to China's political course. Yet this stunning success emerged from a particularly tumultuous period of US–China relations around the turn of the century.

A major diplomatic incident took place a few months after George W. Bush's inauguration. On 1 April 2001, Lieutenant Commander Wang Wei took off from his base in Hainan to patrol the South China Sea. Piloting his streamlined Soviet jet, Wang soon intercepted an American EP-3 surveillance plane, an awkward porpoise of an aircraft covered in appendages to pick up electronic signals.

The Chinese airman had a taste for risk and presumably an unhealthy affinity with *Top Gun*. In previous encounters he had veered within three metres of US aircraft. He'd salute the American crew members, flip the bird at them and even hold up a sheet of paper with his email address on it in case they ever wanted to contact him.[1]

This time, Wang played it a little too close. He misjudged his momentum and slammed into one of the EP-3's propellers. The foolish manoeuvre sliced his plane in two. He was forced to parachute out, plummeting towards the ocean never to be seen again as the EP-3's crew of twenty-four were tossed around inside their fuselage.

The US pilot managed to regain control of his damaged craft and an emergency landing in the sea seemed like the simplest option, but it was risky and the plane was dangerously overweight. They flew instead towards the closest strip of land – Chinese territory. Crew members frantically tried to destroy the literal piles of sensitive equipment and classified information surrounding them – laptops, papers, cassette tapes, and specialised keys for sending and receiving encrypted information. Yet they were untrained for the task, making their emergency landing in Hainan still bearing reams of secrets for Chinese intelligence analysts to dissect.[2]

The American crew were greeted by unsmiling Chinese soldiers who had more of an air of prison wardens than rescuers. As they arrived, the PLA sent out hundreds of search-and-rescue missions but failed to uncover Wang's remains. The pilot was promptly mythologised by Party authorities, while the twenty-four Americans were eventually released after days of interrogation.

It was an unsightly collision between the two countries mere months into Bush's first term as president. It was also the new administration's first major foreign policy crisis. The relationship, still unformed, was on the line, and both sides acted tough. Secretary of Defense Donald Rumsfeld ordered an end to all military contacts with China, and it would take years for the US's relationship with the PLA to again approach normality.[3]

Beijing's foreign policy and security officials must have felt nostalgic for the Clinton White House of the decade before. There had been deep tension over human rights, but the previous administration showed itself willing to make compromises in the name of strengthening other aspects of engagement with China. It dutifully mediated Congress's desire to contain and punish the Party for its suppression of political and religious freedom. What China called the 'little Bush' administration initially made a point of being tough on China and criticising Clinton for not being that. Ahead of the 2000 presidential election, Bush cast China as a 'strategic competitor', as opposed to Clinton's conception of China as a 'strategic partner'. His incoming national security advisor Condoleezza Rice argued the US government should seek to open up China's economy to promote 'internal transition'. The Bush administration believed economic liberalisation would probably lead to 'sustained and organized pressures for political liberalisation' within China, so the US needed to 'strengthen the hands' of reformists in the Party.[4] One can only imagine how such language went down in Beijing.

Then came the September 11 terrorist attacks. A disaster for America looked like a breath of fresh air for China. The CCP jumped at the opportunity to win friends in the new security-focused administration, and Jiang Zemin personally called President Bush to express his sympathy that day. True to its 'united front' tradition of building alliances of convenience in pursuit of a greater strategic goal, China announced its support for the US-led war on terror. Far from merely not disrupting the US's agenda, Beijing supported anti-terror resolutions at the United Nations and may have helped get Pakistan on side with the war in Afghanistan.[5] Around the same time, the MSS set up its own counterterrorism bureau, which became a locus of cooperation with otherwise hostile intelligence agencies.[6]

America responded in turn, designating the East Turkestan independence movement, an Al-Qaeda–aligned Uyghur group, a terrorist organisation. It was a fine pretence for China to justify its repression of traditionally Muslim ethnic minorities such as the Uyghurs, a step down the path that saw a million people held in Xinjiang's re-education and concentration camps under Xi Jinping.

Except there's scant evidence that the group, which mainly operated in Afghanistan and Syria, ever carried out attacks against China. One expert, George Washington University's Sean Roberts, convincingly called into question the very existence of Uyghur terrorist groups with the capacity to launch strikes in China.[7] Nonetheless, bounty hunters kidnapped nearly two dozen Uyghurs in Pakistan and sold them for US$5000 apiece to the US government, which locked them up in its Guantanamo Bay detention facility. Most were later cleared of terrorism charges and released after years of solitary confinement.[8]

In the meantime, America's attention had pivoted away from North Asia and would remain that way for a decade. Finding a convenient issue of mutual concern, the War on Terror helped stabilise the US–China relationship as Chinese strategists and intelligence analysts pondered what the post-9/11 world meant for their country. Chinese security officials, though anxiously watching the US military's awesome force in Afghanistan and Iraq, must have breathed a sigh of relief. CIA Director George Tenet initially briefed the newly inaugurated President Bush that terrorism, arms proliferation and China were the top three threats facing the country, but China had now effectively moved off that list entirely.[9] It was still a foreign policy priority, but dealing with it as a threat seemed off the table. Cooperation, whether on terrorism or North Korea, was the name of the game.

Cognitive bias was at play. Seemingly surrounded by the brilliance and horror of terrorism, people grew desensitised to the CCP's growing power, unabated human rights abuses and authoritarianism. It became easier to focus on China's economic growth and the pockets of liberalisation in Chinese society. As China scholar David Lampton wrote, 'American priorities and threat perceptions changed – the sense of challenge from China declined as dangers from other quarters mounted.'[10] This shift took place equally among the public as it did within the administration: a Pew survey found 13 per cent fewer Americans were concerned about 'keeping close watch on China as a global power' than before the September 11 attacks. Those who believed China should be a priority of America's foreign policy found themselves deep in the minority, 12 percentage points behind those worried about North Korean militarism.[11]

Arms and influence

Zheng Bijian and his MSS colleagues surely sensed the opportunity at hand. This was a crisis and turning point for US foreign policy and the freshly anointed Bush administration's understanding of the outside world. Not only that, Rice had indicated the US government was in search of Chinese reformists it could back, and the MSS excelled at presenting its officers and proxies as reformist. Years, if not decades, of time for China to continue 'hiding its strength and biding its time' were within reach if the Party played its cards right. China Reform Forum had, of course, been probing US politics for years, aided by numerous intelligence officers stationed in DC and New York as diplomats and journalists. In the early days of the Bush administration the forum invited politically connected American China scholars to Beijing, quizzing them on Washington intrigue: who was up for promotion, who might be favourably disposed to China, and so on. Slowly but surely, the MSS was working its way closer to the White House.

Amid the Mid-Autumn Festival of 2002, China Reform Forum flew an old contact out to Beijing. The meeting doesn't appear on the MSS front's otherwise detailed records of over fifty visits and events from that year alone. This was sensitive: the only account of the meeting just describes him as a 'godfather' to National Security Advisor Condoleezza Rice. It was the latest of dozens of trips the man, now in his seventies, had made to China over the decades. This mentor to Rice was also an 'old friend' of Marshall Nie Rongzhen, one of the Party's greatest military leaders and the commander of its nuclear weapons program.[12]

'Their goal was to understand the situation from him, and also encourage him to educate Bush's team on China,' a state-owned magazine later revealed about China Reform Forum's operation. Understandably, there's nothing else that's been revealed about these closed-door chats. The old man left with a box of mooncakes – the rich pastry snack of the Mid-Autumn Festival – and a scroll of Chinese calligraphy to deliver to Rice.

From what little has been disclosed about the exchange, it's clear that the 'old man' was John W. Lewis, the late Stanford University expert on Chinese nuclear weapons and a strong advocate of engagement with China. Though Rice was a Soviet specialist, Lewis was head of the Stanford centre where she worked after completing her doctorate. 'I had wonderful mentors,' one of whom was Lewis, Rice said of her time at the university.[13] Her time at Stanford, where she rose to become the university's youngest-ever provost, was an essential step in her journey towards the world's most powerful jobs.

Lewis's strange dances with the Party's military and security agencies went back to the 1990s, preparing the ground for the MSS's work a decade later. One of his closest collaborators, Hua Di, was a former Chinese military engineer who helped him write detailed and influential histories of China's ballistic missile program, based on 'extensive interviews' with Chinese insiders.[14] Hua was in fact 'one of three people authorized at the highest levels in China to give me material on the history of the strategic weapons program,' Lewis claimed. The Chinese military's leaders wanted the West to better understand its capabilities and strategy, the thinking went. This would reduce the risk of any overreaction to China's relatively small strategic missile program.[15] In 1993, Lewis and Hua also brokered a controversial deal that gave the PLA access to advanced broadband equipment from the United States.

The dance between capitals

When Hua was unexpectedly arrested in China in 1998, accused of leaking state secrets, the turn of events gave the MSS an odd connection to Lewis. After all, it was the MSS to whom Hua turned for guarantees that he would be safe in China. As both an intelligence and a law enforcement agency, tasked with punishing those who leak state secrets, it could have set Hua free. Lewis travelled to China six times the year of Hua's arrest, desperately seeking to resolve the situation. At some point he would have added the MSS to his list of Chinese official contacts.[16]

Rightly or wrongly, the MSS thought it could translate its relationship with Lewis into a connection with the White House and Lewis's former protégé, Rice. Since the Hainan jet incident, their Rolodex for the new White House had been slim. Chinese military intelligence in particular had lost much of its access to the new administration. This was a job for the MSS.

Despite her strong comments on China, 'Condoleezza Rice was still one of the few options we had to work on', explained Li Junru, then a deputy director of China Reform Forum.[17] The scene was set for Zheng to lead the MSS's political influence professionals into Washington.

With an invitation from two venerable DC think tanks, they busily worked their contacts to line up meetings with key decision-makers. This task was made easier by the fact that Zheng was recognised as a leader of Communist Party chief Hu Jintao's new task force on US–China relations. Tellingly, expert theoreticians and narrative crafters like external propaganda official Zhao Qizheng – not diplomats – formed the group's core.[18] This was an influence operation, not a policymaking committee.

For both sides, it was a chance to gauge the waters. In December 2002, the US State Department's head of policy planning, Richard Haass, gave a speech just three days before Zheng's team departed for the United States.

Haass attempted to lay out a 'post-Cold War' agenda for the relationship that would make up for what he called the previous decade's directionless 'fits and starts'. The speech was a defining document of what now feels like the distant history of US–China relations. This new era would be defined by 'tangible actions to build a more cooperative US–China relationship'. Mere 'engagement', Haass argued, was not enough – America's new Chinese mission was to build concrete cooperation on key areas.

And there seemed few bonds as powerful as a common enemy. Just as animosity towards the Soviet Union brought China and the United States together in the 1970s, Haass believed security threats could once again unite them. Haass presented counterterrorism cooperation after September 11 as a model for the two nations' future, raising how they had worked together to label the East Turkestan Islamic movement as a terrorist group.

Yet the Bush administration also believed China could and should be integrated into its international 'system of shared interests and values'. A core but shaky pillar underlying this premonition was the belief that 'prosperity will lead inexorably to demands by Chinese citizens for greater inclusion in their political system'. Haass called for China to move towards political liberalisation and openness, but the coming years showed that the US was willing to leave that up to the Party's discretion. Haass, for his part, was emphatically opposed to competition with China.[19]

China's magi

Zheng and his MSS collaborators arrived that December as the first high-level delegates to study Haass's proposal on the ground. Was this a ploy to distract and undermine China, or could the Party embrace the benefits of US partnership while dallying on the question of human rights and political change? For the MSS, this was an opportunity to analyse the situation in America as it honed and revised its influence operations, seeking to avert attention from signs of the Party's growing misdeeds and ambition.

They couldn't have gathered a better focus group to investigate and test their lines on as they crafted what became the 'theory of China's peaceful rise'. The delegation visited senior congresspeople and officials from the departments of state and commerce. Half a dozen retired officials who continued to shape foreign policy discussions, including Henry Kissinger and Brent Scowcroft, weren't forgotten either.[20]

Condoleezza Rice and Bush's chief of staff were key parts of the agenda. The China Reform Forum team sat down with Bush's young national security advisor, effectively Bush's top foreign policy advisor alongside the secretary of state. According to the Chinese side's rather condescending account, Zheng and Rice got off to a cold start. 'Your qualifications aren't enough to be the US national security advisor,' Zheng said. 'You don't understand China because you've never been to China.' Rice had in fact visited China before, but Zheng pressed the point. He quizzed her on the essence of the Chinese Communist Party and laughed when she claimed it was the 'three represents', Jiang Zemin's recently introduced policy emphasising the importance of the business sector.

Zheng left Rice with three gifts. First was volume three of the *Selected Works of Deng Xiaoping*, which covers most of the 1980s ('to tell her that our internal and external policies aren't tricks, that they're open'). Second were the memoirs of Pu Yi, China's last emperor who was detained and re-educated as a gardener by the CCP (to show China's history of anti-imperialism, class struggle and humanism). Finally, he gave Rice, an accomplished pianist, a copy of the *Yellow River Piano Concerto*, hoping that the score would somehow showcase China's 'vibrant culture and deep history'.[21] Musically, the piece has much of Western romanticism – Tchaikovsky, Rachmaninoff and the like – and remarkably little traditional Chinese influence. Without realising it, this final gift encapsulated an aspect of their influence agenda: show the West that behind our pretence of being uniquely Chinese, China under the Communist Party is also imbued with European tradition as it moves towards modernisation into a liberal democracy.

Zheng's account of the trip, probably a censored version of his report to the Party leadership, was published in a volume edited by MSS officers including Social Investigation Bureau chief Lin Di.[22] In it, Zheng described how his American counterparts often expressed concerns that China was on an inexorable path to conflict with the United States, that it 'will inevitably become a potential threat to the United States'. He rejoined that China would forge a *peaceful* and groundbreaking path to development, relying on socialism with Chinese characteristics. Spicing up the novelty of his approach, Zheng said that his American interlocutors remarked they'd never considered the idea before and told him it was 'very deep'. America's foreign policy giants – 'Kissinger, Brzezinski and Scowcroft' – were all swayed by and in agreement with Zheng's proposal, he claimed. All he requested to take the idea further was approval to focus research efforts on 'peaceful rise' and access to platforms where he could promote it to international audiences, which is where the Bo'ao Forum for Asia fits in.[23]

Versions of the 'peaceful rise' idea had been percolating around academic circles for years, but it was this 2002 tour of the United States that convinced Zheng to advocate and articulate it. The next year's Bo'ao speech took Zheng and his theory to the world. After decades working as a hired pen, he now had a concept to claim as his own – even if he had no power over how the MSS exploited it.

This MSS influence operation was innocently absorbed into the heart of American foreign policy. Speaking in 2005 to the National Committee on US-China Relations, an influential non-governmental group, Deputy Secretary of State Robert Zoellick laid out a new framework for the Bush administration's China policy. He opened his speech by praising none other than Zheng Bijian, with whom he'd 'spent many hours in Beijing and Washington discussing China's course of development and Sino-American relations'. The month before,

Zheng had reiterated his 'peaceful rise' theory in an essay for America's *Foreign Affairs* magazine, and Zoellick presented the new Bush policy as a response to it.[24]

Zoellick could not agree more that China's peaceful rise had so far been immensely successful. He had just wrapped up four years as the Bush administration's top trade official, overseeing China's entry to the World Trade Organization in 2001. 'The dragon emerged and joined the world' as a result of American policies, he quipped, and China was now 'a player at the world table', having entered key international organisations and agreements.

Now that China had taken a seat beside other major powers, Zoellick picked up Zheng's theory and announced that 'We now need to encourage China to become a responsible stakeholder in the international system'. To achieve this transformation, America would have to reject those voices that 'perceive China solely through the lens of fear' and work towards the 'opportunity' that China promised.

Zoellick did not gloss over sources of tension in the relationship. He specifically raised China's military expansion, protectionist tendencies and 'tolerance' of intellectual property theft. Yet further incorporating China into the world order seemed like a remedy to these problems, as if the US only needed to show China the light. Even as these sources of tension only grew over the following decade, they were consistently glossed over in favour of cooperation on international issues like climate change and countering terrorism. It was easier than admitting that decades of China policy had gone wrong.

The early Bush administration's confident language around changing China from within was even more explicit in Zoellick's speech. Cooperating with an emerging China, he said, was a step towards 'the democratic China of tomorrow'. He acknowledged that the concept of 'peaceful rise' would continue to be debated in Beijing and Washington, but this only strengthened the MSS's hand as it positioned its assets and officers as members of a phantom reformist faction. Zoellick appeared to view Zheng Bijian and his undercover MSS associates as exemplifying the forces that would push China towards liberalism, if only they could be further empowered.

The MSS con had worked in a remarkably short period of time. The chief architect of the United States' China policy had name-dropped their top front group, China Reform Forum, and unwittingly endorsed their influence operation.[25]

Turning weakness into strength

Surprising for how much geopolitical stake was placed on it, the vague and loosely formulated concept of 'China's peaceful rise' rested upon several seemingly contradictory narratives. From the outside these might seem like weaknesses but they only enhanced its effectiveness as a propaganda narrative and influence operation, guaranteeing its circulation to this very day.

More than anyone else, it was Chinese scholars who took aim at Zheng's theory. Two professors from Beijing's Renmin University summarised the main critiques, which centred on how the 'Taiwan issue' and America's attitude towards China undermine the idea that China can rise peacefully. For one, China's Taiwan policy officially reserves the right to use armed force to conquer Taiwan, though dressed up in defensive language. This 'sacred right' cannot be limited by the peaceful rise concept. Second, goes the critique, America will try to constrain China's development, peaceful or not. Both countries had their share of folks who believed some sort of confrontation was inevitable.[26]

Though the Renmin University scholars attempted to refute those critiques, Zheng ended up incorporating them into future formulations of his theory.[27] Convening a roundtable at the Bo'ao Forum the year after introducing the concept there, he listed Taiwan among the primary challenges to China's peaceful rise. Peaceful rise, 'by definition, requires the peaceful reunification of Taiwan and mainland China', Zheng maintained. But 'should foreign forces dare to intervene to support "Taiwan independence," the use of force will by no means be ruled out'.

Zheng's retort essentially turned the very contradictions highlighted by his critics into his theory's greatest strength. By emphasising the contingent nature of China's peaceful rise, Zheng was placing the burden of resolving those tensions onto other nations, and America in particular.[28]

It was a wily conceptual *volte-face* that would have made Hu Qiaomu, the Party propaganda chief who once supervised Zheng, proud.

As John L. Thornton, former co-president of Goldman Sachs and board chairman of the influential Brookings Institution think tank pointed out, Zheng's campaign 'demands that the rest of the world help China create an international environment where this sort of rise can take place'.[29] China requires access to 'capital, technology and resources in world markets', Zheng argued, so established powers must support China's integration into the world economy. China needs stronger 'cultural support' around the world for its rise, which also depends on world peace.[30]

The peaceful rise theory 'always had a kind of half threat', an American China scholar who heard Zheng speak recalled. 'It was like, "China will rise peacefully, unless ..."'[31]

The theory's challenges and contradictions create room for ill-informed observers to interpret it differently and map it onto their own aspirations for China. This flexibility allowed 'peaceful rise' to catch on as a kind of unfalsifiable cultural meme that could be conveniently adjusted and elaborated on. It took on a life of its own, far outlasting its official endorsement.

The Chinese government's behaviour, no matter how militaristic, aggressive, abusive or disrespectful of national sovereignty, can never disprove the theory of China's peaceful rise. Instead it becomes proof that China was so bullied and mistreated, its internal affairs so wantonly interfered in, that it had no choice but to diverge from its historical path. China is no longer an independent agent but a reflection of other world powers' thoughts and desires.

Zheng's theory was clearly not a promise. True to the tradition of China's propagandists, he was not so much committing to a direction for the future as he was applying a framework to the past. Although he called peaceful rise a 'new path', it was one he argued China had already been on for a quarter of a century. This was Zheng's analysis of Chinese foreign policy since 1978. One can see in the theory echoes of his deep experience with rewriting official history. As China scholar Robert Suettinger cautioned, 'the concept of peaceful rise was initially intended as something of a propaganda campaign' and 'should not necessarily be taken to have decisive significance for China's foreign policy'.[32]

Rather than a policy position, Zheng's theory represents China's offer to the West: ensure that we aren't provoked into challenging you. For now, we are still growing, but our achievements will soon match and surpass yours. Abandon Taiwan, forget universal human rights, cede your sovereignty, give us control of strategic industries and technologies and you might be allowed a place in the coming century – if we're feeling nice.

Phantom factions

Debate within the Party over Zheng's framework played into the effectiveness of this propaganda narrative. This looked to outsider observers like a struggle pitting the Party's conservative hawks against supposed liberal reformists exemplified by China Reform Forum. China Reform Forum members who were really MSS influence operatives were instead seen as brave voices for change within the Party, glimmers of hope for a westernised China.

Early on, the Party's highest leaders publicly endorsed 'peaceful rise'. Hu Jintao and his premier, Wen Jiabao, both used the phrase in speeches the month after the Bo'ao Forum in 2003. At a Politburo meeting, Hu again endorsed the term. Numerous influential Chinese journals and newspapers discussed or affirmed the idea.[33]

Yet Hu surprised all when he left out the phrase from his speech at the 2004 Bo'ao Forum. From there, Zheng's concept dropped out from the Party leadership's common parlance. 'Peaceful development', which superficially carries fewer connotations of China displacing the United States, has instead become the preferred terminology, while 'peaceful rise' is still used with less prominence.[34]

The rise and fall of 'peaceful rise' may have been the public signs of a high-level political contest. Jiang Zemin still closely guarded foreign policy as his dominion, and this new theory looked like Hu's attempt to place his own signature on China's external affairs. As one story goes, Jiang was curious about Zheng's theory, and Zheng was able to brief the Politburo on it in 2004. But their consensus was that 'while debate should continue on the appropriateness of the idea, party and state leaders need not themselves speak on the subject'.[35]

Regardless, Zheng maintains that 'peaceful rise' and 'peaceful development' are the same thing.[36] Frankly, neither label has any practical bearing on China's actions. Like the political manoeuvring that led to the MSS's creation, the heart of the debate is best understood as one of legitimacy, personality and symbolism. Jiang and Hu's battle over foreign policy, if there was such a clash, looks more like a proxy war over political turf, not substantive differences in grand strategy. It was a struggle the MSS's influence operations could profit from regardless of the outcome.

The peaceful rise meme lives on outside of China, with help from the Party's foreign influence organs. Many foreign China watchers misread the debate over Zheng's proposal as akin to the foreign policy debates familiar to democratic nations, where politicians, academics, media and other stakeholders chip in to formulate policies with concrete consequences. Following this logic, there's one faction of China's leadership that's a better fit for US interests pitted against a hawkish group that's more inclined to intimidate China's neighbours and Washington.[37] Condoleezza Rice merely reflected mainstream views when she wrote that the administration needed to capitalise on the demands that economic growth would bring for political reform in China and 'strengthen the hands' of reformists in the Party.[38]

Zheng's advocacy for peaceful rise and ties to President Hu Jintao placed him and China Reform Forum in the friendlier camp. This image was no doubt buttressed by Zheng's time spent beside Hu Yaobang, a genuine reformist interested in liberalisation. The fact that he'd happily worked across the political spectrum through his career may have escaped people's attention. These looked like the group to back. They were the insiders you talked to in order to understand what a more liberal and peaceful China would look like, to learn how you could help achieve that dream. They were meant to be the good guys.

It was a monumental case of disastrous and misguided mirror imaging. Zheng's influence within China is hard to assess. The symbiotic relationship between Zheng and the MSS makes any attempt to separate disinformation from fact on this matter fraught.

His signature theory is essentially a propaganda framework and not a policy position.

Yet his global influence is undeniable. No less than Henry Kissinger, the giant of American foreign policy who was central to opening US–China relations, praised Zheng in his bestselling 2011 book *On China*. Kissinger, one of Zheng's frequent interlocutors, elevated the peaceful rise narrative to a statement of Chinese government intentions. The fact that Zheng's proposal dropped out of official usage as quickly as it appeared, and for that matter was never about policy anyway, gets left out.[39]

Kissinger's misunderstanding is instead a demonstration of how phenomenal 'peaceful rise' was as an influence operation. Using their skills of deception and manipulation, MSS officers worked hard to promote the assumptions about China that Zheng articulated, assuring their contacts that 'peaceful rise' still had relevance.[40] They combined the theory of China's peaceful rise with intelligence tradecraft to create a new songbook for political warfare.

The 'peaceful rise' narrative cemented China Reform Forum's attractive power. Even if it was only fleetingly heard from the mouths of Party leaders, that seemed to prove that China Reform Forum could shape the Party and not just reflect conservative orthodoxy. It was certainly more than other Chinese think tanks could offer. In the eyes of foreign observers, Zheng was no longer just a former deputy leader of the Central Party School. He was a 'a confidant of Mr Hu', in the words of the *Wall Street Journal*, and a 'consummate Chinese Communist Party insider'.[41] US diplomats concurred, describing him as 'one of Beijing's top foreign policy advisors'.[42]

China Reform Forum could also dangle connections to other powerbrokers in the Party's inner sanctum. According to Bonnie Glaser, an experienced observer of Chinese foreign policy, academics in Beijing who wanted to be heard by the Party leadership would lean on Zheng Bijian to pass their reports up the chain. Scholars in Shanghai would turn to former mayor Wang Daohan, who was Jiang Zemin's mentor and the senior advisor to China Reform Forum until his death in 2005.[43] The group also promised a channel to Zeng Qinghong, then China's vice president and perhaps its third most powerful man.

Zeng's secretary was another advisor to the MSS front and sometimes participated in its meetings with foreigners, such as a dinner with former European Commission president Romano Prodi or a trip to Korea's Jeju Peace Forum.[44]

Yet MSS officers aren't in the business of helping foreigners influence the Party and understand its inner workings. Some if not most of those who've been awarded access to Party leaders are asked to do something in exchange. For example, China Reform Forum and the MSS's Lin Di helped American peace activist Jeremy J. Stone land meetings with Chinese officials as he tried to independently resolve tensions between China and Taiwan by negotiating a unification of the two nations. Lin once even offered Stone an audience with President Jiang Zemin, but there was a catch. He had to firmly take the Chinese government's side on the Taiwan issue. Stone turned down the offer, but we know little of what deals the MSS might have proposed to its dozens of other close contacts.[45]

CHAPTER 9

WIKILEAKS REVEALS THE MSS

THE MSS'S ELITE influence operations are a special homegrown brew. The ability to build and maintain relationships comes first. Actually recruiting an American, European, Japanese or Australian elite is only one end goal. Behind closed doors, MSS officers try to build leverage over their targets, offer favours and cultivate trust that can be exploited later on. We know something about these normally impenetrable exchanges from WikiLeaks.

More so than any other Chinese think tank, the MSS's China Reform Forum could lure in foreign friends from the highest levels of politics and government. While its promises of 'peaceful rise' proved to be a lie, it really did offer access to intermediaries of China's ruling triumvirate, if not a private audience with the men themselves on rare occasions. A spectacular new landscape unfolded before the MSS once it learnt to wield these powers. It could now orchestrate more closed-door discussions and deals with world-class foreign scholars and policymakers than ever before. These private meetings opened up new possibilities for influence operations, the kind China's spies once only dreamt of.

Like how Chinese foreign intelligence officers of the sixties were taught to charm their guests over a Chinese meal, the intimacy offered by confidential gatherings provided a perfect setting for influence and ingratiation. China Reform Forum's staff were often willing and able to give away more of the Party's inner workings to their guests. Foreigners eager to learn about China, some less prepared than others, were convinced they were being brought into a circle of trust by Party insiders. 'There were a lot of people who had interactions with the Chinese that didn't know much about the research organisations and may not have cared very much' about whether they were meeting undercover intelligence officers, one American China scholar said.[1] Some knew the group included spies among its ranks but found the relationship useful and thought they were meeting reformists from within the MSS.

At first glance, there was nothing new or remarkable about this ploy. In the first years of its rule, the Soviet Union ran a masterful counterintelligence operation that used a fake monarchist organisation to lure foreign spies, snagging the intelligence services of Britain, France, Poland, Finland and the Baltic states.[2] The same idea was used at the outset of the 1968 Prague Spring when the KGB dispatched fifteen illegal agents to Czechoslovakia to pose as sympathetic Westerners and thereby uncover local counterrevolutionaries.[3]

What sets China Reform Forum apart from these schemes is how it used similar methods not to catch spies but in an active attempt to guide foreign elites through the intricacies of what Henry Kissinger called 'a beautiful and mysterious land', to implant powerful lies and narratives into global discourse.[4] Official statements that contradicted what they'd said behind closed doors could be swatted away with leisure, dismissed as evidence that a conservative and hawkish faction within the Party was still competing for power, that the West needed to help empower liberals in the leadership, or that China's masters were not yet ready to declare publicly the visions they could share in private with a lucky few. They could never be wrong.

Best of all, these operations needn't run the risk of capture or exposure. There's nothing illegal about chatting up and charming people, no matter how cynical your intentions. There was no reason for China Reform Forum's MSS officers to try to recruit people on their trips to the United States – a dangerous move – because they could simply make their pitch on friendly ground when a target visited China. Most of the time, these officers preferred to play a long game where a recruitment pitch was only one end game. 'Make friends and watch what happens' could have been their motto.

The China experts and policymakers who flocked to China Reform Forum were none the wiser about its schemes. Regardless, law enforcement agencies weren't interested in shining a light on these activities, which seemed at the time inconsequential and hard to prosecute. And there were formidable legal and political reasons not to. Proposals to aggressively intervene in MSS operations on US soil have often been knocked back by policymakers fearful of retribution from China.[5]

WikiLeaked

The WikiLeaks revelations of 2010 shone a light on these operations. The activist organisation rocked the world when it published 251,287 confidential US diplomatic cables stolen by Chelsea Manning, then a US Army intelligence analyst in Iraq. Those documents offered a rare glimpse into internal discussions, disputes and deals, many secret.

The US embassy in Beijing, only one of the diplomatic missions affected by the breach, had been sending back cable after cable to the State Department, National Security Council and CIA. In their search for well-placed sources to read the tea leaves of Chinese politics, American diplomats, like those of any country, spent decades building up friends in government agencies, think tanks, universities, media and business. These contacts are like currency for diplomats, helping them impress seniors back home with information and insights.

Hundreds of Chinese contacts were named in leaked cables from the US embassy in Beijing. Chinese government officials, popular academics, journalists and activists were all included. Worst of all, many were marked as 'strictly protected' sources whose identities should be closely guarded. The consequences looked dire for some.

Party-loving Chinese nationalists were furious. While Chinese media were hesitant to report on the revelations, such as one cable alleging the Chinese government had hacked Google, excited netizens jumped China's online 'great firewall' to access the WikiLeaks website.[6] It didn't take long for lists of so-called 'traitors' and 'US informants' to spread on Chinese forums.[7]

But WikiLeaks also exposed much of the US government's ignorance. Cables show how US diplomats walked themselves into traps: undercover MSS officers were successfully posing as friendly contacts and sources. Through diplomatic cables, MSS officers were being given a channel to speak directly to policymakers in the heart of American power and manipulate their understanding of China. In the eyes of their government readers, the stamp of confidentiality US diplomats placed on these cables must have added to the credibility of their compromised sources. It was so smart an operation that it seems inevitable in hindsight.

This shows why China's authorities didn't act against the US embassy's sources: many were in fact MSS assets or undercover officers. To date, it's unclear whether anyone was seriously punished for being named as a diplomatic contact. Far from being harmful in the eyes of China's security services, these exchanges were a golden opportunity to run operations against the United States.[8]

The MSS had bigger problems to worry about, for that matter. Its counterspies were on the cusp of brutally shutting down one of the greatest threats in the agency's history. First, in 2012, Reuters reported that an aide to MSS Vice Minister Lu Zhongwei had been arrested on suspicion of working for the CIA.[9] Lu, a Japan expert who was once head of the MSS's CICIR think tank, was stood down. His aide's fate is unknown. As investigative journalist Zach Dorfman later revealed, this had merely been the tail end of a bloody MSS campaign that wiped out the CIA's sources in China. More than thirty were executed, including many of the MSS's own.[10] These ultra-sensitive clandestine contacts were precisely the kinds of sources who normally *don't* appear in WikiLeaks files. The CIA has its own, more secure systems for sending messages back to headquarters.

Meanwhile, at least twelve undercover Chinese intelligence officers – only those I have been able to confidently identify – were contacts of the embassy. None were recognised as MSS officers by the diplomats writing about them or the ambassador as he signed off on cables citing them. To government readers back in Washington, these spies were quoted as scholars and think tank experts with unusual insight into Chinese politics. In contrast, numerous scholars from the MSS's 11th Bureau, outwardly known as the CICIR think tank, were quoted by US diplomats, while their affiliation with the agency was usually noted.[11]

The MSS selected some of its most savvy officers for the treacherous duty of engaging with US diplomats. They were chosen in part because they met several basic requirements. First, they all had to be loyal and trusted Party members, especially as they might be targets of recruitment by US spies. Having demonstrated that, they also seem to have been chosen for their expertise in both American and Chinese foreign policy. Finally, they had to be experienced at crafting lies that would stick in American minds.

Three people who tick all those boxes stand out in the forty-one leaked cables that mention China Reform Forum: Ding Kuisong, Xue Fukang and Cao Huayin. All were senior members of the front group. All were undercover senior officers of the MSS, roughly at the level of deputy bureau chiefs.

Ding Kuisong

Ding Kuisong, then a vice chairman of China Reform Forum, is a regular on the academic conference circuit. He's well known to most experienced scholars of Chinese foreign policy. He holds genuine academic credentials and was almost always seen alongside Zheng Bijian. The two formed a complementary pair. Zheng dedicated his career to cultivating theoretical expertise, probing and elaborating on the official line. Ding enhanced Zheng's big-picture thinking, bringing with him the practical knowledge of both a security scholar and a spy.[12]

Ding was charming too. 'I sort of liked him,' said one former US intelligence official. 'His English was good and he had a sort of urbane air about him.'[13] Ding picked up a British accent during his time as a visiting fellow at Cambridge University and an affiliate of the London-based Institute for International Strategic Studies, one of the world's largest think tanks.[14]

With a well-furnished record of publications, Ding is a graduate of the MSS's University of International Relations and spent some fifteen years at the CICIR. Some downplay CICIR's ties to the intelligence agency, but it's officially a bureau of the MSS. Its 400 or so analysts produce intelligence briefs for the ministry and China's leaders. Its role in intelligence gathering is seldom recognised even though many of its scholars, including one who concurrently headed the agency's Counterterrorism Bureau, rotate in and out of operational roles. Ding is one example.[15]

Ding is best known for his time heading Southeast Asian and then American studies at CICIR, but he also worked in a part that's left out of official organisational charts. In name and mission, CICIR's Center for World Personage Studies seems to have spawned from the same tradition of intensive profiling and analysis of influential figures as the MSS Social Investigation Bureau.[16] Very little is known about it except that it produces biographical information on thousands of international 'thought leaders'. What we do know suggests a close connection between its research and actual intelligence operations. Many of those it's profiled have been courted by MSS fronts like China Reform Forum. One of its biographical compilations was even written in partnership with a magazine controlled by the MSS Social Investigation Bureau.[17] Of course, Ding's official biography on the China Reform Forum website doesn't mention his time spent as the centre's deputy director.[18]

Ding must have come to the Social Investigation Bureau in 2000 with high recommendations. His last job at the CICIR was as assistant to its director, Lu Zhongwei, who had just been secretly chosen to run the ministry's Japan-focused Tianjin bureau under the pseudonym Zhong Wei and would return to Beijing as a vice minister.[19] This experience and Ding's high rank within China Reform Forum suggest that he was now a deputy chief of the Social Investigation Bureau.[20]

The promotion certainly showed in Ding's behaviour. 'There was this real sort of air of arrogance and self-importance, that he had taken on a very important position,' recalled one American scholar who met him. 'Ding Kuisong always struck me as an intelligence-like person.'[21] His charm was coupled with a reserved bearing, the caution of one involved in the intelligence community. He stood out among China Reform Forum's staff. The American scholar believed his connections to foreign scholars were unmatched 'because he had come from CICIR and met with so many people'.

As if Ding's status as an MSS officer could not be any more obvious, while working at China Reform Forum he also surfaced as the vice president of another Social Investigation Bureau front, the China Universities Alumni Association, which he led on a trip to Taiwan.[22] Around 2011, Ding graduated from China Reform Forum to lead CICEC, the MSS front group that had taken the lead on operations such as the takeover of Soros's China Fund.[23]

Ding was one of China Reform Forum's most effective agents, successfully ingratiating himself with foreign diplomats and scholars. US diplomats consulting their best sources in preparation for the 2009 meeting of the Party's Central Committee seemed to view Ding as the best of the best. He was an individual with 'access to internal Party discussions' who was able to 'discuss current Party priorities', a September 2009 cable reads. Ding accurately predicted the date of the plenum and advised the US government to pay attention to a forthcoming speech by Xi Jinping, then China's heir apparent, for signals ahead of the meeting. Little did they know, Ding Kuisong was providing what spies call chicken feed – genuine but inconsequential information designed to shore up his credibility as a source and an insider.[24]

Another cable from that year gives one example of the lies Ding's chicken feed helped support. This time, the American foreign service officers wanted to understand the twentieth anniversary of the Tiananmen massacre, which was just around the corner. Perhaps the most tantalising question – a loaded one – they had in their heads was: when would the Party revisit that darkest moment in its recent past? Ding skilfully played to their hopes, describing purged Party leader Zhao Ziyang as 'a good man' who made 'tremendous contributions' to reform and opening. Writing back to the State Department, National Security Council and the CIA, these diplomats took Ding's statement as a demonstration that 'support remains within the Party for ousted General Secretary Zhao'.[25] If it were true then, there's been suspiciously little sign of that since.

Ding seemed to suggest it was just a matter of time before the Party reckoned with the bloodshed it inflicted in 1989 and the broader political consequences that year had for reformists in the Party. The Party had now settled on the path of reform, a vague commitment that, Ding claimed, meant economic liberalisation and even democratic reform were 'the only way forward'.

Exploiting the perception that China Reform Forum was tied to a more liberal faction of the Party, Ding warned his American colleagues of the threat Chinese hardliners posed. He 'expressed some worry that a "minority" within China, such as the "New Left," might attempt to "reverse course"', the cable stated.[26] A category that probably captures those who labelled Ding a traitor for being a 'protected' US government source, 'new leftists' stand for nationalism, Maoism and socialism in opposition to neoliberalism and the West.[27] Those ideas seem to define China more and more under Xi Jinping.

Xue Fukang

Xue Fukang, also a vice chairman of China Reform Forum, was consulted by US diplomats to help write the same cable. More experienced and perhaps more cautious than Ding, Xue nonetheless read from the same script. The Party 'would eventually deal with the Tiananmen problem, but doing so would take time', he insisted. What Xue called the 'Pandora's box' of Tiananmen could only be reopened once China was more stable, something Zheng's theory suggests the United States was responsible for ensuring.[28]

Another cable shows Xue testing out a similar line, this time on Taiwan. It was October 2008 and the United States had just announced a tranche of arms sales to the island. China responded with its usual diplomatic protests and suspended military-to-military contacts with America, a freeze that would only end the following February.[29] Speaking to US diplomats, Xue played down China's reactions as mere face-saving measures made necessary by the population's nationalistic sentiments. China had been reasonable in its response, he claimed, and now the United States needed to prove it didn't view China as its enemy, a tax of sorts on its trade with Taiwan. Washington could demonstrate goodwill by lifting restrictions on exports of sensitive technologies (the kind the MSS and PLA try to steal) to China, he suggested. Again, the veteran intelligence officer was trying to place the onus on the United States for guaranteeing China would rise peacefully while absolving the Party for its feverish countermeasures.

That year, Xue was probably already moving into retirement from the intelligence community he'd joined as an English major at the University of International Relations in 1964. Like most of China's spies, his time during the Cultural Revolution is a black hole. He resurfaced in 1980 as the first Washington, DC correspondent for the *Guangming Daily*, still the MSS newspaper of choice today. As students were gunned down on Tiananmen Square, Xue arrived in Canberra, again posing as a journalist. After six years in Australia, he returned to DC in 1997 for his final overseas posting. During this period, one former foreign intelligence official knew of him as the de facto 'MSS representative' in America.[30] The fact that he was a known yet undeclared intelligence officer to the CIA didn't stop him from securing an interview with President Clinton.[31] Nor did it stop him from posing as a scholar affiliated with the Central Party School in his later dealings with US diplomats.

Cao Huayin

Perhaps the youngest of the three MSS officers, China Reform Forum Deputy Secretary-General Cao Huayin was also one of the US embassy's closest contacts, appearing in fourteen cables between 2006 and 2009. He was an accomplished translator and had been an English interpreter for the MSS's CICEC front group.[32] The Chinese edition of *The Wizards of Langley*, Jeffrey T. Richelson's account of the CIA's scientific and technology program, was one of several publications he had translated.[33] US diplomats thought him 'well connected', and he was willing to entertain discussions on any matter of topics, including the Party's internal affairs.[34] In one cable, he contradicted the official line on China's 'open' National People's Congress, pointing out how various debates had in fact been carried out behind closed doors.[35]

Diplomats often consulted him on North Korea and Taiwan. China Reform Forum had some engagement with North Korea, even delivering flowers to its Beijing embassy for the tenth anniversary of Kim Il-sung's death, and Cao was open to sharing his thoughts on the touchy issue of China–DPRK relations. A few years earlier, Cao travelled to the United States for a stint at Stanford University, where he researched North Korea's nuclear arsenal as a visiting scholar.[36] Another MSS scholar-spy operating under China Reform Forum's cover, Li Peisong, was a visiting fellow at Harvard University in 2006.[37]

China appreciated the issue's sensitivity, sending in assets trusted by the security services to communicate its thoughts on North Korea to Washington. Not one but two suspected MSS officers are quoted in one of the cables, as well as an academic closely associated with China Reform Forum.[38] Unusually, both US embassy cables that feature Cao's comments on North Korean nuclear tests were classified 'secret', as opposed to just 'confidential'. On Taiwan, Cao urged the United States to help China rein in what he called their 'common enemy' – Taiwan's President Chen Shui-bian of the Democratic Progressive Party.[39]

The professionals

While Ding, Xue and Cao led the operation at the working level and built up extensive contacts around the world, several of the MSS's top leaders appear around the edges too. China's agent handlers have a long history of trying to match or outdo the seniority and social status of their targets. If you're recruiting a chaired university professor, you'd best have a bureau chief make the approach, or a division chief for an assistant professor and so on.[40]

So, the MSS elite influence operations – like the PLA's – can draw out remarkably senior officers who might normally be expected to stay behind their desks. These operations are so sensitive that the MSS's headquarters appears to take the lead itself, when other operations are usually passed down to provincial bureaus in Shanghai, Guangdong and so on. If you're being trusted to broker access between foreigners and the Party centre, you'd better get it right.

This meant that the growing ambition of MSS foreign intelligence efforts in the 2000s saw MSS chiefs appear in its front organisations, using a range of aliases. In Western intelligence agencies, such high-level officers almost never dirty their own hands with operational activities. It's risky, unnecessary and inappropriate – the higher up you rise, the more of a manager you become. But in China, even retired MSS vice ministers hang onto their fake identities so that they can help the ministry when needed and maintain their foreign contacts.

So when a new class of MSS leaders rose to power around the turn of the century, they eagerly took part in the operations of China Reform Forum and other fronts. This generation entered the intelligence community after the Cultural Revolution, meaning they cut their teeth on operations in the early years of Deng Xiaoping's 'reform and opening' era. They were a breed moulded by the contradictions of Party-endorsed globalism and capitalism yet seemed to have little more affinity for Western ideas than their hardline, conservative predecessors. Corruption and double agents were rampant, but China's growing ties to and cooperation with Western nations also gave the agency unimaginable opportunities for foreign intelligence operations.

Geng Huichang was the first of the new leadership. In the early 1990s, Geng took charge of the MSS's China Institutes of Contemporary International Relations (CICIR) think tank, giving him extensive access to foreign scholars. He specialised in America, Japan and research related to industrial espionage, yet he disappeared shortly after. In May 1995 he was secretly named a vice minister of the MSS, aged only about forty-four. The last of the agency's generation of Cold War legends began to enter retirement. In 2007, Geng assumed the agency's top job: he was now the minister of state security.[41]

Geng's rise and that of China Reform Forum exemplified a monumental evolution in the MSS's focus. A foreign intelligence expert was in charge for the first time, not a political hack or an internal security specialist. His predecessors were occupied with catching suspected spies and building up the MSS's capabilities, but now it was time to show the Party what the agency could do.

Geng was closely associated with the parts of the MSS involved in influence operations. After disappearing into the MSS's leadership, he resurfaced in several front groups. Photos of a 1999 meeting of the Social Investigation Bureau's CICEC front group show Vice Minister Geng, with his recognisable pudgy face and big round glasses, in attendance.[42] The China International Public Relations Association, which officially reports to the Ministry of Foreign Affairs but is secretly run by MSS officers who use it to interact with multinational corporations, gave Geng another hat as one of its vice presidents.[43]

Geng wasn't publicly associated with China Reform Forum, but his emphasis on foreign operations undoubtedly empowered it. His hand may have been represented by the many MSS officers who surfaced in its ranks. Around the time Geng moved into the MSS's top job, Tao Yijiang and Sun Zhihai became vice presidents of China Reform Forum.[44] Sun is still listed as its executive vice chairman.[45] Both were leaders of the MSS's influence operations.

It's hard to find much more about Tao and Sun than cyclical references to other fronts. CICEC's records say Sun is an advisor to the Chinese Association for the Promotion of Cultural Exchange and Cooperation, which is just another Social Investigation Bureau cover organisation.[46] Sun is also a vice president of the China International Public Relations Association, which describes him as a deputy head of the Chinese government's Asia Africa Development Research Institute.[47] Interesting, but these affiliations reveal little beyond the fact that he's connected to foreign intelligence operations.

This is by design: 'Tao Yijiang' and 'Sun Zhihai' are pseudonyms. Two doppelgangers with similar names to these intelligence officers, Tao Dawei and Sun Yonghai, were delegates to the Chinese People's Political Consultative Conference, the highest meeting place of the Party's united front. Tao Dawei's profile just about gives the game away, describing him as a vice president of CICEC even though only Tao Yijiang is named on CICEC's website.[48] Sun Yonghai's profile is more striking: he's listed as a vice minister of the MSS.[49] Some reports claim Sun used to head the MSS's 5th Bureau, which is responsible for analysing intelligence and coordinating operations with local branches of the agency.[50]

Much can be pieced together from the name 'Tao Dawei'. Now retired, he had a long career in the MSS. In the 1990s, he was second in command of the 10th Bureau, which handles the Party's 'overseas security' work. That means it ensures security for Chinese diplomatic missions and state-owned enterprises but also actively infiltrates overseas Chinese student groups and dissident organisations.[51] Before returning to the MSS's headquarters in 2005 as head of the Social

Investigation Bureau, he worked in the agency's provincial branches in Shaanxi and Henan.[52]

Finally, China Reform Forum also named one of Geng Huichang's old colleagues as a vice president.[53] Lu Zhongwei followed Geng as head of the CICIR and then pulled a similar disappearing act. After some years as the pseudonymous 'Zhong Wei', director of the important Tianjin State Security Bureau, Lu was brought back to Beijing by Geng as one of his deputies.[54] China Reform Forum only describes him as a member of a China–Japan friendship association.[55] If anything, it takes guts and confidence to name so many spymasters on the membership lists of front organisations.

CHAPTER 10

THE REVOLVING DOOR: SCHOLARS AND THE MSS

As GLOBAL THINK tanks innocently posed for photos with China Reform Forum staff and flocked to its events, one American scholar of China policy met firsthand with its underbelly. For the sake of his security, let's call him Barry. It was around 2006, the heyday of China's 'peaceful rise', and just about every major American foreign policy organisation had a relationship with China Reform Forum. Barry, a graduate student, knew its staff well from the sidelines of conferences and dialogues. He was in a better position to handle the situation than most, having lived in China and learnt the language fluently. But his youth and experience in DC marked him out as a target. 'They probably saw the likelihood that I would join government at some point,' Barry said, recalling they once explicitly encouraged him to take that path.[1]

One year, China Reform Forum invited him out to Beijing for a conference that never took place. Instead, after some meetings, they treated the young scholar to a boozy karaoke session. From there they dragged him along to a 'fashion show' of scantily clad Uyghur women. 'We can go upstairs with them if you want,' one of the Reform Forum staff members leant in and suggested. Barry politely turned down the offer, but the MSS officers had a backup plan. They took him to an upmarket spa where the group relaxed in an elaborate indoor water grotto. The boss of the MSS officers even dropped in to say hi and wish them a nice stay. 'After a while we showered off and went upstairs and we got massages,' Barry recounted. Then, halfway through, 'the girl asked me if I was alright with a rub and tug, which I declined'. He was, no doubt, being watched and filmed by hidden cameras in the massage suite. 'All the other guys were in other rooms … who the hell knows what they're doing in there.' He guessed the MSS officers were trying to compromise him while also getting in on the fun themselves.

When Barry visited Beijing a few years later, the undercover MSS officers were 'genuinely excited' at the prospect of taking him out for another massage. Sexual entrapment might have failed, but there are many other ways to get at a man. This time he visited a pub in Beijing with one of the China Reform Forum staff. Barry was only acquainted with the man, so he was shocked to hear him suddenly lament that he was in love with a colleague even though he had a wife and child. 'He doesn't love his wife and he wants to be through with it, but he can't … and he really wants to run away with this woman,' the story went. It was a bizarre confession, and all Barry could do was try to console the man over pints of Guinness. 'You're the only one I can tell because you don't know anybody,' the MSS officer moaned. But sympathy wasn't what the MSS was after, of course. The spy had spun his yarn, pretending to drop his guard in the hope that his guest might do the same. 'It did seem to me that he was trying to get me to open up to him,' Barry recalled. 'He even asked me, "Oh, did anything like this ever happen to you?"'

Then there was the money. One of the China Reform Forum officers met with Barry to hand over a cash reimbursement for some travel costs. The money came in a sealed envelope, tapping Barry's knee as the officer tried to pass it to him under the table. 'He did it in a way that was totally sketchy.' Barry assumed someone was watching, ready to snap a photo of a suspicious transfer of cash between him and the MSS. It was kindness dressed up as debt he might have to repay one day, but it didn't even contain the full amount he was owed. To this day, China's premier intelligence agency owes Barry money.

The MSS Social Investigation Bureau's approaches to Barry were downright polite compared to how lesser wings of the ministry treated him. In his assessment, China Reform Forum never asked him to do anything that would 'bring the situation to a head'. They wore their cover as think tank scholars like skin, patiently building a relationship with him and asking for insight into American politics and policy without ever stepping beyond the bounds of what a Chinese scholar might say or do. Never did they 'drop cover', revealing they were intelligence officers in an attempt to recruit him. Barry guessed they were 'largely in a collection mode and a kind of co-option mode'. They wanted him to know that China was going to be 'this great democratic paradise', and they wanted to use him like a focus group to help adjust talking points and influence operations to American tastebuds.

China Reform Forum's MSS officers come from the agency's headquarters, where staff are usually the cream of the crop. Many are transfers from other agencies, like the police or military, or top-tier graduates of specialised MSS training institutions like the University of International Relations and other elite universities in Beijing. Capable graduates with local connections and somewhat lower grades might find jobs in Shanghai, Guangdong, Zhejiang and Tianjin. Woe to those who end up in the landlocked Henan State Security Department, under-resourced, undertrained and overlooked.

While Henan province's intelligence officers may have had the same mission as their comrades in Beijing, they had more rustic ways of going about it. One officer, posing as a scholar at the local Academy of Social Sciences, tried to blatantly honeypot Barry, bribe him and recruit him without so much as trying to strike up a rapport. The spy even explained how he would give Barry access to an email account where Barry could discreetly send in reports as email drafts. Chinese intelligence officers could then log into the same account and read his messages. 'How stupid do you think the Americans are?' Barry asked him. A second local agency – the 'pain in the ass' Shanghai State Security Bureau – also harassed him along similar lines. Was this the muscle called in to prop up China's strained pretence of 'peaceful rise'? Other foreign scholars and policymakers, perhaps because of their seniority, were treated more delicately as targets for influence.

Weak points and revolving doors

Other US think tanks envied the Carnegie Endowment for International Peace's unusual connections in Beijing. One of the largest American think tanks, Carnegie runs a joint centre in Beijing with Tsinghua University, an elite institution that's also Xi Jinping's alma mater. But Carnegie's presence in China goes back even earlier to a partnership with China Reform Forum.

Cables released by WikiLeaks, mostly from between 2006 and 2010, reveal only one aspect from the twilight phase of China Reform Forum's influence operations. Although the MSS still uses the front group to go after easier targets than the United States, the cables are from the front's last days as a highly active and effective intelligence front. And MSS officers were busily exploiting the group's warm and fuzzy reformist aura to do far more than interact with American diplomats.

America's think tanks have long been of interest to Chinese intelligence agencies. Numerous spies from both the MSS and People's Liberation Army have held posts as visiting scholars in DC think tanks with varying degrees of transparency and awareness about their backgrounds.[2] Even before the MSS was created, Chinese intelligence analysts were compiling open-source studies of influential think tanks in the Reagan era.[3]

Closer to the present, MSS Vice Minister Yu Fang travelled to America in the 1990s to carry out fieldwork on the Washington think tank community using his pseudonym, Yu Enguang. Surveying both the Democratic Party–aligned Brookings Institution and the Republican-leaning American Enterprise Institute, the experienced operative queried them on their funding, staff and policy influence. 'These think tanks could be called storage houses or training institutions for government officials,' he concluded, counting up the many former senior officials among their ranks. 'Their status and influence mustn't be downplayed. If we're to understand American politics, we can't be indifferent to think tanks.'[4]

Yu understood that think tanks are open, revolving doors of people and ideas, connecting governments to civil society and academia. They pay little heed to security – after all, they generally don't deal with classified information. Physical security might be practised by some institutions, but warding off influence operations and misinformation is largely up to the discretion of individual analysts. They are exactly the kind of weak points intelligence agencies hope to exploit in democracies. Cultivating and recruiting scholars who might end up in positions of power is orders of magnitude less risky than trying to target serving government officials.

Another advantage for the MSS is that some scholars and consultants can be more valuable intelligence assets than government officials. Most government officials work in narrow lanes and wouldn't normally interact with politicians or colleagues working on unrelated topics on a whim. Their spy handlers need to painstakingly prepare secure channels, as well as backup options, for meeting them, often through third countries. For an academic, on the other hand, jumping between research topics and meeting bureaucrats and politicians for coffee is just part of the job. Regular trips to China for fieldwork don't raise any eyebrows, even if a few leisurely chats with intelligence officers pop up in one's itinerary. Writing confidential reports for various clients is also a common part of think tank work and consultancy.

So the MSS had long known that think tanks were an ideal operating ground for influence operations, and now with China Reform Forum it had the team it needed to breach and enter. Its entanglement with the scholars of not just America but the world goes deeper than any other covert MSS operation of its kind. While MSS US specialists dominated the front group, many of its staff had studied in France and spoke the language. For example, the forum held numerous conferences with the prestigious French Institute of International Relations, giving MSS officers excuses to probe European scholars and policymakers.[5] In 2016, one of China Reform Forum's staff members reappeared in the Chinese embassy in Paris as a 'press attaché'.[6]

The Carnegie Endowment for International Peace

Fittingly, it was at a conference on China's 'peaceful rise' that the Carnegie Endowment announced the opening of its new branch in Beijing. Already in 2004 Carnegie boasted the largest China program of any DC think tank, one that would more than double in size by the decade's end.[7] The two-day conference that September drew together leading voices on American China policy like former national security advisor Zbigniew Brzezinski and J. Stapleton Roy, a former ambassador to China.[8] It was, in the words of one speaker, 'the best conference on China I've had in my professional career'.[9]

The Carnegie Endowment had much to be excited about. After several years of collaboration with China Reform Forum, it could now reveal it had inked a deal to deepen that partnership and set up Carnegie's first Beijing office within the premises of China Reform Forum. It was the first American think tank with a permanent presence in Beijing. Carnegie's Chinese partner, which program director Minxin Pei stressed was 'an independent NGO', would also kindly appoint a local coordinator to help run seminars and meetings in Beijing. Perhaps as a gesture of goodwill, several members of China Reform Forum, like Ministry of Foreign Affairs think tank chief Ruan Zongze, travelled to DC for the conference.

This was, in Pei's words, an unrivalled chance to 'reach the Chinese policy community' and engage in honest discussion with the Party. Carnegie thought it was expanding its influence within China, blind to the fact that it was taking part in an MSS influence operation.

Once again, dreams of shaping China were turned on their head, transformed into opportunities for the Party's own foreign influence operations.[10] The blunders of Soros's China Fund, and Wang Chi and Chas Freeman's US–China Policy Foundation, were doomed to be repeated. China Reform Forum's access to Party insiders and reformist guise proved irresistible.

Carnegie's China experts were not fools who would happily repeat Party lines. Minxin Pei, now a professor at Claremont McKenna College, is an experienced and perceptive observer of Chinese politics. Writing in 2005, he argued the Bush administration needed to toughen up on China and push the country to implement policy changes that would 'assuage American anxieties about the nature of the Chinese regime and its aspirations for power'. Pei had no illusions about China's authoritarian ruling Party, which he assessed was 'entrenched in power and shows no willingness to embrace democratic reforms'.[11]

But entering a partnership with a front for the MSS Social Investigations Bureau risks far more than ideological compromise.

Nestled in Massachusetts Avenue in central Washington, DC, the Carnegie Endowment's headquarters speaks to its engagement with policy and politicians in America. Even without relying on classi-fied information, the insights scholars gain from living and breathing Beltway culture can help the MSS track US politics and guide its intelligence operations. The kinds of exchanges and discussions that are a routine part of any policy analyst's work become fraught when your interlocutor is a covert political influence officer. It's not a game that genuine think tanks – the kind that aren't run by the MSS – can safely play.

The Carnegie Endowment wasn't just sending its own China scholars into the MSS's arms but bringing other organisations and policymakers along for the ride, opening them up to the kind of targeting Barry experienced. China Reform Forum already wielded Zheng Bijian's magnetic power and the Central Party School as tools for drawing in foreigners, and the Carnegie Endowment was essentially adding to its armoury, lending its name and reputation to the MSS. For example, the Carnegie Endowment introduced the MacArthur Foundation to China Reform Forum when the philanthropic organisation, one of America's largest, was scoping out prospects for a presence in Beijing.[12] In one meeting, Carnegie gathered scholars from India who shared their analysis of Indian foreign policy with undercover MSS officers.[13]

One meeting organised by the Carnegie Endowment and China Reform Forum, on Taiwan, saw MSS officers affiliated with a total of three different fronts attend.[14] This relationship extended into the United States too, such as when Carnegie hosted China Reform Forum's vice president for a speech in Washington, DC.[15] After Obama's election in 2009, the same MSS officers organised a conference with Carnegie's China program, then headed by former National Security Council staffer and US Taiwan representative Douglas Paal, to learn the latest on American political developments.[16]

A few years after the Carnegie Endowment's bargain with the MSS, its China program was in full swing. Carnegie Endowment bosses in DC and New York rewarded it with an additional US$3 million grant to expand its engagement with China. The US needed more research to help 'redefine the nature of its relationships with major and emerging powers', the Carnegie Corporation's president explained.[17] China Reform Forum's peddling of insider access continued to deepen the global think tank community's compromise.

The Carnegie Endowment was far from the only American think tank that unwittingly wrapped itself up in the MSS's influence operations. Two China representatives for the Asia Society, an influential institution based in New York, were named as members of China Reform Forum's council.[18] Washington, DC's Center for Strategic and International Studies was often a host for visiting China Reform Forum delegations, as was the Brookings Institution, which published an English edition of Zheng Bijian's collected works.

Scholars, think tanks and diplomats from India, Korea, Japan, Singapore, Canada, Taiwan, Germany and the United Kingdom were frequently drawn to the MSS group. The Australian embassy invited Ding Kuisong, one of the most senior MSS officers running China Reform Forum, to give a presentation to Australian defence officials. Later, the embassy took a visiting Australian intelligence analyst to meet China Reform Forum scholars.[19]

Analysts at geopolitical intelligence firm Stratfor considered a China Reform Forum staffer as one of their best sources, while noting with puzzlement that he sometimes 'drops totally off the radar'.[20]

The RAND Corporation

It was China Reform Forum's partnership with RAND that should have raised the most eyebrows.

If you've ever windsurfed, then you've literally stood upon the RAND Corporation's work – the sport was invented by one of its engineers. That's just one example of how RAND's achievements speckle twentieth-century history. Its analysts have left their mark on the full spectrum of government policy, from nuclear weapons strategy, counterterrorism efforts and healthcare to the earliest computers and government-sponsored LSD testing.[21]

Nearly all its work is published and unclassified, but its critics still see it as some mix between the 'deep state' and the Cold War military-industrial complex. Pravda, the Soviet Union propaganda outlet, branded it an 'academy of science and death'. In 1971, RAND unwillingly galvanised the anti–Vietnam War movement when RAND analyst Daniel Ellsberg leaked a top-secret study of US involvement in the country to the press. Soon dubbed the *Pentagon Papers*, the report revealed how successive presidents had deceived the public about the plans and motivations behind the conflict.

For these reasons, the MSS quickly homed in on RAND as a priority for influence and espionage operations. It surely helped that RAND is headquartered in California, the state with the most mature MSS networks. And, like any decent think tank, RAND had a healthy interest in China, employing some of America's leading experts on the country.

Through China Reform Forum, RAND also had some of the strongest and longest-running ties to the MSS of any American institution. For over a decade starting in the mid-nineties, the groups partnered to hold high-level conferences, gathering the US investor community with undeclared MSS officers and the Chinese scholars and officials they chaperoned. Funded in part by the US Department of Defense, the meetings gave the MSS a chance to focus attention on China's economic rise and build elite contacts in the United States with RAND's help. A 2003 conference even gained support from Capital Group, one of the world's largest investment fund managers, which sent senior executives to participate.[22] Alongside respected Chinese academics like international relations scholar Wang Jisi, a vice president of the MSS front group, Chinese intelligence officers posing as think tank scholars sat opposite RAND analysts, American government officials and investors at these meetings. The MSS seemed happy to share its bounty: an otherwise low-profile general from China's military intelligence agency sat in on one of the meetings.[23]

Esteemed RAND economist Charles Wolf Jr was one of China Reform Forum's best contacts, an old friend and a frequent collaborator. 'The Chinese had clearly sought out someone of pretty high prestige at RAND,' which led them to Wolf, said former RAND analyst James Mulvenon.[24] Despite years of engagement with China, Wolf was oblivious to the think tank's true nature and introduced it as 'the think tank of China's Central Party School'. Wolf simply didn't want to know, and neither did RAND's leadership. 'China is too important to be left to the sinologists' was a common saying in those circles.

In fact, Wolf 'deliberately cockblocked all of the China people at RAND from attending the meetings' with China Reform Forum, as Mulvenon put it. The decision was so unusual that even the Chinese questioned why RAND's well-known China specialists didn't show their faces when they visited the organisation's offices in Santa Monica. RAND's culture was heavily biased towards economic analysis, Mulvenon explained. The thinking was that econometric tools could be used to unravel tough problems of strategy, nuclear weapons and defence, and 'you didn't need area specialists'. With the China experts out of the room, China Reform Forum's staff and scholars had more room to push deceptive narratives and peddle disinformation.[25]

But when Mulvenon, a junior researcher at RAND in the early 2000s, got his hands on a list of the Chinese visitors, it became clear they had other reasons for coming to America. In the RAND meetings, talkative Chinese economists like Hu Angang and Huang Fanzhang, who were senior members of China Reform Forum, sat alongside undercover intelligence officers who hardly uttered a word. MSS bureau chief and US specialist Lin Di was one of them, but to RAND he was known as a vice president of the Chinese think tank. Mulvenon alerted the FBI to Lin's presence, sending its counterintelligence agents into overdrive. It turned out that while Lin Di went through the motions of attending RAND sessions by day, he was bouncing across Los Angeles to meet assets by night. His contacts were numerous enough that some evenings he was having second or even third dinners around town. Katrina Leung, the FBI source who was conclusively outed a few years later as an MSS spy, was one of Lin's agents (see chapter 4).

Mulvenon tried to warn RAND executive Michael D. Rich, later the institution's CEO, about China Reform Forum. 'I was able to tell him definitively that they were, if not an official part of the MSS, a platform for MSS officers to conduct intelligence operations abroad,' Mulvenon says. He maintains Rich brushed off the concerns, emphasising both Charles Wolf's experience and pre-eminence, and the importance of RAND's relationship with the Chinese think tank.

Undaunted, Wolf continued to deepen RAND's exchanges with China Reform Forum. He proposed the two organisations team up to connect former US government officials, each leaders in the areas of diplomacy, intelligence and economics, with their Chinese counterparts. Rich also backed the idea. After all, as Wolf argued, China Reform Forum, now headed by Central Party School leader Li Junru, offered unparalleled 'opportunities for top-level networking in China'.[26]

Over several meetings with the think tank's MSS officers in 2011, Wolf drafted plans for task forces that would bring together influential Chinese and American thinkers to work on common goals. Robert Gates, the recently retired secretary of defence and a former CIA director, as well as former World Bank president Paul Wolfowitz, were two of the names Wolf floated. China Reform Forum couldn't quite match the monumental status of Wolf's nominees, instead offering the names of respected academics it had long worked with, as well as MSS officers like former *Guangming Daily* US correspondent Xue Fukang. China Reform Forum also nominated two more MSS officers to coordinate activities on their side. Wolf hoped the fruits of these exchanges would influence US–China relations, including through joint reports submitted to both governments and opinion articles in leading outlets such as *The New York Times*.

Mindful of China's developing economy but oblivious to the MSS's resourcing, Wolf proposed that RAND would scrape together the funds for 80 per cent of the project's bill, amounting to over a million dollars. In essence, he was offering to help out with an MSS elite influence operation and pay for the privilege. The money would be used to bring the task force members to each other's country, carry out research, and hold more conferences that the MSS could use as cover for meeting assets.

It would have been one of the greatest breakthroughs in the history of MSS influence operations had it gone ahead. In the end, two things may have come together to foil to Wolf's plans, neither of them a US government intervention. First, a billionaire Wolf turned to for funding was initially supportive of the project, but his staff had the foresight to ask a friend with intelligence experience for advice on China Reform Forum. The former intelligence official came back with damning findings. 'At best the initiative is a talk shop with relatively little impact,' they wrote. 'At worst, funders of the project would be paying Chinese intelligence to influence US policymakers discreetly and to give Chinese intelligence access to former senior officials' who maintain US government advisory roles and might take up office in future administrations. 'The MSS is not a pathway to influence' within China, they cautioned.[27] Second, it was around this time, 2011 or 2012, that the MSS dismantled the CIA's networks in China. In the process, several MSS officers were executed, and the ministry may have lost confidence in China Reform Forum's cover.[28]

Chinese scholars lend a hand

Zhu Feng had travelled to America many times. This trip in 2018 seemed no different to the others as he rushed to board his flight home at Los Angeles airport. An international relations professor at Nanjing University, Zhu is no stranger to government circles but was surprised when two FBI agents stopped him at the boarding gate. They took his passport, crossed out his American visa and told him he'd 'receive a notification' once he was back in China. His visa had been cancelled.[29]

Zhu revealed to the *New York Times*'s Jane Perlez that the FBI had also met him when he arrived in America. They quizzed him about ties to the Chinese military and Ministry of Foreign Affairs. They asked him to hand over what he knew about his colleagues' connections to Chinese intelligence agencies, but he said he didn't know anything. No cooperation, no visa, seemed to be the message. Zhu is well known to American scholars and journalists, many of whom were shocked by what they considered to be an inexplicable and unwarranted intervention.[30]

The professor admitted to the *New York Times* that he'd worked with a group overseen by the China Association for International Friendly Contact, which the newspaper described as an organisation of the 'ruling Communist Party that seeks to promote Chinese interests abroad', but that's less than half the truth.[31]

The association is a well-documented front group for the Liaison Bureau of the Chinese military's Political Work Department. The agency's obscurity – it doesn't even have an English-language Wikipedia page – makes it easy to miss its importance. Simply put, it's a military counterpart to MSS political influence units like the Social Investigation Bureau, specialising in using political warfare to win wars without fighting. The professor is still listed as a council member of its front group and a researcher at its think tank, alongside numerous undercover military officers.[32] In 2017, Zhu worked with Xin Qi, secretly a major general in the political warfare unit, to organise a conference in China that placed Xin alongside American China experts and security thinkers like Dennis Blair, the former director of national intelligence who had also been targeted by the MSS's CICEC influence front.[33]

The FBI probably had an interest in Zhu's MSS ties too. Zhu produces an academic journal in partnership with a Chinese government think tank, the Development Research Center's Asia-Africa Development Research Institute. Ranked among China's top research institutions, the Development Research Center is one of the go-to stops when foreign scholars visit Beijing, but few know that several of its institutes are covertly run and staffed by the MSS.[34] Their exact operational role remains mysterious, but intelligence officers and secret agent handlers returning from overseas often reappear as researchers there.

Not long after Zhu left the United States for perhaps the last time, Wu Baiyi, head of American studies at the Chinese Academy of Social Sciences, had his visa cancelled in a similar encounter with the FBI. Likewise, Wu's biography reveals his involvement in both covert Chinese military and MSS organisations. He's been a long-time member of China Reform Forum and also maintains an affiliation with another part of the Development Research Center that's run by the MSS, the Institute of World Development Studies.[35]

China Reform Forum is nothing without these reputable names. While the MSS directly employs many scholars as intelligence analysts at CICIR, it's is widely recognised as part of the MSS; US embassy cables dutifully note the fact whenever they quote CICIR researchers. This limits its effectiveness for influence and espionage (although it still participates in those activities). MSS operations therefore rely on genuine and internationally recognised academics to open doors, make introductions and gather intelligence. At the very least, MSS officers have accompanied these scholars on international trips with the purpose of meeting agents after each day's meetings.

What's remarkable about the involvement of these Chinese thinkers is that many of them are widely considered to be leading reformists and moderates. They're often well liked by their peers in Australia, the United States, Japan and so on. Like China Reform Forum as a whole, the West has often looked to them as the kinds of people who, it was hoped, would gain more influence inside the Party and push it towards reason, liberalism and tolerance. For decades, they've been widely consulted by foreign diplomats in China.

Cases like Zhu Feng's raise the unnerving possibility that many Chinese scholars owe their survival, or even their success, to relationships with intelligence agencies. As China expert Peter Mattis says, 'The MSS is not so foolish as to not see value in someone like Zhu' as a tool in their operations.[36] Well-regarded academics with foreign connections are allowed a spectre of autonomy to the extent it benefits the MSS. It's a symbiosis that gives the scholars relative freedom and security, and spies influence and cover. Zhu even hinted at this Faustian bargain in his interview with *The New York Times*: 'When a national security official comes to my office, I have no way to kick them out,' he explained.[37] The MSS playbook appears to recommend fostering friends with helpful opinions rather than changing the minds of dissenters, but China Reform Forum and the MSS's cynical role in Zheng Bijian's 'peaceful rise' theory should lead us to pause before taking Chinese foreign policy debates at face value.

Wang Jisi, a long-standing and senior member of China Reform Forum, exemplifies this strange duality. As president of Peking University's School of International Studies, Professor Wang is often considered among the country's leading and most reasonable foreign policy scholars. No 'America worshipper', he is nonetheless wary of overstating China's power and ability to challenge the United States. He often emphasises the space for cooperation between the two countries and practises this himself, serving on the board of the International Crisis Group, as a fellow at New York's Asia Society, and as a Princeton University scholar.[38]

At the same time, Wang has been closely associated with the MSS for decades. He became a member of the Social Investigation Bureau's CICEC front group in the early 1990s, joining its strange medley of scholars, artists and undercover officers, like future Minister of State Security Geng Huichang.[39] Even before then, Wang was joining

MSS officers on trips to Japan (including one who had previously been declared *persona non grata* while posing as a journalist) and the United States.[40] As head of American studies at the Chinese Academy of Social Sciences in the early 1990s, Wang was a colleague of MSS US operations guru Lin Di, who covertly managed the academy's foreign exchanges for many years. In 1998, Lin, then operating as CICEC's secretary-general, accompanied Wang to workshops in Tokyo and Washington. In 2003, Wang would join Lin and other MSS officers, now acting as researchers in China Reform Forum, at a RAND Corporation conference. These were the same events Lin used as cover to rendezvous with his Californian agents.[41] Wang also headed the Central Party School's Institute of International Strategic Studies at the peak of its deep collaboration with China Reform Forum. Similarly, leading reformist economist Fan Gang took part in many of these activities while a member of at least two MSS front organisations.[42]

Jin Canrong runs a more hawkish line than Wang Jisi but has equally strong MSS connections. The man known affectionately to Chinese nationalists as 'Political Commissar Jin' has gained a large following for brash pronouncements like 'China is a dragon. America is an eagle. Britain is a lion. When the dragon wakes up, the others are all snacks'.[43] As associate dean of Renmin University's School of International Studies, he's among China's most prominent scholars of international relations. He was also interviewed by the FBI on a recent trip to the United States and blasted the measures as 'ridiculous'.[44] And he has connections to the MSS's front groups: he's been a member of China Reform Forum and the China International Public Relations Association.[45]

Reformist or conservative, hawkish or dovish, the MSS seems to have an in with many while keeping a watchful eye on the rest. This is an intelligence agency able to reach across China's society to orchestrate operations against the most sensitive of targets – world leaders.

CHAPTER 11

'CHINA NEVER FORGETS ITS FRIENDS': ELITE CAPTURE

ZHENG BIJIAN AND the MSS's peaceful rise bandwagon drew an incredible crowd of admirers. In 2004, the year after he introduced the concept at the Bo'ao Forum, a who's who of the Indo-Pacific gathered once more in Hainan for a special roundtable on 'China's peaceful rise'. This time, Zheng surely had little to worry about when it came to the international appeal of his operation. 'Against the backdrop of wave upon wave of theories about "China threats" and "China collapse" ... I have noticed lately that people are quite interested in the topic of China's peaceful rise,' he remarked.[1] Though his concept had already fluttered out of the rhetoric of Party leaders, the elite audience before him was a testament to its remarkably immediate and resounding success. To the MSS, this itself was enough proof of concept.

Rounding off his speech with a message of 'peace, development and cooperation', Zheng returned to the row of coffee-brown lounge chairs reserved for VIP speakers. Next in line were Fidel Valdez Ramos, Ernesto Zedillo and Bob Hawke, respectively the former leaders of the Philippines, Mexico and Australia. Former US president George H. W. Bush, who had served as the top American representative in Beijing nearly three decades earlier, was another guest, praising China's peaceful rise as 'very reassuring and very, very important to the Asian horizon and Asia's landscape'.[2]

Before them sat a few dozen of the world's leading statespeople, business figures and scholars on an enormous circle of tables surrounding a mound of potted flowers. RAND Corporation economist Charles Wolf Jr, whose exchanges with China Reform Forum were used by the MSS to facilitate intelligence operations, was one of the first speakers that day. Other frequent DC interlocutors for China Reform Forum followed, including John Hamre, CEO of the Washington, DC Center for Strategic and International Studies and a former deputy secretary of defence, and then John L. Thornton, the former Goldman Sachs co-president who's one of the Brookings Institution's largest donors. Senior Chinese officials and scholars were interspersed among them, including MSS officer Ding Kuisong and many of the agency's old friends. Peking University international relations scholar Wang Jisi was there, as was Liu Changle, CEO of Hong Kong's Phoenix Media empire and a former PLA officer.[3]

The roundtable's agenda reads like a checklist of target areas and narratives for MSS influence operations. After heavy discussion of China's economic growth, the participants moved on to US–China relations and the barriers to Chinese development, as well as the role of media in promoting 'peaceful rise'. Over dinner, the topic shifted to the role multinational corporations could play in the Party's schemes. Philips, the Dutch electronics giant, sponsored the event and sent its CEO to speak on the topic alongside the MSS's Ding Kuisong. The year before, China Reform Forum helped the Philips CEO secure an audience with Chinese Premier Wen Jiabao.[4] Continuing the next day, China Reform Forum ran dedicated sessions on France and Japan, both top priorities for the MSS Social Investigation Bureau's intelligence operations.[5]

The MSS was making the most of the Bo'ao Forum's opportunities. China Reform Forum drew an equally impressive crowd to its peaceful rise roundtable the next year. This time they partnered with New York's Asia Society to run the event, which included speeches by Singaporean statesman Lee Kwan Yew, Nepalese deputy head of government Kirti Nidhi Bista, French presidential advisor Jérôme Monod and Korean presidential advisor Moon Chung-in.[6] Just about every major American foreign policy research organisation sent a senior representative. On the sidelines of the conference, Zheng Bijian and his MSS entourage arranged individual meetings with key international contacts such as John L. Thornton (see chapter 12).[7]

Whether they meant it or not, these global luminaries were lending their reputations to a misguided hope that the Chinese Communist Party would follow the path Zheng described. They may have differed in their exact belief in the proposal, but the respect they afforded China Reform Forum cemented its worldwide ties and the currency of its undercover MSS officers. Certainly, almost none were aware that the theory of China's 'peaceful rise' wasn't just a propaganda narrative but a deliberate influence campaign by the Party's covert agents, some of whom were sitting right beside them.

Of all the speakers China Reform Forum mustered at the Bo'ao Forum, Bob Hawke best exemplified the MSS's patient and persistent manipulation of elites and their good intentions. He also shows how the agency peddles access to the Party's highest leaders as its greatest tool for influence and compromise.

Bob Hawke

Hawke, Australia's prime minister from 1983 to 1991, was an ardent believer in close ties to China, seeing that Australia too might dine on the fruits of China's economic reforms. Australia had in fact arrived late to the game. It only established diplomatic relations with the People's Republic of China in 1973 and had a lot of catching up to do. Successive Australian prime ministers travelled to the country to build personal ties to Party leaders. In the mid-eighties, Hawke welcomed Hu Yaobang and his premier, Zhao Ziyang, in what Australian China scholar Geremie Barmé dubbed a 'burgeoning bromance' between the two nations' chiefs. This was the most optimistic period of recent Chinese political history. 'Reform and opening' seemed to be materialising right before one's eyes in those days. Many of the men at the top of the Party were easygoing, upstanding and invested in economic – maybe even political – liberalisation. 'I found it personally easy to get along with [Zhao],' Hawke said. 'We were on the same wavelength.'[8]

Hawke's friends in the Party leadership were the losers. Early signs of the storm to come, such as the Party's 1983 campaign against 'spiritual pollution', were 'downplayed by many at the time as nothing more than a side-show to the real story of China's economic reforms', writes Barmé. Two years after Hu was ousted for exercising his own initiative and sympathising with calls for political reform, the protests in Tiananmen Square sparked by his death had now been horrifically quashed.[9] It was a physical refutation of every principle Hu stood for, striking the Australian prime minister deeply. Hawke remembered Hu ('he looked like a little bright bird'), who once travelled with him to the remote Mount Channar iron ore mine in Australia's Pilbara desert, as 'a lot of fun' with a habit of ignoring prepared materials to speak off the cuff. '[Hawke] was devastated for two reasons. One was the horrendous, horrendous reported loss of life, and the other was that he saw it would be a disaster for China,' said Hawke's biographer and wife.[10]

Hawke wept as he went over gruesome details of that Sunday's Tiananmen massacre. A Chinese funerary wreath stood before him, marked in black ink with the character *dian* for 'mourning', as he addressed a memorial service of hundreds inside Canberra's Parliament House. 'Thousands have been killed and injured, victims of a leadership that seems determined to hang on to the reins of power at any cost – at awful human cost,' he said in a trembling tone. Then, a few paragraphs into his prepared speech, the prime minister reached for another set of notes and began to read directly from a classified cable sent by the Australian embassy in Beijing. In the chaos and shock of that week, the number of dead was widely estimated at over 10,000, an overly precise translation of a Chinese word that often means something more like 'many thousands' or simply 'a huge number'. Accounts from the time claiming military vehicles drove back and forth over the bodies of students, turning them to pulp, were probably wrong. But the overall picture of murder was true. Hundreds of innocent civilians had been gunned down, their blood staining the streets of Beijing. Some were killed in their homes by excited soldiers firing at random into the buildings around them. Twisted bodies lay on the city's central avenue, pressed in their bikes by tanks.[11]

The Tiananmen massacre was an inflection point in Australia's relationship with China. A few days after his speech, Hawke surprised his cabinet when he acted alone to announce that the government would be extending the visas of all Chinese nationals in Australia, and 42,000 ultimately gained asylum. It was the most significant event in the history of Australia's Chinese community. 'I have a deep love for the Chinese people,' Hawke later explained.[12]

It was this emotion that kept him connected to China and led him to see the best in the country even after 1989. Hawke had planned to visit China later that year before calling it off because of the massacre. 'The personal relationship went into a deep freeze,' said Hawke.[13] In 1991, he lost office. The final chapter of his career – now as a businessman – had begun, and the same allure of Chinese economic reform that drew him in as a statesman and politician retained its powerful pull on him.

Back in Beijing

Four years after the Tiananmen massacre moved Bob Hawke to tears, he received an unusual message from the Chinese consul in Sydney, asking if they could meet. He hadn't been to China since 1986 and wasn't sure what the diplomat had in mind when he arrived at Hawke's office in the city centre. After awkward pleasantries, the Chinese official told Hawke he'd been instructed to ask if he would be willing to visit China. Finally, the Party's leadership was reaching out once more – not just to Hawke but to the world. Hawke leapt at the opportunity. Still mindful of 4 June, he nonetheless 'wanted to go forward because the relationship was so important.'[14]

Arriving in Beijing that July, Hawke reflected on the significance of the invitation. 'It shows something about the deep intelligence and thinking of the leaders,' he later commented, seeing in it a profound pragmatism and willingness to set aside differences. He was offered the chance to meet General Secretary Jiang Zemin, a quirky and charismatic man fond of reciting the Gettysburg Address in heavily accented English, and waited in the Diaoyutai State Guesthouse until the leader was ready.[15] Finally, he was whisked to a meeting room in the Party leadership compound. He saw not just Jiang but his inner cabinet too seated before him, about six people in total.

As Hawke recounted, 'I walked in, walked across the room and Jiang Zemin got up and he walked out towards me and he said, "Mr Hawke, there's one thing I want to say to you." And I thought, "Shit, what's this?"' Jiang surely remembered his condemnation of the Tiananmen massacre. He would have been aware of Hawke's past friendship with his purged predecessors as general secretary. The capacity of Party officials to lecture and berate foreigners was as well known as their occasional magnanimity. Instead, Jiang extended his hand and said, 'Mr Hawke, China never forgets its friends, and we want you to know that we regard you as one of our best friends.' All Hawke's nervousness, built up by the long wait and the meeting's imperial setting, must have evaporated at that moment. 'They'd understood that my tears had been out of love for China and the Chinese people. And they'd understood this and they were welcoming me back. It was a marvellous moment,' he recalled.[16] Just a week earlier, Prime Minister Paul Keating had visited Beijing too – Australian embassy officials described his agenda as 'business, business, business'.[17] The *People's Daily* featured Hawke's visit on its front page, describing how Jiang Zemin praised his 'far-sightedness and perceptiveness' in emphasising Australian cooperation with the Asia-Pacific.[18] In January 1989, Hawke had proposed the creation of what became the Asia-Pacific Economic Cooperation meeting.

The special bromance between Chinese and Australian leaders was back on track. Hawke thought the fate of Zhao Ziyang, who eventually died in house arrest, was 'extremely sad', but the importance of building ties to the Party leadership came first. After all, most assumed that China's economy would grow and with it Chinese politics would naturally grow more agreeable.[19] The question of the Tiananmen massacre was swept under the rug, for it would have been impossible for Hawke to move forward with China otherwise.

The Party's leaders had their own agenda. Alongside Jiang Zemin, Li Peng, the conservative premier known as the 'Butcher of Beijing' for his part in the Tiananmen massacre, was almost certainly there to greet Hawke. The massacre was the defining moment of Jiang and

Li's political careers, cementing their power within the Party. Few benefited more from it. They knew what happened to Party leaders who were inclined towards political reform and against the Party's own misconduct.

For all Jiang Zemin's reputation outside of China as a reasonable leader with unusual fondness for the West, especially compared to Xi Jinping, the general secretary struck a remarkably different tone internally. A newly uncovered internal document shows a different perspective on the man. Speaking to a secret nationwide MSS conference months after Hawke's visit, Jiang declared that 'The West indeed hopes to see China in turmoil'. He believed 'capitalism ultimately seeks to defeat socialism', and to this end the United States was 'fighting a global war without smoke'. Jiang's answer to this, much the same as Xi Jinping's today, was to emphasise the sanctity of communist rule. 'If we don't have a solid political regime and we don't have a vigorous people's democratic dictatorship, then there's no point discussing anything else,' Jiang told the intelligence officers gathered before him, reminding them of the Soviet Union's inglorious demise. 'If we lose the realm carved out for us by countless martyrs, then what's the use of having greater economic development?'[20]

The China in Hawke's eyes and the Party's China were two very different things. There's no more striking demonstration of this than the untold details of how Hawke's return to Beijing was arranged. Though the invitation came down through the consulate-general, it was an 'unusual' research society called the China Institute of Strategy and Management (CISM) that officially hosted Hawke.[21] The group was acting as a conduit for Beijing's effort to rebuild its international status by befriending world leaders. On the same day he entertained Hawke's audience, Jiang Zemin met with former Thai prime minister Chatichai Choonhavan, who had also travelled to China at CISM's behest.[22]

CISM named Hawke its first foreign advisor and held an international conference for his visit. 'The future should give East Asia a chance,' went his speech, which became the lead article of the first edition of the institute's influential journal.[23] The 'vicious xenophobe' Wang Xiaodong was a regular contributor to the group and the translator of Hawke's article.[24] Its journal became a hotbed of

contributions from red royalty like Xi Jinping, then a local official in Fujian province. Importantly, the group's secretary-general,
Qin Chaoying, was the son of a senior propaganda official and close
to Xi Jinping's family.[25]

Hawke almost certainly didn't recognise that his well-connected
friends at CISM were in fact deeply involved with the intelligence
community. Qin himself later became a member of the MSS Social
Investigation Bureau's China Reform Forum front group.[26] China's
post-Tiananmen embrace of world leaders such as Hawke was a
professional influence operation.

MSS officers were all over the group. A photo that appears to show
Hawke's appointment as an advisor to CISM includes a curious set of
faces. Secretary-general Qin grins as he hands a gift to Hawke in the
foreground. Behind them, Yu Enguang looks on with a steely expres-
sion from behind his trademark shaded glasses. The institute's records
describe him only as one of its senior advisors and a member of China's
National People's Congress. Under his real name, Yu Fang, he was the
vice minister in charge of MSS efforts to manipulate foreign elites.

In the same photo, Qin Chuan, another senior advisor to the group
and the father of its secretary-general, sits beside Yu. Best known as the
former editor-in-chief of the *People's Daily*, Qin was chairman of an
MSS front called the China International Culture Publishing Company
at the time. While he served as the company's figurehead, MSS Social
Investigation Bureau officers used the business to provide cover for operations in the United States, Singapore, Hong Kong and Japan, including
handling FBI asset Katrina Leung.[27] Luo Qingchang, an MSS advisor
and the head of its predecessor agency, was another CISM member.
Also affiliated was an MSS officer who worked in India and Hong Kong
before becoming manager of an MSS trading company.[28]

Military figures were heavily represented too. CISM started its
existence as the internal think tank of the PLA's Academy of Military
Science, where it served to gather experts from across the intelligence
community for workshops and to write reports. Two weeks after the
Tiananmen massacre, it was upgraded to an 'externally open' group
permitted to carry out international exchanges. Former vice premier
Gu Mu, an architect of China's economic reform, was its president

(his son was a senior military intelligence officer).[29] Xin Qi, a rising star in the Chinese military's influence operations and political warfare department, was another CISM member.[30]

By befriending Hawke, CISM had now added an operational side to its history of intelligence analysis. And Hawke was one of many targets. The same year as his visit, the organisation established partnerships with America's RAND Corporation and Atlantic Council, both prominent defence think tanks. Later, former Japanese prime minister Hata Tsutomu joined Hawke as one of the group's foreign advisors.[31] More recently, Japanese counterintelligence officers found a suspected MSS officer using CISM as cover in an operation to infiltrate Okinawa, which hosts a US military base, and access sensitive technology.[32]

Cash for access

The former prime minister's wealth was always something of a mystery. The signs of his success were easy to see. After leaving politics, Hawke developed an exclusive seafront property in Sydney's inner north into a four-storey mansion, complete with a rooftop putting course.[33] The house sold for over A$9 million shortly before his death in 2019.[34] Over his lifetime, he travelled to China more than a hundred times on business trips.[35] But, 'quizzed on any particulars over the years, Hawke has always demurred on giving any detail', stated Australia's *Crikey* magazine.[36] Exactly who the former prime minister was working for in China was a commercial secret.

It all began with that 1993 return to Beijing. Hawke appreciated the warm welcome he received from Party leaders but was also interested in business opportunities. As if by sheer chance, when Hawke was waiting in his hotel lobby on the same trip, a man with an 'elfin face' introduced himself to the former prime minister. The man, Jiang Xiaosong, had recently returned from studying and working in Japan's film industry. His mother was among China's greatest movie stars. They exchanged greetings and cards and moved on. A few years later, the two reconnected.[37] Jiang, now at home as an entrepreneur and investor, wanted to transform the Hainanese fishing village of Bo'ao into an international conference venue. Signing up Hawke, former Filipino president Fidel Ramos (also an advisor to CISM) and former Japanese prime minister

Hosokawa Morihiro as the faces of his new venture, Jiang launched the Bo'ao Forum for Asia in 2001.[38]

While Hawke lent his considerable reputation to the Bo'ao Forum, now among the most important channels for CCP elite influence, he also stood to profit considerably from CISM. 'They wanted to set up a commercial arm and asked me to be chairman, and I accepted,' Hawke said of his 1993 visit.[39] Everything fell in place smoothly. The next year, Hawke flew to China once more to work out the details of the joint venture. Over a few days of meetings, the two parties worked out the business's name, ownership structure, areas of work and other matters.[40] Hawke wanted to call it 'China Strategic Investment Advisory Co Ltd' but had to settle for 'Lanmo Strategic Investment Advisory'. Normally, only major state conglomerates are allowed to use 'China' in their name, but Hawke's company still received special treatment. The usual requirement that businesses include a location, such as Beijing, at the beginning of their name was waived.[41]

What business did CISM, a research society for Chinese spooks, have setting up a commercial wing? CISM secretary-general Qin wanted to commercialise his elite status and the political connections his organisation offered. 'Qin was a member of the princelings, and at the time still a researcher at the Academy of Military Sciences,' said one of his colleagues. He was 'typically rather quiet and spoke little at public gatherings, but if you conversed with him in the right setting the broadness of his thought, insightfulness of his cognition and sharpness of his analysis left you with a deep impression. This was a man with great political aspirations.'[42] And he needed Hawke's help.

The company's aim was to market Hawke and Qin's door-opening abilities to foreign companies hoping to make deals in China and assist Chinese companies going abroad. Hawke was widely known in China and among its political class but could never have matched Qin's intricate understanding of the Party's elite culture. 'Lanmo's niche was that it exploited Hawke's enormous resources internationally, integrating them with the rather large domestic political and government resources of the Institute of Strategy and Management,' explained one of the company's former executives.[43] Hawke bragged to *The Sydney Morning Herald*, 'I have a very good rapport with the Chinese. I have very good contacts with the government, I know where to go and who to see. I think I'm better known in China than just about any other Australian.'[44]

Years later, Hawke casually remarked that he'd 'spent quite a bit of time with the Chinese International Institute of Strategic Studies, which is an extremely high-level body'. The group, in fact an arm of the same military intelligence agency that funnelled illegal donations to Bill Clinton's 1996 presidential campaign, was run by 'the last head of security intelligence in the PLA', he said.[45] Hawke felt he was influencing China through these expert spy handlers and influencers. 'You're talking with people who help to make decisions there,' he argued.[46] Meanwhile, Australian diplomats in Beijing were placed in an uncomfortable position: obliged to welcome the former leader to Beijing and help set up meetings when asked but concerned by the company he kept.

The consultancy got off to a great start. General Alexander Haig, previously President Ronald Reagan's secretary of state, worked with Lanmo to help explore nuclear energy projects in China. They also engaged Australian mining companies, a Japanese recycling business and numerous Chinese state-owned enterprises as clients. One of their earliest projects was a successful effort to ensure that delegates from the Conference Board, a peak body for America's largest corporations, could land meetings with Party leaders and high-level officials in Beijing.[47] Hawke also recommended the Communist Party legalise gambling so that he might ride the expansion of the country's horse-racing industry.[48]

Lanmo was dissolved sometime in the 2000s, despite its early successes. 'I do some of my work in China through them, but not all,' Hawke said in 1998. Of course, he had his own ventures with both Chinese and foreign companies and sat, for instance, on the China Advisory Board of Australian mining giant Fortescue Metals.[49] But the significance of Hawke's dealings with Qin Chaoying and his odd bunch of intelligence community insiders has been overlooked and is remarkably hard to dig up.[50]

It was CISM that acted as a cut-out for Party leaders when it invited Hawke back to China, operating in tandem with Beijing's efforts to win key friends among foreign statesmen. And it's doubtful Hawke fully understood his Chinese partner's agenda: they were just doing business. Chinese intelligence officers like Yu Enguang would never have attempted to recruit Hawke as an agent. There simply wasn't any point.

Instead, Hawke's value was that he sold China to the rest of the world, reframed Australia's image of the nation after the Tiananmen massacre, and gifted his reputation to influence vehicles like the Bo'ao Forum. He was personally taking part in the story of China's incredible economic rise with his consultancy. Through the fruits of his 'marvellous' return to China, he helped craft an image of a modernising and liberalising China.[51]

To many Australians, Hawke still symbolises a golden era of Australia–China relations and a model for engaging with the Party-state. In 2020, Labor Party shadow minister Jason Clare invoked Hawke's legacy to criticise the Australian government's failure to secure meetings and phone calls with Chinese leaders. Disputes over China's economic coercion against Australia 'should be able to be sorted out on the phone or face to face. That's what Bob Hawke would have done,' he said.[52]

CHAPTER 12

THE PARTY YOU CAN'T LEAVE: TRUMP, BIDEN AND BEYOND

INFLUENCE VEHICLES AND intelligence fronts like the China Institute of Strategy and Management are often short-lived. A serious blow was dealt to these groups when the MSS began to uncover CIA infiltration of its ranks around 2010. The number of exposed CIA assets within China reportedly numbered in the dozens, including the aide to an MSS vice minister involved in China Reform Forum. The MSS's frantic and merciless destruction of these networks sparked a painstaking re-evaluation of its own foreign operations to determine whether they'd been exposed.[1] Scores of plots, methods and operatives had been ruined by the CIA's moles – which were they? Given its prominence among the MSS's operations and the positions held by some of the moles, China Reform Forum was almost certainly tainted. Its value for highly sensitive operations in risky terrain such as the United States was vastly diminished.

Today's China Reform Forum is but a husk of its former self. Even before the MSS realised the extent of CIA penetration among its officers, the front group was on a downward spiral. Zheng Bijian's departure in 2007, perhaps due to his advanced age, left China Reform Forum without its greatest asset.[2] The group still keeps up an impressive list of exchanges with policymakers and research organisations around the world but has passed its peak as an influence platform.

Whatever China Reform Forum's fate, the MSS never let go of Zheng Bijian. It wasn't about to give up on its most useful door-opener and affiliate. China Reform Forum was only one part of Zheng's exchanges with American elites, which have since touched on presidents Trump and Biden. At the same time, the MSS has attempted to compromise key local politicians in the United States.

Zheng goes platform hopping

Within a year of stepping down as China Reform Forum's leader, Zheng appeared out of the blue as chairman of CISM. It was no coincidence that Zheng had been selected to lead the group.[3]

On top of Zheng's presence, traces of MSS influence operations specialists were all over the organisation. A decade earlier, the very same body spearheaded the Party's efforts to befriend and enrich former Australian prime minister Bob Hawke. Yu Enguang, the charming former vice minister of the MSS in charge of political influence operations, used his well-worn alias to serve directly under Zheng as the group's senior vice chairman.[4] A few years earlier, the group's secretary-general had been named a senior council member of China Reform Forum.[5]

If CISM was being primed for another elite influence operation then what was its target? After a year of careful preparation, in October 2009 the institute joined hands with Washington's Brookings Institution to hold a major conference on clean energy at Beijing's Diaoyutai State Guesthouse.

Fighting climate change through clean energy still seems like an obvious area for cooperation between the United States and China. The two countries are leading emitters of greenhouse gases but also at the cutting-edge of renewable energy technology. Just as mutual interests in countering terrorism provided a foundation for warm relations under the Bush administration, this similarly global threat might pave the way towards realising China's peaceful rise. After the 2008 global financial crisis, US public opinion reflected a major jump in positive attitudes towards China. The percentage of Americans reporting a favourable opinion of China rose by eleven points to 50 per cent in 2008.[6]

Both organisers of the forum had clear government support and attracted the kind of high-level attendees that suggested greater forces were at play. Just as the Party's leaders used CISM to rekindle their relationship with Australia's Bob Hawke, this bilateral energy forum looked like a chance to set an optimistic tone for relations with the newly instated Barack Obama White House. The United States sent former vice president Al Gore, an outspoken advocate for climate change action, and ambassador John Huntsman to speak at the event. Former president Clinton's national security advisor, Sandy Berger, delivered a keynote address over dinner. Key White House appointees, including Secretary of State Hillary Clinton and Secretary of Energy Stephen Chu, spoke via video link.[7]

In turn, the CCP rolled out some of its most senior officials, particularly those typically chosen to engage with foreigners. Many had MSS ties. Li Keqiang, future premier of China, gave the opening address while Premier Wen Jiabao spoke to a closed-door gathering of attendees. Liu He, the senior Chinese financial official who is now one of Xi Jinping's key interlocutors with the United States, spoke too. Liu was also a senior member of the MSS's CICEC front group. Tung Chee-hwa, a vice chairman of the Chinese People's Political Consultative Conference and former chief executive of Hong Kong, gave another address.[8] Described by China expert Peter Mattis as one of Beijing's key 'proxies' for influence abroad, Tung has been a prolific donor to American foreign policy institutions and universities, sponsoring exchanges in conjunction with a Chinese military influence front.[9]

John L. Thornton: The middleman
Zheng Bijian's clean energy forum contributed to a much more specific effect: empowering Brookings chairman John L. Thornton as a communication channel between the two nations. The former Goldman Sachs co-president built his career on investing in long-term relationships, chiefly in China, and has since become a key intermediary between the leaders of China and the United States. In the process, he unwittingly fell into the sights of an MSS influence operation.

In the late nineties, Thornton built connections to key Chinese economic officials who have since risen into national leadership roles.

Wang Qishan, who led Xi Jinping's crackdown on corrupt political rivals and occupies a central position in China's US diplomacy, is one of his oldest and most important contacts.[10] To this day, those relationships have earned him a secretive role shuttling messages between the White House and Zhongnanhai.

When Thornton announced his surprise resignation from Goldman Sachs in 2003, he was travelling in China. He explained to the media that he would be taking up a professorship at Beijing's prestigious Tsinghua University (Xi Jinping's alma mater) to direct a leadership training program there. He'd grown tired of being co-president at Goldman Sachs, where he was known for his ambitious personality, and his prospects for the chief executive job were slim. The immense potential of China's rise promised a greater legacy than any investment bank presidency.[11]

Thornton continued to advise Goldman Sachs on China but found new institutions to stand on. He was elected chairman of the Brookings Institution board, placing him at the top of one of America's most prestigious think tanks, traditionally a Democratic-aligned organisation. Shortly after, he gifted US$12.5 million to the institution's China program, now called the John L. Thornton China Center.[12] He also served as a special China advisor to the president of Yale University.[13] Like every other major American foreign policy institution, Brookings had already been engaging with China Reform Forum, hosting Zheng Bijian and the MSS as they tested out the 'peaceful rise' theory on its target audience.

The group's well-advertised elite connections would have immediately stuck out to Thornton. It was affiliated with the Central Party School and headed by a man with General Secretary Hu Jintao's ear. Its staff had new ideas, a reformist agenda, an unusual air of free agency, and a willingness to talk about the Party's inner workings that was uncharacteristic of Chinese think tankers. They were the kinds of people Thornton learnt to gravitate towards in his banking days – interfaces between outsiders like Thornton and the inner circle of the Party leadership.

Thornton soon became one of the group's top American contacts, and he was often in Beijing for his duties at Tsinghua University.

Zheng Bijian was the main attraction when he met with China Reform Forum, but MSS Social Investigation Bureau chief Lin Di sat in on at least three meetings with Thornton. Wang Xuejun, another senior MSS officer, was present at many of the meetings.[14] Thornton also attended and spoke at the group's Bo'ao Forum 'peaceful rise' roundtables.[15]

With these undercover MSS contacts among his Chinese interlocutors in the 2000s, Thornton gradually built what journalist Josh Rogin calls 'one of the most reliable and high-level networks with the families that run the CCP'.[16] Thornton undoubtedly felt he was being given the chance to glean the inner workings of China's Communist Party as he picked up more accolades within China. The China Reform Forum website once listed dozens of world leaders and kingmakers as advisors, but almost all look like they were added without consent: people like Lee Kuan Yew and Hillary Rodham Clinton who may have met Zheng's delegations once or twice but don't appear to have done any more than that. John L. Thornton is the exception. He's included the title in some of his online biographies.[17]

Thornton also accepted an advisory role at China's sovereign wealth fund as well as the Chinese government's Confucius Institutes program, which seeks to influence universities around the world. In 2008 he was awarded China's 'Friendship Prize', the highest award bestowed upon foreigners.[18] Today he's chairman of the Silk Road Finance Corporation, an investment fund dedicated to financing activities under the Belt and Road Initiative, a key strategic policy of Xi Jinping.[19]

By 2009, the beginning of Obama's presidency, Thornton was well and truly entrenched as a leading interlocutor between America and China. According to a former Trump administration White House official, Thornton 'lobbied very hard' to become ambassador to China during the Obama years but was passed over for the governor of Utah, Jon Huntsman Jr, a Republican who in his youth had been a Mormon missionary in Taiwan.

Thornton still sought to play the middleman. After the success of the first bilateral clean energy forum he'd organised with Zheng, they held an encore in Washington, DC's Mandarin Oriental Hotel. Ambassador Huntsman spoke at the conference's opening but it was Thornton who had the privilege of reading out a message from President Obama to the audience. Zheng followed with a statement from China's President Hu Jintao. In spite of their parallel roles as messengers for their nations' leaders, the differences between Thornton and Zheng ran deep. One was an ambitious former banker working above and around the US government, the other was an old Communist Party insider who had spent the past decade secretly assisting China's top intelligence agency.

Thornton's importance to China only grew after Donald Trump's election in 2016. At face value, Steve Bannon, Trump's campaign manager and chief strategist, couldn't have been more opposed to Thornton's views on China. Bannon helped craft and animate Trump's campaign-trail attacks on China and globalist elites. He once compared China to 1930s Germany, arguing it was poised to unleash conflict upon the world and locked in an economic war against the United States.[20] Thornton, with his Goldman Sachs pedigree and Chinese inroads, seemed to personify everything Bannon was against.

Nonetheless, Bannon reached out to Thornton after Trump's election victory. The pair in fact had a long history, starting in 1985 when Bannon worked alongside Thornton at Goldman Sachs after a career as a US Navy officer.[21] He viewed Thornton as a kind of mentor. According to journalist Josh Rogin, Bannon asked Thornton for help on China 'because China is the whole thing'. Thornton replied, 'Steve, I've been waiting for thirty years to hear someone in that chair make that comment.' He'd played a role in the Obama White House's relations with China, but now he was being offered a whole other level of influence. Thornton elected to stay out of the administration, preferring to work behind the scenes with Bannon and Trump.[22]

Bannon mistook Thornton's access for expertise. He was right in thinking few could match Thornton's connections within the Party aristocracy, but he may not have recognised how that privilege warped Thornton's vision. He certainly wasn't aware that China Reform Forum and Zheng Bijian were fronts for the Party's intelligence agency. As one senior Trump-era White House official said, they never received any warnings from US intelligence agencies that Thornton had unwittingly engaged with the MSS.[23]

Thornton's beliefs about China's future have been characterised by the same false narratives the MSS Social Investigation Bureau pushed

THE PARTY YOU CAN'T LEAVE: TRUMP, BIDEN AND BEYOND   159

on foreign scholars, diplomats and elites. In 2008, he argued in an essay for *Foreign Affairs* magazine that the Party was actively considering moving towards democracy. While Thornton held no illusions of a hasty transition to a genuine multiparty system with elections for all leaders, what he heard from his Party contacts was encouraging. 'A senior Communist Party official I know marvelled privately that ten years ago it would have been unimaginable for someone in his position to even be having an open discussion about democracy with an American,' he wrote. Opening up to Thornton, this Party official advocated direct elections of provincial-level officials but stopped short of supporting fully open multiparty elections.[24]

As they did with countless others, Zheng Bijian and China Reform Forum guided Thornton's assessments of China, although the details of Thornton's interactions with Party insiders are confidential. Unknowingly, American peace advocate Jeremy J. Stone had similarly relied heavily on MSS contacts for access in China and described China Reform Forum's Ding Kuisong, in fact an undercover intelligence officer, as 'one of those few free agents in China with good connections but without any bureaucracy sitting on him'.[25] As Thornton penned his essay on Chinese democracy, Ding was privately claiming to US diplomats that democratic change in China was inevitable.[26] Aside from organising exchanges and conferences with Zheng and MSS fronts, Thornton arranged for the Brookings Institution to publish a translated volume of Zheng Bijian's speeches, the first in a planned series of works by leading Chinese thinkers.[27] To Thornton, Zheng Bijian was the definitive living Chinese thinker. Introducing him at their joint clean energy dialogue in Washington, DC, he described Zheng as having been 'the most innovative and deepest thinker on public policy issues in China for a very long time'. Not the kind of praise one hands out lightly. 'We could have no better, no more influential voice,' he added, 'than Chairman Zheng Bijian.'[28]

Importantly, Zheng reinforced Thornton's belief in the importance of actively friendly and positive relations with China. 'Zheng's concept of a peaceful rise doesn't depend on China alone,' he wrote in his foreword to Zheng's speeches. 'It also demands that the rest of the world help China create an international environment where this sort of rise can take place.' In other words, the burden lies in large part with the United States to ensure the CCP chooses to behave respectfully and responsibly on the world stage.[29]

Thornton's writings reflect the same optimism about China that Party leaders and the MSS learnt to capitalise on decades earlier. With George Soros in 1988, they accepted him and led him to believe they would protect and foster his efforts to promote open society in China. Dubbing their front group China Reform Forum, the MSS clearly hoped to play on visions of an economically and politically open China. Speaking to Washington, DC's National Press Club in 2001, undercover MSS bureau chief and China Reform Forum leader Lin Di claimed China was becoming a more 'democratic' nation.[30] Paradoxically, officers and fronts of the MSS, one of the most conservative and anti-American parts of the CCP, were uniquely poised to present themselves as friendly liberals and reformists.

In his 2012 *Foreign Affairs* article on China, Thornton declared that 'How a country manages the transfer of power at the very top sends an unmistakable signal to all levels below'.[31] By this standard, Xi Jinping has since dashed any hope of democratic change in China for the foreseeable future. His rule has been characterised by the end of presidential term limits, vicious purges of his political rivals, extreme oppression in Xinjiang and Hong Kong, and a crackdown on the freedoms and powers of private sector leaders. Though Chinese democracy now seems an unlikely prospect, the importance of ensuring China's peaceful rise and building close personal relationships with Party figures remain core to Thornton's beliefs.

These misplaced hopes shaped Thornton's advice to the Trump administration. Thornton impressed upon Trump the importance of befriending Xi Jinping and framed the chance to 'recast the US-China relationship' as a defining opportunity for Trump to secure his legacy.[32] 'He had this whole thing that the relationship between Xi and the president had to be just right and that they had to love each other,' said one former senior White House official. 'His view is that … like it or not, China is going to be the one that dominates the future so let's try to benefit from that.' Thornton also stressed the need for Trump to make a goodwill gesture to Xi Jinping, claiming the Party leadership was incredibly reasonable and Xi himself was trustworthy. Trump was a fan of the idea, and Thornton soon visited Beijing where he passed on these messages to Xi Jinping and Wang Qishan.

Using Thornton to convey these messages to Beijing had its advantages. He could do it reliably, and discreetly. 'The official channels included too many people to be leakproof,' explains Rogin.[33]

Thornton's shuttle diplomacy had some initial successes. The Trump–Xi summit, held in April 2017 at Florida's Mar-a-Lago resort, was an outcome of his advice.[34] Even Bannon briefly adopted a more diplomatic tone. In a 2017 speech to business figures in Hong Kong, he stressed Trump's admiration for Xi Jinping and the need for the two countries to 'work out' their differences.[35] After Bannon left the White House less than eight months into Trump's presidency, Thornton brought him to Beijing for a friendly meeting with Wang Qishan.[36]

One of Thornton's main efforts was to position those who were more favourable to China as the administration's interlocutors in the trade dispute. Tensions between the two capitals were growing over China's unfair trade practices and theft of American intellectual property, and the Trump administration threatened a trade war. 'His mission was to find the most pliant interlocutor in the administration that the Chinese could negotiate with,' argues a former senior White House official.[37] He tried to promote Jared Kushner, Trump's son-in-law, as well as treasury secretary Steve Mnuchin and commerce secretary Wilbur Ross for the role.

But Thornton could only forestall what looked like an increasingly inevitable correction in US–China relations. 'In the end, no amount of smooth operating was going to paper over the fact that China wasn't making any concessions on theft of our intellectual property,' said the former White House official. Instead of Kushner or Mnuchin, China ended up with a 'hardliner' as their negotiating partner in the form of Robert Lighthizer.[38]

Biden and China

While Thornton's influence over the Trump administration's China policy was short-lived, he's continued to act as a high-level backchannel during Joe Biden's presidency. In September 2021, an unidentified individual revealed to Hong Kong's *South China Morning Post* that Thornton had just completed a six-week tour of China, comparing it to Henry Kissinger's secret China visit in 1971, which set the foundations for US–China relations.[39] US climate policy envoy John Kerry and Deputy Secretary of State Wendy Sherman also separately travelled to China in the early months of the Biden administration, but Thornton's trip was different. Kerry and Sherman received frosty receptions and were only allowed to visit the coastal city of Tianjin, not the capital itself.[40] According to China scholar Dean Cheng, the US official visitors had effectively been humiliated by their counterparts and 'the Biden administration risks signalling to Beijing that Washington is desperate for a deal' to improve relations.[41]

The treatment the CCP afforded Thornton could not have been more different. Despite holding no formal role in the US government, Thornton met face to face with one of the CCP's most senior leaders, Han Zheng. A meeting with Zheng Bijian, of course, was on Thornton's itinerary too.[42] Thornton also took up an offer to visit Xinjiang, the site of extreme and ongoing human rights abuses against the region's non-Chinese ethnic groups, against the warnings of a White House official who believed the trip would be seen as an endorsement of the Chinese government's policies there. Han pressed a list of complaints and asks on Thornton, iterating China's demands and telling him to share what he had seen in Xinjiang, where the CCP claims its genocidal policies are counterterrorism efforts.[43] The Party's leaders were re-appointing Thornton as their go-between with the White House.

It's clear who Thornton backs. Though John Kerry is nominally the US climate change envoy, Thornton reportedly told Chinese leaders that Kerry is Biden's lead on China policy.[44] Aiming to force the United States to choose between minimising climate change and challenging China, the CCP has driven a wedge into Biden's foreign policy team.

As Biden's climate and energy policy chief, Kerry has used his newly created executive position in an attempt to position climate policy at the heart of US–China relations. In their meetings with Kerry shortly after Thornton's visit, Chinese officials refused to cooperate on climate change until the United States rolled back its criticism of China's human rights abuses and other issues, according to *The Washington*

Post. Returning from China empty-handed and embarrassed after the Chinese foreign minister only offered to meet through a teleconference, Kerry has shifted his focus to building a strong personal relationship between President Biden and Xi in the hope of overruling the all-or-nothing offers made by Xi's officials.

Thornton's positions are echoed by many others. He reflects the sentiments of a group of top Wall Street bankers who have emerged as the most influential American believers in China's peaceful rise. If they're right, they seek to gain from China's economic growth. On top of that, promoting policies of cooperation with a genocidal, totalitarian and increasingly anti-capitalist political party has benefits in and of itself. As Rogin explains, Blackstone Group CEO Stephen Schwarzman and Blackrock CEO Larry Fink were among 'the most active set of outsiders trying to get Trump's ear on China'. Of these, many 'depended on Beijing's good graces for billions of dollars in annual revenue' and compete for access to China's financial services sector. Schwarzman, for his part, worked hard behind the scenes to stop Trump from enacting tariffs on China. He funds an eponymous program at Tsinghua University where outstanding Chinese and foreign students study alongside each other. Rogin characterises him as 'perhaps Wall Street's top dealmaker with large Chinese corporations'.[45]

During the Trump administration, Thornton worked with China to invite these bankers to exclusive 'China-US Financial Roundtables' that gave them access to key Party officials like Wang Qishan. All those in attendance understood that their business interests depended in part on preventing greater competition between the United States and China. 'Those of us in the financial industries of both countries realise that we have an obligation to help improve US-China relations,' one participant told the *Financial Times*. 'This relationship is too important to be wrecked by a few people.'[46] Beijing was hoping to resurrect high-level economic dialogues with the United States. Within the Trump White House, these dialogues were seen as stalling mechanisms that delayed real action against China.[47]

Since Biden's election, this Wall Street faction has reconvened. Again, its backroom talks with Party leaders go beyond finance and straight to the topic of US–China relations.[48] However, China's complicity in Russia's invasion of Ukraine has hardened the Biden government, which is focusing its efforts on strengthening alliances in China's wake.[49]

The China Institute for Innovation and Development Strategy

At the elite level, the MSS's long-term investment in Zheng Bijian continues to pay off. After serving as the face of influence operations by China Reform Forum and then the China Institute of Strategy and Management, in 2010 Zheng set up a new vehicle: the China Institute for Innovation and Development Strategy (CIIDS).

The MSS's involvement in CIIDS is harder to spot than in China Reform Forum where serving MSS officers administered the group, but this probably reflects the MSS's improved operational security rather than a loosening of its ambition. Lin Di, the former MSS bureau chief who led US operations and was Katrina Leung's handler, is a senior advisor to CIIDS. Likewise, some of CIIDS's staff were brought over from MSS fronts: one CIIDS secretary-general has maintained a second job as manager of China Reform Forum's office.[50] In addition to Zheng, many of CIIDS's senior council members have also been key figures in MSS front groups.[51] One of the MSS Social Investigation Bureau's front groups, run by a former China Reform Forum officer, helped CIIDS produce promotional videos for its conferences.[52]

CIIDS's activities follow in China Reform Forum's footsteps but are more narrowly focused on targeting political elites. One of its first major events saw Zheng Bijian shift his focus to Australia. In 2011, CIIDS held a high-level forum on 'trade and friendship' with Australia that attracted Australia's deputy prime minister as well as its ambassador to China.[53] While it's unclear whether anything concrete came out of the conference, it added to the status and mystique of Australian Chinese billionaire Chau Chak Wing, who partnered with CIIDS to organise the event. The forum was the first international event held in Chau's Imperial Springs resort in the southern province of Guangdong, Chau's homeland. The *People's Daily*, the official mouthpiece of the Party, dubbed it the 'Guangzhou Bo'ao Forum', a new venue for China to entertain and befriend elites the world over.[54]

Chau was at the peak of his influence and repute in Australia. Over the previous decade he'd earned himself a place in Australian politics through steady donations to politicians and public institutions and was known for being extraordinarily well connected in China.[55] Australian political leaders credited him with helping seal a A\$25 billion deal to export natural gas to China.[56] After migrating to Hong Kong and Australia in the 1990s, Chau gave millions to both sides of Australian politics and landed his daughter a job in the office of New South Wales premier (and future foreign minister) Bob Carr. The University of Sydney's museum is named after him, as is a postmodern building designed by renowned architect Frank Gehry at the University of Technology Sydney.[57] More recently, he gave millions to Australian veterans' charities and the Australian War Memorial.[58]

One incident in particular hints at Chau's unusual behind-the-scenes power. In 2011, Australia's then foreign minister Kevin Rudd, a Chinese speaker, made a last-minute rendezvous with Chau. As reported by *The Sydney Morning Herald*, one Australian diplomat called Rudd's behaviour 'extraordinary' because of how little notice Australian officials were given of his sudden trip to Guangzhou on the way back from meetings in Europe. 'The meeting with Dr Chau, which was not part of the official schedule, came as Mr Rudd was mounting his guerrilla campaign to undermine Prime Minister Julia Gillard,' wrote journalists Nick McKenzie and Angus Grigg. 'It has been suggested Mr Rudd was seeking Dr Chau's continued support' as he prepared to eventually retake Australia's top job in 2013, they reported.[59]

After mounting controversy over Chau's ties to Australian politicians, and Australian counterintelligence agency ASIO's warning to both major parties that Chau's political donations may be a conduit for interference, the Australian Labor Party announced it would no longer accept donations from Chau or Huang Xiangmo, another billionaire property developer accused of working with the CCP.[60] Then, Australian parliamentarian Andrew Hastie used parliamentary privilege to allege that Chau was a co-conspirator in a plot to bribe United Nations officials, which had been exposed by the FBI.[61] In 2022, the late Labor Party senator Kimberley Kitching also used parliamentary privilege to suggest that Chau was the unnamed 'puppeteer' behind a foreign interference plot revealed by ASIO earlier that year.[62]

Despite this, Chau won a defamation suit against the two journalists who initially reported on his ties to the CCP, John Garnaut and Nick McKenzie.[63] And former Australian prime minister Rudd, now president of the New York–headquartered Asia Society, has kept up exchanges with Chau's partners from the 2011 Australia–China forum, Zheng Bijian and his CIIDS.[64] Chau remains a leader and financial backer of the Club de Madrid, a not-for-profit composed of dozens of former world leaders including past presidents and prime ministers of New Zealand, Canada and Latvia.[65]

The homeless billionaire: Nicolas Berggruen

German American investor Nicolas Berggruen is a natural partner for CIIDS. Speaking English with an accent that's 'more French than anything else', he's known as the 'homeless billionaire' for once shedding his properties (but not his private jet) to live from a suitcase in luxury hotel suites. Nicolas, the son of German art dealer Heinz Berggruen, made billions from savvy private equity investments and now dedicates himself to political causes.[66] Famously private and far from a household name, he has found his niche in the geopolitics of China.

His personal intellectual project, the Berggruen Institute, helps connect CIIDS to global elites and is key to its success. Berggruen's mission? Only to improve global governance and save democracy. California, where he has proposed setting up a committee of prominent figures to propose policies directly on the state ballot, is one of his main focuses.[67]

But at the global level, China is Berggruen's primary interest.[68] The circumstances of the institute's founding in the aftermath of the 2008 global financial crisis set the tone for its activities today. According to its website, Nicolas Berggruen and scholar Nathan Gardels established the think tank to examine 'the widespread perception of failing political institutions and Western democracies, and the question of how China's rise would affect international cooperation and governance in the 21st century'.[69] The answer they propose is a future that depends heavily on learning from China and appreciating its rise. In the process, their institute has become what scholars Clive Hamilton and Marieke Ohlberg dub 'the most shamelessly pro-Beijing think tank'.[70]

The Berggruen Institute's emphasis on understanding the cultural and philosophical origins of a society pushes it into orientalism when it comes to China. Gardels claims that democracy is unsuited to Hong Kong, while Nicolas Berggruen characterises the CCP as a 'service organisation' driven by the needs of the Chinese people.[71] He writes that China 'is dedicated to the ancient Confucian traditions of stability and harmony', seeing the CCP as a reflection of these imperial habits rather than its unabashed Marxist–Leninist principles. He also believes that 'the Party is largely meritocratic and competitive', a common trope that has little grounding in the reality of Xi Jinping's China, where the family ties of princelings define elite politics. It's a claim that also overlooks the fact that entry to this supposedly meritocratic system is dependent on one's acceptance of Party rule and all that it entails.[72] Similar ideas were promoted through *The Washington Post* and *The Huffington Post*, which until recently hosted dozens of articles curated by the Berggruen Institute including some by Zheng Bijian.[73]

As it ponders the benefits of one-Party rule, the Berggruen Institute convenes its own collection of world leaders called the 21st Century Council. CIIDS's Understanding China conferences double as a meeting place for this council, which is how Zheng draws in such a crowd to these events. They're the centrepiece of CIIDS's efforts. First held in 2013, not long after Xi Jinping's formal rise to power, Understanding China encapsulates the MSS approach to elite influence. Through CIIDS, the Party invites retired world leaders, respected academics and business leaders to this exclusive event. They're granted rare audiences with a series of senior Party leaders including the general secretary himself. Practised barbarian handlers like foreign affairs official Fu Ying and the economist Liu He, a vice premier and former vice president of the MSS's CICEC front group, also attend the conference to deliver speeches and make connections with their foreign guests. As the gathering's name indicates, the conference aims to help its high-level attendees 'understand China' on the Party's terms. With the kind of privileged access they're offered, CIIDS's guests might not only be encouraged to take softer positions on China but are also given greater credibility around the world. Not many people have the right to say, 'I caught up with Premier Li Keqiang last week.'

In 2013, two former Australian prime ministers – Rudd and Paul Keating – as well as the former leaders of Mexico, Pakistan, the United Kingdom, Spain, Chile and Italy attended. Big tech leaders like Google's Eric Schmidt and scholars such as Singapore's Kishore Mahbubani attend too. In the words of Berggruen Institute co-founder Nathan Gardels, these world leaders 'had the opportunity to take off Western lenses and understand China's strategy from their own perspective' through meetings with Party leaders, who claimed that strengthened political control and greater economic and social liberalisation in China were 'two sides of the same coin'.[74] (Xi Jinping has since made reasserting state control over the economy and Chinese society core parts of his agenda.)

Grassroots honeytrap: The Christine Fang case

As well as trying to influence the highest levels of politics, the MSS helps the Party influence an unguarded force in American policymaking: local politics. Katrina Leung, the MSS's star agent in California, played this game in the 1990s, involving herself in Republican circles (see chapter 4). But it's the case of Christine Fang, an alleged MSS agent in California whose work was exposed by journalists Bethany Allen-Ebrahimian and Zach Dorfman in 2020, that best illustrates the MSS's work in this space.[75]

Moving from China to enrol at California State University, East Bay in 2011, Fang became president of the Chinese Student Association. She was active in student life and eager to become involved in politics, receiving an award from the university for her student leadership. Joining the local chapter of a public affairs association for Asian Americans, she built connections into state politics. What stood out to acquaintances was that she was older than most students and, with her white Mercedes, seemed unusually wealthy. She was also liaising with a diplomat at the Chinese consulate in San Francisco, suspected by the FBI of being an undercover MSS officer.[76]

In just a few years, Fang managed to cultivate friendships and relationships with several politicians and position herself as a conduit to the Chinese community. She was unusually active for a student, let alone one who's not an American citizen, becoming a staple at political events in California's Bay Area and helping out with fundraising. As Allen-Ebrahimian and Dorfman write, 'Fang's Facebook friends list is a virtual who's who of local Bay Area politicos.'[77] In one photo she was pictured beside Russell Lowe, another alleged MSS asset and a staffer of Senator Dianne Feinstein at the time.[78]

Fang played a long game. She didn't push policy positions and seemed more interested in networking. Any direct influence she gained in the Bay Area wouldn't be particularly consequential in the scheme of things. Local politicians don't have access to any classified information either.

Instead, the MSS is interested in personal intelligence on up-and-coming politicians. It aims to study, compromise and influence those who are on the path towards greater things. By targeting politicians at the beginning of their careers, spies have a better shot at success as they avoid the heightened scrutiny that senior politicians are subjected to from the public and security agencies. These freshly elected politicians are much less likely to be on guard either, as few would appreciate why the MSS would be interested in them. Politicians like Eric Swalwell.

When Fang arrived in California, Swalwell was at the lowest rung of politics. Things changed quickly. The former Dublin City councillor was only thirty-one when he began his bid for a seat in Congress as a Democrat, winning against a well-established incumbent from the same party. Fang became a frequent contact of his and was even friends with his father and brother on Facebook. She helped fundraise for his re-election campaign in 2014 and arranged for an associate to intern in his office.[79]

Swalwell wasn't the only politician Fang grew dangerously close to, nor were her targets limited to California. According to Allen-Ebrahimian and Dorfman, she was also seen at political conferences and a Chinese embassy event in Washington, DC. At one conference, 'an older Midwestern mayor "from an obscure city" referred to Fang as his "girlfriend" and insisted the relationship was genuine despite the clear age difference between Fang and himself'. The FBI also listened in as Fang had 'a sexual encounter with an Ohio mayor in a car', who she'd said she wanted to practise English with.[80]

By 2015, Swalwell was appointed to the House Permanent Select Committee on Intelligence, which oversees the CIA. The FBI had to act and began warning Swalwell and others about Fang, prompting Swalwell to immediately sever ties with her. Later that year, she left the country suddenly. As with Katrina Leung two decades earlier, Fang 'was just one of lots of agents' operating for the MSS in America, a senior US intelligence official told reporters.[81] This is only the tip of the iceberg.

CHAPTER 13

THE GODDESS OF MERCY: BUDDHISM AS A TOOL OF INFLUENCE

T HE BODHISATTVA'S TOWERING and brilliant shape juts out from a vast ocean. Her tons of painted titanium sit some yards off the shore, like an Atlantean ruin bleached bone-white by centuries of sun. The only interruption between sea and statue is the golden lotus-blossom platform she rests upon, looking down from 108 metres high with a cryptic smile. She is a modern image of the timeless Goddess of Mercy and Compassion, the most revered Buddhist deity in China. To the Chinese she is Guanyin, Kannon to the Japanese, Chenrezig to Tibetans and Avalokiteśvara in the ancient tongue of Sanskrit.

This Guanyin of Nanshan Temple stands close to the southernmost point of Hainan Island off China's south coast. Like Hainan's annual Bo'ao Forum, the gigantic statue is positioned in a geographical gateway to China. Depending on how you view it, the island is also a vantage point for China to look upon the rest of the world. Guanyin's gaze traces down to Malaysia and Indonesia before landing somewhere on Australia's north coast.

Guanyin's full name in Chinese, Guanshiyin, means 'perceiving from high the world's sounds'. In one legend, she was on the cusp of ascending to a celestial realm but turned back at the last moment upon hearing the suffering of the world, vowing to end all pain. Other Buddhist divine beings are seen as representations of happiness, light, demon-smiting or even the end of time, but Guanyin has intimate appeal as one who listens to each being's lamentations.

She is the great uniter of Buddhists. Unlike other higher beings worshipped in China, Guanyin is a feature of the Theravada traditions of Sri Lanka, Thailand and Myanmar too. When the Hainan statue was unveiled in 2005 after six years of construction, more than a hundred senior monks from China, Taiwan, Hong Kong and Macau gathered in resplendent robes to celebrate its completion.

A political message was enshrined at its very opening: the monks assembled that day prayed 'for world peace, and the peaceful reunification of China'. The king of Nepal attended too, bearing a gold-plated statue of Sakyamuni Buddha (approximately one-seventieth the height of the Guanyin colossus) to commemorate fifty years of China–Nepal relations. None other than the most senior Party leader in charge of united front work was sent down from Beijing to show his face, reminding attendees of the stake the world's most powerful communist party holds in Buddhist affairs.[1] This was politics, diplomacy and influence riding on the back of religion.

The ceremony's hidden meanings mirrored the Guanyin statue itself. She is presented as a triptych of beings, one facing China, another Taiwan, and lastly the rest of the world. Each manifestation holds an object with its own significance. The main, China-facing Guanyin holds a scroll that represents wisdom. The Taiwan Guanyin's lotus, of course, stands for peace and 'peaceful reunification'. To the rest of the world, Guanyin bears a string of pearls symbolising mercy.[2]

In history, Guanyin has been understood in equally amorphous terms. Originally depicted only as a man, she is now generally portrayed as female. In archetypal terms, some see her as a mother figure not unlike the Virgin Mary. Others view her as an androgynous deity, surpassing the barriers of gender. In many statues she has eleven faces and a thousand arms, or sometimes six, but often just two.

Though its physical form is unchanging, this Hainanese incarnation of Guanyin has a backstory as phantasmagorical as the goddess herself. The true story of its creation lays bare how China's intelligence agencies covertly exploit religion and united front work in their attempts to influence foreign societies and build clandestine networks.

The Shanghai connection

Ji Sufu stood proudly before Guanyin, out of place in his stark white dress shirt and black pants. The statue was a dozen metres taller than the Statue of Liberty, he liked to point out, and he had built it. The site would soon become a 'centre of worship for the Southeast Asian Buddhist masses and a hot destination for global Buddhist cultural tourism', he told the reporters gathered before him.[3]

Ji had been at the heart of the scheme since its inception in the 1990s. There were all sorts of matters to sort out, even though the island's top leader, the Party secretary, was a supporter. It needed approval from the religious affairs authorities in Beijing, not to mention experts on Buddhism, artists, metallurgists and architects to contribute to the final design. Most importantly, it needed a site – a community of monks, a temple and, crucially, a respected Buddhist master to partner with.

But why was Ji, a nondescript businessman from Shanghai with little apparent interest in Buddhism, conducting this orchestra? The truth is that he was secretly working for the Shanghai State Security Bureau (SSSB), one of the most aggressive and internationally active units of the MSS. The Shanghai bureau is notorious for running long-term operations to infiltrate foreign governments and also boasts substantial cyberespionage capabilities. In 2004, it pushed a Japanese diplomat to suicide after blackmailing him over his affair with a karaoke bar hostess.[4] Not long after, it paid an American university student in Shanghai to apply for jobs in the CIA and State Department, which scared the US intelligence community off hiring people with significant experience in China.[5] In recent years it's approached numerous US current and retired government officials, as well as scholars and journalists, successfully recruiting some and paying them to hand over sensitive information.[6]

Ji has an engineering background, starting his career at a top-secret military laboratory that specialises in developing infrared missile-guidance systems.[7] In the 1980s, cadres whose political reliability and discretion had been proven through years of military work made good recruits for the newly created MSS. So from engineering he made a sudden career shift, surfacing as a manager in Shanghai trading companies – all of which eventually trace back to the SSSB.

The companies are officially owned by the Communist Party's Shanghai Foreign Trade Committee, but this is a simple trick to hide the immensity of the SSSB's business empire. Most of them connect up to the agency through using buildings owned by it, 'business executives' who upon closer examination turn out to be intelligence officers, and front groups that are also used to cultivate foreign scholars and policymakers. Once you find a pinhole – a single solid connection to Shanghai's businessperson spies – a vivid moving image of cash, corruption and covert operations pours out.

Across China, both civilian and military intelligence agencies have numerous units in each major city. For routine corporate matters like purchasing office furniture or contracting builders, they often use predictable forms of what's known as 'administrative cover'. If you chance upon a charming military intelligence officer at a Shanghai bar, she might claim to be from the Shanghai Municipal Government Fifth Office, for example.[8] (Shanghai has at least thirteen of these numbered cover offices, and Guangdong has eighteen.)[9] Armed with this knowledge, it's a simple matter of cycling through searches of different numbered offices. Odds are, you're either looking at military spies or MSS spies.

In Shanghai, the little-known municipal government's Fourth Office ticks the right boxes. An official study of Shanghai's economy mentioned that the Fourth Office's 'cover companies' were involved in 'special industries' but not commercial activity.[10] One employee of the Fourth Office simultaneously worked at a cultural front organisation for the city's intelligence services.[11] This is the SSSB.

Business records reveal more about the metropolis's spy networks. One company owned by the Fourth Office, a large trading corporation, is registered to a Spanish-style residence built at the height of the city's Art Deco period. The Anting Villa, once home to a Nationalist Army general, was confiscated when the Communist Party took the city, then passed down to the city's newly created security services.[12]

But the trading company isn't the only front organisation calling the Anting Villa home. Whether because of thrift, laziness or overconfidence, Chinese intelligence agencies often reuse addresses for their fronts. A charity called the Shanghai New Century Social Development Foundation also shares an address at the Anting Villa. While it now tries to hide its mission, its goals haven't changed from those recorded in an old government record: 'to support and encourage the whole of society's active cooperation with state security work' and 'to fund state security activities'.[13] Official records also show that the charity reports back to the Shanghai International Culture Association, a local branch of the MSS's long-standing front group for influence operations, CICEC.[14]

As a charity, the organisation has to abide by the government's transparency and disclosure rules, unlike front companies that often have little online presence. Importantly, some of its public filings were written with little heed for the SSSB's secrecy. For example, records show many of the charity's board meetings are held at 1 Ruining Road, a towering office building on the banks of the Huangpu River that bisects Shanghai.[15] Strangely, for a complex with enough floor space for more than 10,000 workers, there's almost no information about it.[16]

One local taxi driver was equally puzzled by the building, writing on an online forum:

> Today I dropped off a passenger at the entrance to 1 Ruining Road. The tower looked quite beautiful, narrow at the top and bottom yet wide in the middle, but there wasn't any nameplate at the entrance. So I asked my passenger, 'What unit is this?' He told me it was a government unit. When I turned my car around, I rolled down the window to ask the guard what unit it was. Incredibly, he replied: 'It's best if you don't know and don't understand what unit this is. You won't be able to ask what unit this is – even if someone replies they'll only say it's a government unit.'

The taxi driver asked his fellow forum users, 'What sort of unit dabbles in such secretive things?' User milk19860911 replied: 'State Security.'[17]

Out of convenience, this low-profile Shanghai charity's board members have been meeting in the same classified facility where they work: the SSSB's very own skyscraper.[18]

What exactly does the charity busy itself with? Its official reports, though vague, hint at a covert agenda. One year, almost half its budget went to helping 'special talents' fluent in Uyghur and Tibetan 'settle into their jobs' in Shanghai. Though it's on the opposite side of China to the homelands of Tibetans and Uyghurs, the SSSB's prominence means it carries out operations across the country and probably targets overseas diaspora communities from those regions. The foundation also rewarded individuals who 'distinguished themselves' – presumably star intelligence officers – with family health retreats outside of Shanghai to help them 'feel the organisation's care and praise'.[19]

The only public references to the foundation's activities lead to an annual competition for students from countries along the Mekong River (known in China as the Lancang River). Working with Shanghai's prestigious Fudan University, the charity has brought hundreds of bright young men and women from Vietnam, Myanmar, Thailand, Laos and Cambodia to China. The students team up to tackle the ecological and social problems challenging their shared river, which gushes out of the glaciers of Tibet.

Chinese state media captures the event through the lens of the Belt and Road Initiative and the 'Lancang-Mekong Cooperation' framework – China's scheme to stake its influence over the region – describing the competition as 'a high-end external propaganda project'. But, as with much of the Party's united front and propaganda work, intelligence operatives come along for the ride too. It's a perfect scheme for the SSSB to identify and cultivate the Mekong region's future leaders.[20]

The donors to the charity are just as intriguing as the dozens of intelligence officers who run it.[21] The regular givers are generous companies that agree with its mission. That is, they're front companies for the SSSB, channelling profits from property development, international shipping and telecommunications equipment back into the agency. These businesses probably have an operational function too – managing safe houses and other facilities for the bureau, providing surveillance equipment to officers and providing cover when officers need to travel abroad or recruit an agent.

One of those donor companies brings us back to Guanyin. Hainan Island's Sanya Nanshan Gongde Foundation has given close to

¥6 million (A$1.3 million) to the SSSB charity in recent years, accounting for almost a third of its funding.[22] Its chairman isn't a shadowy intelligence officer but a holy man named Yinshun, a Zen master, vice chairman of China's official Buddhist Association, frequent speaker at the international Bo'ao Forum, and abbot of Nanshan Temple, which houses the colossal Guanyin statue.

This 'Buddhist' foundation is an alms bowl for the SSSB's pet projects and influence operations, filled by millions who've come to worship the Goddess of Mercy. What did the atheistic officers of the MSS do to deserve Guanyin's blessings?

Manufacturing holiness

According to official accounts, Hainan's provincial Party secretary first gained an interest in setting up a major temple on the island in the early nineties. He had the name 'Nanshan Temple' in mind, inspired by tales of a medieval Chinese monk from the Nanshan sect of Buddhism. Attempting to reach Japan, this monk's ship was blown off course and ended up in faraway Hainan. Only on his sixth attempt did he finally reach his destination, becoming an influential preacher and spreader of Chinese Buddhist culture in Japan. It was a powerful tale of friendship and exchange between the two countries.

The Party secretary spotted a suitable location on a trip to Sanya – a scenic spot backed by mountains with few established farmers – and got to work. Within a few months, he secured the backing of China's Buddhist leaders and united front officials, who oversee the Party's religious policy. Local authorities drew up their plans for the temple and eventually came up with the idea of a colossal Guanyin statue as the project's heart.

Money was a problem in those early days. Thankfully, generous Buddhist leaders offered their support; Taiwan's Nan Huai-chin contributed a million dollars to the Party secretary's dream. (Master Nan also acted as a secret backchannel between the Party and Taiwanese authorities, handled by the father of state security minister Xu Yongyue.) After many years of planning, negotiation and hard work, the goddess was completed in 2003, ready to withstand the fiercest tropical cyclones.[23]

In reality, corruption, mystery and spies defined the Nanshan Guanyin project from the beginning. The Party secretary had his own connections to China's security apparatus: a decade earlier he ran the Ministry of Public Security, a counterpart to the MSS that carries out counterintelligence work. Before then he was a leading official in Shanghai, which perhaps explains why the SSSB's prints are all over the temple.

Shanghai State Security Bureau business figures like Ji Sufu joined the project in its early days. Their front companies could foot the bill the Hainan government struggled to pay on its own. Accountants from the Shanghai bureau were brought over, their experience at managing complex and costly operations coming in handy.[24]

Today, the company that owns and runs the temple complex is filled with an odd assortment of Shanghainese men and women. Xu Yuesheng, general manager and Communist Party secretary of the company, also sits on the board of the SSSB charity that's funded by Nanshan Temple. Government records show he's attended charity meetings held inside the agency's headquarters building.[25] Another document claims that he works for a technology company, Shanghai Tianhua Information Development Co., which has also used the bureau's Ruining Road headquarters as its address.[26] If someone turns up behind an intelligence agency's closely guarded walls and works for one of its front companies, they're probably an intelligence officer.

Four other suspected SSSB agents sit among the company's leaders in Hainan. Feng Fumin is one of them. He once headed the agency's Political Department, a senior leadership role overseeing the smooth operation of the SSSB Party committee as well as domestic propaganda to improve the agency's image. As one of the bureau's most senior Communist Party officials, Feng would be trusted to maintain discipline while covertly dealing with religious organisations and companies.[27]

Despite the bureau's leading role in the Nanshan Guanyin company, business records make it look as if it only owns a meagre 0.7 per cent stake through one of its front companies. The rest is owned by two investment firms from Shanghai and Hong Kong.

Both trace back to Wu Feifei, who started her business career as an executive in what remains one of the MSS's main front companies,

China National Sci-Tech Information Import and Export Corporation. Wu owns the corporation's Shanghai branch and controls more than two dozen subsidiaries that specialise in property development, investment and Buddhist tourism.[28] As for the Hong Kong company, Wu and SSSB officers such as Xu Yuesheng own most of it.[29]

All roads, it seems, lead to the SSSB, which reaps income from Guanyin and the Nanshan Temple. While the Nanshan Temple makes regular donations to the bureau through its charity, those are dwarfed by the large payments it makes to the agency's front companies. According to the Nanshan foundation's financial reports, it paid out ¥174 million (A$37 million) to SSSB-controlled companies in 2019. About ¥3 million (A$600,000), in contrast, went to the temple itself.[30]

Marx's monk

Master Yinshun, the abbot of Nanshan Temple and head of its MSS-backed charity, is the face of a new breed of Chinese Buddhists. More in tune with the pronouncements of Xi Jinping than Buddha's word, Yinshun stands out with his unabashed flattery of the country's communist leadership. After the 19th Party Congress in 2017, he bragged that he'd hand-copied Xi Jinping's tedious speech three times. 'I'm planning to write it out ten more times,' he added in an address to Hainan's peak Buddhist association, which he chairs. One needn't speculate at the comparison he was making to sacred sutras, which the faithful often transcribe as a kind of meditation, for Yinshun believes 'the 19th Party Congress report is a contemporary Buddhist scripture'. Assuming he writes a rapid forty characters a minute, he must have set aside a full day for each copy of Xi Jinping's doctrine.

If this is the new Xiist sect of Buddhism, Yinshun is its high priest and international ambassador. Yinshun concluded, after meditating on Xi Jinping Thought: 'Buddhist groups must consciously protect General Secretary Xi Jinping's core status, practising the principles of knowing the Party and loving the Party, having the same mind and morals as the Party, and listening to the Party's words and walking with the Party.'[31]

Yinshun has added a litany of political titles alongside his Buddhist honorifics. As a vice president of the China Buddhist Association, he is effectively a senior co-optee of the United Front Work Department, which controls the association. Yinshun also chairs the official Buddhist associations of Shenzhen and Hainan province.[32] Most importantly, he's a delegate to the Chinese People's Political Consultative Conference, the country's peak united front forum.[33] The role technically makes him a political advisor to China's Party-state. In practice, he is merely a cog in its united front machine, faithfully working towards the Party's goals – a cadre in monk's robes.

Buddhism made in China

The MSS was also behind another bold Buddhist venture, Yinshun's Nanhai Buddhist Academy.

In 2017, Buddhist leaders from across Asia visited Hainan Island to celebrate the opening of the academy, situated in the same complex as the Guanyin statue. Guests gathered before a temporary stage in the construction site that was to become an institution of Buddhist learning. The shells of many of the complex's buildings stood around the visitors, but it was hard to imagine the full splendour Yinshun planned for his school. Sheets of green mesh were strewn across the newly excavated hillside to keep dust down. Already, over 6000 controlled explosions had been deployed to carve out terraces and pathways for the academy.

Mock-ups showed a stunning complex of modernist but unmistakably Chinese buildings, with secluded meditation halls and dormitories to house more than a thousand monks from faraway nations. A central promenade faced the sea, leading down the hillside before ending in a jetty where visitors would arrive by boat. More than 200 monks had already signed up for the academy's degree program.[34]

Like the Guanyin and Yinshun's Nanshan Temple, this state-of-the-art academy owes its existence to the SSSB. Between 2019 and 2020, at least RMB66 million (A$14 million) of the academy's funding has come from the temple charity controlled by the SSSB.[35]

To Indian observers, the announcement was an embarrassing reminder of their government's failed bid for international Buddhist influence. Nanhai Academy compares itself to Nalanda, a famous medieval Indian Buddhist university that once received visitors from as far away as Korea.[36] A few years earlier, the Indian government had tried to resurrect Nalanda, drawing in high-profile figures like Nobel laureate Amartya Sen as advisors. Yet the university opened with a mere eleven teachers and fifteen students and no campus. In the meantime, classes were held in a government-owned convention centre while students stayed in a hotel.[37] Construction carried on at a snail's pace in India, while the Nanhai Academy's main structures were already in place upon its unveiling in 2017.[38] The symbolism of China beating its southern neighbour in the race to resurrect an ancient Indian Buddhist institution is painfully clear.

As a further snub to India, the Nanhai Academy eschews Sanskrit, a canonical language of Buddhism. In fact, Sanskrit lexicon has left a significant mark on modern Chinese because Chinese Buddhist sutras are believed to mostly be translations of Sanskrit originals. The academy instead offers programs in the Chinese, Tibetan and Southeast Asian Pali traditions of Buddhism.[39]

China has a more specific reason for keeping Indian influence out of the Nanhai Academy too. *Nanhai* means 'South China Sea', the region where China has illegally occupied and militarised coral reefs, simultaneously angering and belittling countries like Vietnam, the Philippines and Malaysia, which also have claims to the waters.[40] The nine-dash line, a vague yet ludicrously expansive border China claims over the South China Sea, represents a touchy dispute that the Party wants to keep the Indian government out of.

As scholar Jichang Lulu writes, 'The Academy's international orientation does not conceal its PRC patriotic character,' and Xi Jinping's political agenda defines its activities. Its creation has coincided with the emergence of 'a bolder global Buddhist policy' under General Secretary Xi Jinping.[41] Through its international exchanges, the academy functions as a base for Buddhist influence efforts designed to sign up Buddhist leaders to the CCP's strategic vision.[42] The United Front Work Department, as the agency in charge of religion in China, sits at the heart of China's Buddhist influence program. Under Xi, it has formally subsumed the country's religious affairs agency in a move designed to strengthen the Party's control over religion.[43] The department currently supervises an ungodly mix of Buddhism, Christianity, Islam, communism and political ambition. While it uses holy men to peddle the Party's agenda abroad, it runs informant networks within Chinese temples, mosques and churches, working with security agencies to stamp out foreign influence over religion in China.[44] Officially, the Nanhai Academy is subordinate to Hainan's UFWD. Its deputy dean is not a priest but a local united front system official.[45]

While the UFWD's agenda is clear – to manage and spread China's global Buddhist presence – exactly what MSS officers gain from their stake in the academy is kept tightly under wraps. Even Yinshun is unlikely to be informed of the operations they run through his temples and the academy. Nonetheless, it's hard to imagine spies missing the opportunity to profile and recruit foreign Buddhist students from across Asia. They would be stupid not to ride on Yinshun's coat-tails, watching if not actively guiding his political influence operations throughout the region.

Indeed, China's Buddhist influence activities in the region are growing much more targeted and state-driven, according to Southeast Asia scholar Gregory Raymond.[46] By training the next generation of monks and building personal relationships with influential abbots and temples in the region, Yinshun has declared that the Nanhai Academy will 'create a sinicised Buddhist system', reinventing Communist China as the sole global axis of Buddhism.[47] Just as China seeks dominance over the South China Sea, Yinshun explained that his 'South China Sea Buddhism' concept is one 'with China's Buddhism as its core, radiating out broadly' across the region and exporting schools of 'Made in China Buddhism'.[48]

China's history of Buddhism, shared with much of the region, helps it claim shared values, or even a shared future, with other Asian nations.[49] 'South China Sea Buddhism establishes the cultural foundation for the South China Sea region's community of common destiny,' Yinshun wrote in a detailed report to the Chinese government.[50]

To this end, Yinshun convenes an annual gathering of world Buddhist leaders, including those from Taiwan, the United Kingdom, the United States and Canada, called the South China Sea Buddhism Roundtable.[51] Designed to promote the Party's political vision, the event has little focus on Buddhism except as it's relevant to Party ambitions. In 2019, former Japanese prime minister Hatoyama Yukio, who has repeatedly been feted by Party influence agencies, issued the roundtable's opening address, reportedly offering his full support for the Belt and Road Initiative.[52] Yinshun's speeches at the event are framed around Xi Jinping's trademark foreign policy concept: building a 'community of common destiny for mankind' with China at its core.[53] As China expert Nadège Rolland explains, the clunky phrase 'reflects Beijing's aspirations for a future world order, different from the existing one and more in line with its own interests and status'.[54]

Yinshun seeks to implement the spirit of Xi Jinping's ideology by 'raising the discourse power of China's religious sphere on the international stage'.[55] He claims that attendees to the roundtable have 'confirmed the position that the South China Sea is China's, and that China has already become the core of world Buddhism'. In reality, the memorandum signed by attendees contains no such language.[56] That's not to say many wouldn't wholeheartedly agree with Yinshun's claim. Foreign delegates to the roundtable often issue praise of the Belt and Road Initiative and 'Buddhism with Chinese characteristics' or pledge their commitment to the 'One China Principle'.[57]

One Buddha, one China, one thousand targets

Yinshun primarily targets countries such as Mongolia, Thailand, Cambodia and Myanmar with deeply Buddhist populations. In those lands, religious leaders often legitimise political leaders or speak out against them, such as when monks in Yangon refused to accept donations from the state's military.[58]

Mongolia's Sainbuyangiin Nergüi is one of Yinshun's closest foreign contacts. He is the abbot of a temple in the capital of Ulaanbaatar and sends many of his monks to train in China.[59] Yinshun has appointed him a guest professor at the Nanhai Academy and invited him to the South China Sea roundtables. At the 2017 roundtable meeting, Nergüi spoke more of international relations and economics than religion, tying the event to politics in ways that might make even Yinshun blush. After emphasising Mongolia's adoration for the Belt and Road Initiative, he praised China as 'the leader of world Buddhism'. Nergüi sees Yinshun and the Party as ushering in a new era of Buddhism, asking them to 'further and more tightly unite the world's Buddhist groups and formulate policies' on the religion. He highlighted one of the policies in particular: 'All lamas and countries that believe in Buddhism support the one China policy,' he said. 'We only have one Buddha and we support the one China policy, therefore we attend this event.' In other words, agreement with the Party's policies is tantamount in importance to belief in Buddhism, and attendees to Yinshun's events are hitching their religious credibility to the Party's political beliefs.[60]

Detailed in the research of independent scholar Jichang Lulu, Nergüi's case highlights how Buddhist influence quickly reaches the profane realms of politics and moneymaking.[61] The abbot belongs to a large and well-connected family, and his siblings have flourished as local elites. During one of Yinshun's visits to Mongolia, he was greeted by representatives of a major construction company headed by one of Nergüi's brothers, who was an Ulaanbaatar city councillor until his conviction on embezzlement and abuse-of-powers charges in 2009. Not the most virtuous company for Yinshun to keep, but the potential for political influence opportunities is undeniable. Another brother, previously posted to China as a diplomat, has risen to the top of Mongolian politics. After serving as mayor of Ulaanbaatar, he was appointed deputy prime minister in 2021, taking the lead on Mongolia's relations with China.[62]

While these operations are most effective in Buddhist nations, Buddhism has a strong appeal and following in the Western world too. And Chinese abbots have a unique ability to disarm foreign guests, despite China's history of religious repression and the scandals rocking its Buddhist establishment, notably when the head of the national Buddhist Association resigned after sexual harassment allegations in 2018.[63]

In particular, Yinshun has maintained ties to the United Kingdom; former prime minister Tony Blair delivered a video message to Yinshun's 2020 South China Sea Roundtable.[64] Yinshun first travelled to the country in 2015, speaking at the House of Lords and touring Cambridge University.[65] The Nanhai Academy has since signed a partnership with Cambridge to set up a joint digital Buddhist museum. Yinshun couldn't resist claiming a political victory for China here. After the museum project began, he unveiled a 'Cambridge Research Institute for Belt and Road Studies' in Hainan even though Cambridge's website makes no reference to its existence.[66]

Yinshun has also visited Australia several times. On one trip he met billionaire united front figure Huang Xiangmo, a prolific donor to Australian political parties and head of an organisation advocating for China's annexation of Taiwan. According to media reports, Huang's visa was later cancelled by Australia's counterintelligence agency because they found him 'amenable to conducting acts of foreign interference'.[67]

In fact, the MSS isn't the only intelligence agency that works with Yinshun, nor the only one cultivating foreign religious groups. A front group run by Chinese military intelligence, the China Association for International Friendly Contact, has included the abbot in its international exchanges.[68] This military intelligence front has for decades maintained close ties to a Buddhist-inspired Japanese New Age religion called Agon Shū.[69]

It's not humour or faith that lies behind the SSSB's embrace of Yinshun and Hainan's Buddhist community but cold calculus. From a relatively undeveloped place without any notable history of Buddhism, Shanghainese intelligence officers quite literally built Hainan Island into a leading platform for Buddhist influence efforts. The Guanyin colossus is a testament to the agency's creativity, resourcefulness and long-term planning. Buddhism is a window into how the MSS seeks to use religion as a tool for influence and infiltration in countries with different political environments to the United States. The case is one of many that indicates intelligence agencies covertly drive those who already raise eyebrows for their international influence efforts and united front work.

CONCLUSION

FACING UP TO THE MSS

S ET ON A quiet road in the western hills of Beijing, the Cold Spring Base is the MSS's newest spy school. And it's massive. With around 80,000 square metres of floor space, it's larger than Australia's counter-intelligence headquarters. It features lecture theatres, table tennis rooms, classified briefing rooms, a large artificial lake and multistorey villas. A building directory, indiscreetly shared online, shows the complex has its own halal restaurant, indicating just how many ethnic Uyghur and Hui recruits the MSS has.[1] An exclusive hotel sits at the centre of the complex, operated by the same state-owned company that manages other MSS guesthouses.[2]

As they study Party doctrine and methods of persuasion, surveillance and recruitment, these spies will also be honing their physical fitness.[3] Across the ridge from the base they can look over the Chinese military's eavesdropping headquarters. Walking an hour to the south they can pay tribute at the tomb of Larry Wu-tai Chin, the first MSS mole in the CIA who was outed in 1985.[4]

It's an incredible step up from older MSS training facilities across China. The Jiangnan Social University, a secretive MSS academy an hour's drive from Shanghai, has its own shooting range but none of

Cold Spring Base's grandeur.⁵ Other MSS bases in Beijing's environs are starting to look old and certainly can't accommodate the agency's newly enlarged ambitions.

The MSS has come a long way since 1983. For decades it was the People's Liberation Army that most interested observers of China's intelligence apparatus. Deng Xiaoping was a fan of these soldier-spies too and let them manage hundreds of overseas military attachés while the MSS was kept out of embassies. MSS officer Yu Qiangsheng's defection to the CIA in 1985 only made things worse, cutting short the inaugural minister of state security's career. Mindful of this, the dozens of MSS officers posted abroad as journalists had to be painfully cautious. Several Chinese 'journalists' were publicly banned from countries such as Japan and India for espionage and subversion in the 1960s, but things were different now.⁶ China was opening up to the rest of the world and trying to do business with the West. As an MSS officer, it was better to complete one's tour uneventfully than to be arrested in the United States, blamed for setting back China's diplomatic relations and doomed to an inconsequential desk job.

It's only now becoming clear how the MSS thrived in spite of these circumstances. Though it couldn't roam free abroad, it made sure it was everywhere within China. No foreign power could beat them on home ground. So when foreign targets or potential threats like George Soros arrived in China in the first decade of reform and opening, MSS officers had everything in place to monitor and control them. The ministry's Social Investigation Bureau has been at the forefront of these efforts. It alone has directly managed dozens of front organisations and companies, and seeded spies into many more. MSS officers were plugged into all kinds of 'people-to-people' exchanges with China: political, musical, literary, economic, scientific, journalistic or academic. You name it.

And as China's economy, military and ambition grew, so did the MSS. During the 1980s it was only beginning a long process of building front groups and networks. Already, it was during this period that the MSS recruited FBI asset Katrina Leung and several others whom the US intelligence community believed were its own informants. Hong Kong, Japan and France were other priorities for these network-building operations. The agency ramped up its infiltration of Chinese communities in the aftermath of the Tiananmen massacre.

Towards the turn of the millennium, the MSS found its forte. It still lacked the skill of organisations like the CIA or Russian intelligence agencies when it came to clandestine operations but finally began to get its head around the US foreign policy system and appreciate the benefits of targeting weak points like think tanks, retired officials and the business community. After the embarrassing public failure of PLA influence operations targeting President Bill Clinton's 1996 re-election campaign, it was the MSS's turn to show what it could do. Finally, it was allowed to run operations out of Chinese embassies and now had a solid network of bureaus across China to back up its efforts. At the same time, a new generation of experts in the Western world rose into the leadership of the MSS, turning its focus from roughing up dissidents and watching foreigner visitors to actively shaping the world. Yet it was the same Social Investigation Bureau of the MSS that led the way with its unrivalled networks in the United States and in international Chinese communities, largely independent of any provincial bureaus or diplomatic missions.

The first key feature of these efforts was that instead of trying to play a Russian game of hardcore operations designed to flip CIA officers and break into classified facilities, the Social Investigation Bureau's officers were careful and patient, and they wore their cover stories like skin. They became foreign policy scholars, cultural exchange officials, poets, filmmakers, businessmen and book publishers. Lin Di, the bureau chief in charge of these operations, spoke English, held a master's degree from Johns Hopkins University and was well-known to many American China watchers. Like Lin, many of his subordinates were fluent in foreign languages, had books and journal articles to their name and often held credentials from world-class universities in Britain, the United States and France. Chinese spies of generations past couldn't match the comfort with which they moved in Western capitalist circles. They could, quite literally, go to RAND Corporation conferences by day and eat dinner with their American agents by night. Unlike spies posted to embassies, Social Investigation Bureau officers were based in

China and served in the same positions for years, meaning they built up and maintained international connections well beyond the usual three-year cycle of diplomatic assignments. Their contacts were almost exclusively among those who made regular trips to China, making them safe targets.

These methods meant MSS officers were playing a different game to Western intelligence agencies, striking at unprotected parts of democratic systems. When the FBI was looking for sophisticated espionage operations or the theft of defence technology, China Reform Forum and other influence operations seemed insignificant. At the same time, China work was under-resourced across Western intelligence agencies, and there was scant political will to take a hard stance against Beijing, so MSS operations faced little opposition. Counterintelligence agencies were also lulled into a false sense of ease by the fact that these MSS officers usually weren't using the kinds of sophisticated tradecraft that might indicate they were engaging in high-risk operations.[7]

The second key to the MSS's success was that it had long been signing up prominent Chinese officials and scholars to give its front groups a degree of verisimilitude and ensure it had plenty of informants among the kinds of people important foreigners interacted with. The networks it had built among pro-CCP Chinese community figures abroad, long dismissed by Western intelligence officials as unimportant and 'only' targeting pro-democracy activists and other enemies of the Party, were another launchpad for foreign operations. Once the MSS was ready to actively operate against the West, these friends became even more useful. Well-known Chinese academics accompanied MSS officers on trips abroad, shoring up their cover stories and expanding their access in foreign capitals.

But perhaps the MSS's most brilliant decision was to bring on board leading Chinese thinkers who were seen in the West as liberal and reformist. China Reform Forum, the think tank tailor-made by the MSS for influencing the outside world, was at the centre of these operations, drawing together talented officers from across the agency and sometimes even gaining the participation of Party leaders.

This was a long-term game of building up relationships, bartering access to the Communist Party's inner workings and elites, and distorting perceptions of China's direction.

The MSS was taking the West's dream of a more free and open China and turning it into a weapon that gave China valuable time to build up its power and ability to challenge the existing world order. To many of the people targeted for influence, these undercover MSS officers and scholars stood out as the kinds of people who wanted to push China towards political and economic liberalism. They were 'free agents' who could help you get meetings with important Chinese liberals, sometimes even Party leaders, and were willing to share gossip. It worked not just on China scholars but also on Western diplomats and policymakers, who cabled back information and disinformation passed on to them by undercover MSS officers. Every now and then they also tried to blackmail their American contacts and make deals, offering greater access to Party leaders in exchange for siding with China on key issues like Taiwan. Few were any the wiser. Those who realised their friends at China Reform Forum were more than they seemed some-times genuinely believed these were reformists within the MSS who were willing to help foreigners influence the Party.

Zheng Bijian, the veteran Party ideologue serving as China Reform Forum's chairman, transformed the MSS front group into flypaper for foreigners eager to learn about and shape China. His 'theory of China's peaceful rise', which he coined after working with the MSS to study American attitudes towards China, lives on in today's 'peaceful development' policy and gave a brand to the MSS's influence operation. They were no longer just promoting friendship and sympathy towards China but pushing the theory of China's peaceful rise. This schema for understanding China was praised and adopted by no less than Henry Kissinger and former Goldman Sachs co-president John L. Thornton, two backchannels between Party leaders and the White House. Those whom many in the West placed their greatest hopes for China's future in turned out to be serving a covert agenda.

Today's political environment, where overt coercion and aggression towards Western nations is an increasingly normal part of the Party's behaviour, has further unshackled the MSS.

What went wrong?

Faced with such an enormous and poorly understood host of intelligence agencies, how can governments and societies around the world hope to push back?

It's worth first considering what went wrong, because the circumstances that allowed past MSS operations to thrive haven't gone away. Why was MSS bureau chief Lin Di allowed to build close friendships with influential Americans and speak at Washington, DC's National Press Club? Why did no one intervene when former Australian prime minister Bob Hawke entered business with an MSS affiliate? Why did diplomats from around the world continue to treat undercover MSS officers as sources when their colleagues in intelligence agencies should have stopped it? Why did experienced scholars of China fail to sound the alarm on these activities? Why, for so long, has the challenge posed by the CCP and its intelligence agencies been downplayed in the West? Reckoning with these absurdities will be the first step in defeating China's intelligence and influence operations.

There's no easy answer to these questions, especially when the MSS's operations are themselves part of that answer. It's a cyclical problem. Intelligence agencies are ultimately accountable to their governments, which set priorities and targets for information gathering. If political leaders fail to appreciate the significance of China's rise then the resources they allocate to studying China naturally decline. The global War on Terror also drew attention away from China at a key moment and even became a driver of cooperation between Western intelligence agencies and the MSS. At the same time, the onus is largely on intelligence and foreign affairs agencies to assess the CCP's activities and educate policymakers. They failed to effectively do this.

Mindful of these complexities, a few key failures and mistakes stand out.

1. The failure to appreciate influence efforts by the CCP

The CCP's political influence mechanisms remain poorly understood, but the situation was far worse in the past. Intelligence agencies and scholars have chronically overlooked the overseas aspects of united front work. Very few recognised that the MSS wasn't just playing a game of espionage but rather tasked some of its best officers to convince influential foreigners that China would rise peacefully and gradually liberalise. The MSS's involvement in promoting such narratives should have also hinted that the Party may have had other intentions and was simply buying more time to build its power. Instead, American foreign policy took on board the idea that the United States should encourage China's peaceful rise as formulated by Zheng Bijian. The US government sought to deepen China's involvement in international governance and focus on areas of cooperation while downgrading concerns over matters such as human rights, unfair trade practices and theft of intellectual property.

Had the significance of CCP political influence efforts been appreciated, they should have triggered very different responses from governments and their intelligence agencies. Countering political interference is fundamentally different to countering espionage and terrorism because the CCP's influence operations tend to focus on individuals without access to classified information and often don't involve traditional attempts to recruit agents. Rather than intervene to stop the MSS from building friendships with those individuals, intelligence agencies usually preferred to watch and see what happened. They might have stepped in once these efforts touched on senior government officials but the need to prevent the MSS from influencing scholars and retired leaders wasn't appreciated. Furthermore, many countries lack laws to prosecute political interference, and there isn't anything necessarily illegal about being manipulated by an undercover intelligence officer.

Together with anti-interference laws, targeted actions by security agencies and clear government policies on the matter, sunlight is the best disinfectant. Transparency is an essential pillar of responding to political interference. Governments and media can cut off the legs of many an influence operation simply by publicly exposing it. The earlier the better. But first they need the capabilities to accurately identify and understand CCP influence.

Now that the threat of political interference is widely recognised, governments need to foster a community of experts in the CCP and its intelligence agencies. This will be a decades-long effort. Analysts in the government should be encouraged to specialise and cultivate their expertise on China rather than being moved between assignments every three years. University programs need to be established to train a new generation of fluent Chinese speakers with strong open-source research skills. The flexibility and creativity of independent research institutions will be a key part of this.

2. The belief in misleading stereotypes about China and its intelligence agencies

Stereotypes and misconceptions were widespread among observers of Chinese intelligence agencies until recently, and these biased them towards downplaying or misunderstanding the threat. Over many decades, this has allowed the CCP to build entrenched intelligence and influence networks in many countries.

The 'thousand grains of sand' theory, whereby China purportedly uses masses of ethnic Chinese amateur spies to hoover up vast amounts of information that are then pieced together into useful intelligence, has perhaps been the most widespread of these misconceptions.[8] At first glance, this vivid idea might seem to encourage an active and well-resourced response to Chinese intelligence activity. But any attempt to uncover some essential character of Chinese intelligence is danger-ously wrong. China expert Peter Mattis criticises the theory because 'if "Chinese intelligence" includes everything from the intelligence services to a corporation to a criminal entrepreneur, then the term becomes almost meaningless'. Mattis points out that it fails on empirical grounds because it grossly understates the role of professional intelligence agencies and wrongly focuses attention on ethnic Chinese people when the MSS has a long history of targeting foreigners too.[9] Nonetheless, versions of this idea have been common among intelligence analysts and in the broader China-watching community.

A related mistake has been the belief that CCP efforts to infiltrate and influence Chinese diaspora communities, particularly through united front work, are relatively harmless. The MSS's foreign operations have always been hotly focused on suppressing what it calls the 'five poisons': Uyghur activists, Tibetan activists, Taiwanese activists, democracy activists and Falun Gong practitioners.[10] Until very recently, intelligence agencies didn't pay attention to these activities. They were seen as insignificant ethnic community affairs even as they impinged upon the freedoms of citizens.[11] This has its roots in ignorance and ambivalence towards ethnic Chinese communities.

Today, the failure by governments around the world to care about united front work in Chinese communities is leading to serious and broad consequences. The diversity of Chinese community organisations and media has collapsed in many countries. Where most groups were independent or aligned with Taiwan in the past, today many of the loudest community bodies in countries such as Australia and Canada are run by CCP-aligned individuals who have been courted by the Party's united front work agencies. Recent political interference cases in Australia show that these united front networks now serve as an infrastructure for espionage and covert influence beyond Chinese communities and into mainstream politics. This also forms a vicious self-sustaining cycle when CCP influence over traditional media and dominance over Chinese social media platforms like WeChat stymies efforts by anti-CCP groups to push back, and by governments to educate affected communities on foreign interference.[12]

3. Risk aversion in bureaucracies and intelligence agencies

Intelligence agencies are hoarders. To protect these hoards, they strictly compartmentalise sensitive information, and little is more sensitive than information gathered on intelligence agencies in foreign countries. This process of gathering and protecting information is an art, but so is knowing how to share and act on it. When it comes to sharing intelligence on China, insular culture and political sensitivities have helped the MSS's influence operations flourish.

Excessive compartmentalisation of information hindered efforts by intelligence agencies to cooperate with other members of their own communities – the CIA with the FBI, for example. In the case of MSS agent Katrina Leung, this made it almost impossible to pick out and remove or flag the information she passed on while posing as an FBI source, information that sometimes made it to the White House. With China Reform Forum, it allowed diplomats to cable MSS disinformation straight to Washington, DC.

Even worse, it predisposed intelligence agencies against intervening in these MSS operations, which was also exacerbated by the lack of understanding towards political influence efforts. This explains why foreign diplomats in China continued to rely on information from China Reform Forum even when some of their colleagues in intelligence agencies knew the think tank was an MSS influence front.

If even US government employees weren't being warned then it's little wonder that many scholars, retired officials and business leaders weren't either. While intelligence agencies often do warn and debrief those they see coming into contact with MSS officers, they're reluctant to do so when high-level retired officials, politicians and business leaders are involved. One concern is that these warnings might end up in the press, which could lead to a change in MSS tactics. Even worse, some worried that warnings given to the wrong people would be ignored or even passed on to the MSS, so it wasn't worth doing. To some, the access and opportunities offered by the MSS are too valuable to pass up.

Bureaucratic risk aversion has probably been an even greater factor in the weak response to Party influence operations. In consensus-driven bureaucracies where hearts and minds change at a snail's pace, nothing is more risky than making an arrest or exposing an operation that reflects poorly on your political masters. As one former US intelligence officer explained, 'The [FBI leadership] hate dealing with political cases because they feel like either way you're going to piss off half the people no matter what you do,' because neither major party wants to be exposed as the target of a concerted influence operation.[13] This way, influence operations become self-reinforcing. By spreading its influence operations broadly across the world's political, business and academic leadership, the Party forestalled any response to those activities.

Another problem is that intelligence agencies have chronically underutilised open-source intelligence – information collected from publicly accessible sources. Intelligence gathered through secretive channels has a powerful mystique, even when similar findings could be made with Google searches. As this book demonstrates, many Chinese government secrets can be pieced together by carefully reading Chinese-language books, newspapers, journals and websites. Amazingly, no country (with the exception of China) has seriously invested in this approach to intelligence gathering, and open-source intelligence is viewed as a lesser calling and a bad career choice within intelligence agencies. While there's much you can't access from analysis of open information, its distinct advantage is that it's low risk, it's cheap and it comes with a lower level of security classification. This means open-source intelligence is easily shared within governments, and even outside of them. It's an essential tool for countering foreign interference but one that is largely untapped.

Recognising the special characteristics of influence efforts should change these approaches. If you're trying to disrupt an influence operation, sometimes a headline newspaper story is exactly what you want. Educating the public about the CCP's political influence methods and narratives should be a priority. Releasing information about the scale and nature of the MSS will help encourage people to take its activities seriously. Raising the transparency of foreign interference through public reporting and prosecutions has to be hard-wired into the response. Having high-quality open-source intelligence on hand makes that much easier to do.

4. The vacuum of research on Party intelligence organisations and the rise of the Access Cult

Let's not forget the importance of one of the main targets of MSS influence operations: scholars, commentators and other non-governmental observers of China. Though they're not experts on intelligence agencies, they profess to be experts on China, yet the degree of obliviousness and recklessness with which some of these people have treated the CCP is astounding. The case of the RAND Corporation, which continued to help China Reform Forum access the United States even after it was warned that the group was an MSS front, is symptomatic of a broader problem.

China's intelligence and security agencies are generally left out of histories and analysis of the country in a way that would be unimaginable when writing about the Soviet Union, for example. As intelligence historian Christopher Andrew points out, 'The intelligence community is central to the structure of the one-party state.' It's one of those forgotten lessons from the Cold War, and one that has been slow to sink into discussions about China.[14] China's intelligence community continues to be glossed over when scholars write about contemporary

China. One recent 650-page report about the CCP's influence operations only devoted two pages to the MSS.[15]

Part of this might be chalked up to the inherent difficulty of studying intelligence agencies, but this excuse holds little water. Scant scholarly attention has been applied to the dozens if not hundreds of biographical articles and memoirs by retired Chinese intelligence agents. Government archives in many countries provide another angle on Chinese intelligence operations, yet little attention has been paid to them.[16] You'll be hard-pressed to find any substantial references in academic literature to the CCP's Central Investigation Department, a predecessor to the MSS, even though it was a driving force behind China's early diplomatic missions and foreign relations.[17] Today, when the US government prosecutes Chinese spies or hackers, few follow up on the leads littered in court records and indictments that often name front organisations for the MSS and PLA.[18]

Instead, there is minimal scholarly interest in Chinese intelligence agencies. As a field, China studies research into the structure and operation of Party organisations has largely given way to theoretical or quantitative approaches that leave little room for studying the MSS. Open-source investigative methods haven't featured enough in academic research on China, although this is beginning to change. Since the gradual reopening of the People's Republic of China after Mao's death, it's simply been more fruitful to work in the fields of study that emerged from that liberalisation. Demographic statistics and economic records that had never been accessible could suddenly be studied by foreigners. New opportunities for fieldwork opened up across China to interview everyday people. For those interested in Party politics, some officials were now willing to sit down for interviews and share their perspectives with American scholars.

These were all worthy avenues for inquiry but had the effect of drawing attention away from less fruitful and more sensitive areas of study. And when scholars managed to interview MSS officers, they often didn't realise it because their interviewees were undercover. When they understood they were meeting with MSS officers, often through the MSS bureau outwardly known as the China Institute of Contemporary International Relations, those they met were carefully selected individuals trusted to push the Party line, promote influence narratives and not give away the secrets of the trade.

Another explanation is that scholars know well what happens to those who cross into verboten topics or are too politically incorrect for the Party's liking. China experts like Professor Andrew Nathan, who helped publish and edit a collection of leaked documents on the Tiananmen massacre in 2001, have been barred from entering China. I was publicly banned from China in 2019. No one likes to self-censor, but it's a reality for many who want to continue to visit the country. As Professor David Shambaugh, often viewed as an authority on the CCP, reportedly told a group of young scholars: 'At some point, you'll receive a call from a journalist, who will ask you about Taiwan, or Tibet, or Tiananmen … And when that happens, you should put down the phone and run as far away as possible.'[19] The impact of this self-censorship upon China research, and particularly on the West's understanding of sensitive aspects like the MSS, cannot be understated.

Self-censorship is the sibling of another source of ignorance and laxity towards the Party's underbelly: the Access Cult. In a relatively closed-off political system, those who can access its inner sanctum gain credibility and authority. A cohort of scholars and retired policymakers such as former Australian prime minister Bob Hawke have built careers and business upon their ability to meet with decision-makers in the Party.

But the MSS is all too aware of the power of access, and it's a phenomenon the Party as a whole exploits to great effect. The MSS has explicitly offered to help individuals land meetings with senior officials as part of its recruitment pitches.[20] While not all who take part in the Access Cult are involved with Chinese intelligence agencies, all accept its bargain of access in exchange for compromising their freedom and integrity. They rely on access for their reputations and income and will never knowingly cross a line that might compromise their continued good standing with the Party or the proxies they rely on to organise high-level meetings. As the case of China Reform Forum shows, what China whisperers learn through the Access Cult is of little value. At best, they're fed trivial information. At worst, they're pawns in a covert influence operation.

The MSS's China Institutes of Contemporary International Relations is another key part of these MSS efforts.[21] Many know that it's 'affiliated' with the MSS, but its contribution to intelligence collection and influence operations as the 11th Bureau of the agency is recognised by few.[22] In fact, the institute was originally established as the outward-facing nameplate of an intelligence bureau that specialised in open-source analysis. The reason for its establishment was to give Chinese intelligence a channel for engaging internationally, and it actively helps the rest of the MSS target and recruit foreigners.[23]

Nonetheless, this MSS bureau's international relationships are some of the most extensive of any Chinese research institution because many assume it offers insight into the Party's thinking. It holds dialogues and conferences with think tanks like the Center for Strategic and International Studies in Washington, DC and London's International Institute for Strategic Studies.[24] The Australian Strategic Policy Institute previously ran exchanges with CICIR with the aim of seeking 'common ground' on cybersecurity by encouraging the Chinese government to limit cyber attacks.[25] The Australian government once sponsored one of its economists to complete a joint PhD at CICIR and the Australian National University. The same university also partnered with CICIR to produce a significant report on Australia–China relations.[26]

The backlash

Despite the world's past mistakes, the MSS now faces the toughest backlash in its history. The agency that once prided itself on never having allowed an officer to be captured abroad saw one of its own arrested and hauled before a jury in the United States. Xu Yanjun, an officer in the Jiangsu State Security Department, fell into a trap laid by the FBI after it cottoned onto his efforts to steal American jet engine technology. Captured in Belgium, he was extradited to the United States in 2018. Other arrests that year dismantled the network of agents he'd been building up in America.[27] And in November 2021 he was convicted of economic espionage. The US government was announcing loud and clear that MSS officers, previously only watched but never arrested, were now fair game.[28]

That's not the only disaster that's keeping MSS officers up at night. Numerous governments are in the process of fundamentally reconfiguring their foreign policies as the charade of China's peaceful rise crumbles.

Australia was an unlikely first to cross the point of no return. The country is heavily reliant on trade with China, although US companies still lead in investments.[29] Xi Jinping toured the country in 2014, and Australia's political establishment boasted strong ties to Chinese officials and Party-linked businesspeople. Political interference and united front work were a distant and obscure vocabulary. That is, until a series of contingent events in 2017 jolted the country into action. Early in that year, backbench politicians rebelled against ratifying an extradition treaty with China.[30] In June, investigative journalists produced what were then the most detailed and revelatory reports the public had seen into CCP-backed interference in Australian politics.[31] By the end of the year, the prime minister, armed with findings from a classified study into the Party's covert influence operations, tabled new laws that gave security agencies powers to intervene in such activities.[32] The government also began contemplating banning Huawei from the nation's 5G network.[33]

This was much more than a readjustment of the Australia–China relationship. It was a tectonic realignment, the effects of which continue to play out. Waking up to the threat of political interference called into question the Party's intentions and goodwill. It also brought understanding the CCP and its ideology into the heart of discussions about China, when their contemporary relevance had long been downplayed.[34] Recognising the innocence with which much of the country previously engaged with China meant that the field was now open for a re-evaluation of the place of economic ties, research collaboration, education exports and human rights in the China relationship. Nothing about waking up to this was easy or inevitable. China's retaliation – economic coercion, arbitrary arrests of Australians and ending high-level exchanges with the Australian government – only confirmed that Australia's growing reliance on China was fraught.[35] This new paradigm doesn't mean giving up on the benefits of exchanges with China. As John Garnaut, a key architect of Australia's foreign interference strategy, explained, 'It's about sustaining the enormous benefits of engagement while managing the risks.'[36]

Australia is now seen as both a model for countering foreign interference and a canary in the coalmine, sending out warnings of the CCP's coercion and covert activity.[37] Slowly but surely, the misguided assumptions and narratives that informed decades of engagement with China are being discarded. The MSS operations that propped them up for so long are being unwound. Even in Australia, this process still has many years to go. The country's capacity to shine a light on interference, enforce foreign interference laws, deter covert operations and build the resourcing and expertise needed to inform those efforts is still being developed.

Though no other political system has 'reset' its relationship with China as suddenly as Australia, aggressive responses to the Party's espionage are ramping up across the globe. In 2021, the CIA, still struggling to collect intelligence after the MSS dismantled its networks a decade earlier, announced the creation of a new mission centre dedicated to China operations.[38] Daring spy-catching operations have seen FBI agents go undercover to pose as MSS officers to meet with suspected spies.[39] (The bureau has come a long way. More than two decades ago it directed an employee who only spoke Cantonese, and not Mandarin, to impersonate an MSS officer.)[40] Several current and former US government employees have been charged with spying for China in recent years. Baimadajie Angwang, an officer of the New York Police Department, was charged in 2020 with acting as an agent of the United Front Work Department.[41] US prosecutors have also accused more than a dozen MSS hackers of committing espionage, although it's almost certain that none will ever face court.[42]

The United States is not alone as it clamps down on Chinese espionage. In 2021, governments around the world teamed up to point the finger at the MSS for widespread hacks of Microsoft Exchange servers.[43] All large nations hack each other, but the MSS 'crossed a line', in the words of Australian cyber chief Rachel Noble, by letting cyber criminals move in behind it to steal and extort.[44] Australian authorities have accused a Melbourne-based united front figure of working with the MSS to influence a sitting politician. Many other suspected foreign agents, including two Chinese academics, have had their visas cancelled.[45] The UK government has expelled three MSS officers who were pretending to be journalists.[46] It officially named lawyer and political donor Christine Lee as an agent of influence for the United Front Work Department.[47] German authorities have charged a political scientist with working for the Shanghai State Security Bureau.[48] Japan, which still lacks laws against espionage and interference, publicly blamed the Chinese military for cyber attacks and announced the creation of new police units to counter technology theft and cyberespionage.[49] In 2021, Estonia, a Baltic state normally under constant threat from Russia, convicted a spy for China.[50] Other PRC intelligence agents and covert influence plots have been exposed in France, Taiwan, New Zealand, Belgium, Poland, India, Afghanistan, Sri Lanka, Kazakhstan, Singapore and Nepal.[51] All that in a few years.

This list of counterintelligence actions is at once reassuring and unsettling. For every MSS spy who's caught or whose case is leaked to the media, dozens if not hundreds continue to operate. Out of all these cases, few touch upon the CCP's influence operations.[52] But maybe that's about to change.

ACKNOWLEDGEMENTS

This book would not have been written were it not for the encouragement and feedback I received from John Garnaut. Peter Mattis also encouraged me and taught me much about studying China. I owe a great debt to four friends in particular, for bringing me into their trust, sharing their wisdom and acting as sounding boards: a Chinese-Australian scholar who prefers not to be named, Jichang Lulu, and two old friends with unrivalled expertise in the field.

Clive Hamilton always offered his support to me, and the confidence and knowledge I gained from working with him at the very beginning of my career were essential for this project. Bob and Dimon have also been generous teachers and friends.

At Hardie Grant, Arwen Summers, Julie Pinkham and many others put in an enormous effort to see through the realisation of this book. I would also like to thank the editors who helped cut and refine its drafts.

Murong Xuecun taught me much about being a writer and how to let go of manuscripts and place them in your publisher's hands.

Many others from Australia, Europe, the United States and Asia helped through their friendship and guidance or by agreeing to talk about their experiences of China's intelligence operations. I am grateful to them all.

Finally, I would like to thank my family and close friends for supporting me during the largely solitary experience of writing a book.

About the author

Alex Joske was the youngest-ever analyst at the Australian Strategic Policy Institute and is known for meticulous Chinese-language investigations grounded in authoritative and independently verifiable sources. His research on Chinese Communist Party influence and intelligence efforts has withstood intense scrutiny and shaped the thinking of governments and policymakers globally. He lives in Canberra, Australia, and previously lived in Beijing for six years.

INDEX

NOTES

Introduction

1 Quotes and description of Lin's talk come from 'The beginning of new relations' [video], *C-SPAN*, 23 April 2001, 1:18:00, www.c-span.org/video/?163854-2/beginning-relations&event=163854&playEvent.

2 Mark Stokes & Russell Hsiao, *The People's Liberation Army General Political Department: Political warfare with Chinese characteristics*, Project 2049 Institute, Arlington, VA, October 2013, pp. 38–9, project2049.net/wp-content/uploads/2018/04/P2049_Stokes_Hsiao_PLA_General_Political_Department_Liaison_101413.pdf.

3 'US charges three Chinese hackers who work at internet security firm for hacking three corporations for commercial advantage', United States Department of Justice, 27 November 2017, www.justice.gov/opa/pr/us-charges-three-chinese-hackers-who-work-internet-security-firm-hacking-three-corporations.

4 For an overview of key agencies in China's intelligence community, see Peter Mattis & Matthew Brazil, *Chinese Communist Espionage: An intelligence primer*, Naval Institute Press, Annapolis, MD, 2019, pp. 10–22.

5 Alex Joske, 'Secret police: The Ministry of Public Security's clandestine foreign operations', *Sinopsis*, 25 January 2022, sinopsis.cz/wp-content/uploads/2022/01/mps0.pdf; Aruna Viswanatha & Rebecca Ballhaus, 'New details revealed of RNC fundraiser's lobbying for China', *Wall Street Journal*, 24 August 2020, www.wsj.com/articles/new-details-of-chinas-efforts-to-remove-critic-in-u-s-revealed-in-hawaii-court-11598294289.

6 Peter Mattis, 'The analytic challenge of understanding Chinese intelligence services', *Studies in Intelligence*, vol. 56, no. 3, September 2012, pp. 47–57. Overlooking the political and strategic significance of intelligence services is not limited to discussions of China. See Christopher Andrew, 'Intelligence,

international relations and "under-theorisation"', *Intelligence and National Security*, vol. 19, no. 2, 2004, pp. 170–84.

7 The thousand grains of sand idea was thoroughly dismantled in Mattis, 'The analytic challenge' and William C. Hannas, James Mulvenon & Anna B. Puglisi, *Chinese Industrial Espionage: Technology acquisition and military modernisation*, Routledge, Abingdon, 2013, ch. 8. Starting in the 1990s, the idea was promoted by commentators and gained popularity inside many intelligence agencies, and is still believed by some today. See David Wise, *Tiger Trap*, Houghton Mifflin Harcourt, Boston, 2011, pp. 5–19; Paul Moore, 'China's subtle spying', *New York Times*, 2 September 1999, www.nytimes.com/1999/09/02/opinion/ chinas-subtle-spying.html. For a recent use of the grains of sand theory, see Ian Williams, 'How China spies on the West', *Spectator*, 23 January 2022, www.spectator.co.uk/article/how-china-spies-on-the-west.

8 Mattis, 'The analytic challenge'.

9 Interview with a former US intelligence officer.

10 Gerry Groot's research was a rare exception. See Gerry Groot, *Managing Transitions: The Chinese Communist Party, United Front work, corporatism and hegemony*, Routledge, New York, 2003.

11 John Garnaut, 'Chinese spies keep eye on leading universities', *Sydney Morning Herald*, 21 April 2014, www.smh.com.au/national/chinese-spies-keep-eye-on-leading-universities-20140420-36yww.html.

12 Alex Joske, 'Incident at university pharmacy highlights a divided Chinese community', *Woroni*, 26 August 2016, www.woroni.com.au/news/incident-at-university-pharmacy-highlights-a-divided-chinese-community/.

13 Clive Hamilton, *Silent Invasion: China's influence in Australia*, Hardie Grant Books, Melbourne, 2018.

14 Jichang Lulu, 'Repurposing democracy: The European Parliament China friendship cluster', *Sinopsis*, 26 November 2019, sinopsis.cz/ wp-content/uploads/2019/11/ep.pdf; Bethany Allen-Ebrahimian, 'This Beijing-linked billionaire is funding policy research at Washington's most influential institutions', *Foreign Policy*, 28 November 2017, foreignpolicy. com/2017/11/28/this-beijing-linked-billionaire-is-funding-policy-research-at-washingtons-most-influential-institutions-china-dc/; Anne-Marie Brady, 'Magic weapons: China's political influence activities under Xi Jinping', Wilson Center, September 2017, www.wilsoncenter.org/article/magic-weapons-chinas-political-influence-activities-under-xi-jinping.

15 Jamil Anderlini, 'China-born New Zealand MP probed by spy agency', *Financial Times*, 13 September 2017, www.ft.com/content/64991ca6-9796-11e7-a652-cde3f882dd7b; Matt Nippert, 'Jian Yang didn't disclose Chinese intelligence connections in citizenship application', *NZ Herald*, 13 October 2017, www.nzherald.co.nz/nz/jian-yang-didnt-disclose-chinese-intelligence-connections-in-citizenship-application/ JLU7VTF5L44X3TLINU4MOBLRXY/; Brady, 'Magic weapons'.

16 Stephanie Peatling & Fergus Hunter, 'China scandal: Embattled Labor senator Sam Dastyari resigns from Parliament', *Sydney Morning Herald*, 11 December

2017, www.smh.com.au/politics/federal/china-scandal-embattled-labor-senator-sam-dastyari-resigns-from-parliament-20171211-h02ddn.html; Nick McKenzie, Richard Backer & Phillip Coorey, 'Sam Dastyari's South China Sea comments exposed on tape', *Australian Financial Review*, 29 November 2017, www.afr.com/politics/sam-dastyaris-south-china-sea-comments-exposed-on-tape-20171129-gzv57l.

17 See, for example, Lulu, 'Repurposing democracy'; Andrew Chubb & John Garnaut, 'The enigma of CEFC's Chairman Ye', *South Sea Conversations*, 7 June 2013, archive.ph/vvQb3; Jichang Lulu, 'China's state media and the outsourcing of soft power', *University of Nottingham China Policy Institute Blog*, 12 July 2015, archive.ph/lnRst; John Garnaut, Deborah Snow & Nic Christensen, 'Behind the mysterious Dr Chau', *Sydney Morning Herald*, 4 July 2009, archive.ph/wp1F9.

18 薛钰, '周恩来与党的隐蔽战线: 试谈民主革命时期周恩来对我党情报保卫工作的贡献', 人民网, no date, web.archive.org/web/20180309073811/http://www.people.com.cn/GB/shizheng/8198/9405/34150/2544000.html.

19 上海市国家安全局, 江苏省国家安全厅 & 华东情报史边审委员会办公室 (eds), 华东情报史专题选集, no publisher, 1994, p. 1.

20 See, for example, titles held by Yan Tingchang (严廷昌). 中共江苏省委组织部 (ed.), 中国共产党江苏省组织史资料 1922.春-1987.10, 中共党史出版社, 1993, pp. 545–6. For a 1990s example, see Fujian State Security Department officer Zhi Dujiang (智渡江), who was concurrently deputy director of the Fujian Overseas Chinese Affairs Office. '人事与机构', 福建政府公报, no. 11, 1998, archive.ph/MBSdM; '人事与机构', 福建政府公报, no. 8, 1998, archive.ph/CsdH6. See also Stokes & Hsiao, *The People's Liberation Army General Political Department*, fn. 217.

21 Myra MacPherson, 'All governments lie', *New York Times*, 1 October 2006, www.nytimes.com/2006/10/01/books/chapters/1001-1st-macp.html; Eric Alterman, 'I. F. Stone was no spy', *Daily Beast*, 22 April 2009, www.thedailybeast.com/if-stone-was-no-spy.

Chapter 1 George Soros, the China Fund and the MSS

1 梁恒, 《与索罗斯一起走过的日子》, 广东经济出版社, Guangzhou, February 2012, p. 1; Liang Heng & Judith Shapiro, *Son of the Revolution*, Random House, New York, 1983.

2 梁恒, 《与索罗斯一起走过的日子》, p. 14; Michael T. Kaufman, *Soros: The life and times of a messianic billionaire*, Knopf, New York, 2002, p. 213.

3 See also Judith Shapiro, 'The rocky course of love in China', *New York Times*, 13 December 1981, www.nytimes.com/1981/12/13/magazine/the-rocky-course-of-love-in-china.html.

4 梁恒, 《与索罗斯一起走过的日子》, p. 1.

5 George Soros, 'Remarks delivered at the World Economic Forum', *George Soros* [blog], 24 January 2019, www.georgesoros.com/2019/01/24/remarks-delivered-at-the-world-economic-forum-2/.

6 梁恒, 《与索罗斯一起走过的日子》, pp. 1–5.

7 Interview with a former colleague of Chen Yizi (head of the Economic System Reform Institute and the first Chinese co-chair of Soros's China Fund), 15 July 2021; 朱嘉明, 《中国改革的歧路》, 联经文库, Taipei, January 2013, p. 40.

8 See Catherine Keyser, *Professionalizing Research in Post-Mao China: The System Reform Institute and policy making*, M. E. Sharpe, New York, 2003, pp. 78–9.

9 Kaufman, *Soros*, p. 215.

10 Interview, 15 July 2021. The Ford Foundation, which the Chinese government likewise suspected of being run by the CIA, was funding similar exchanges between Chinese economists and counterparts in socialist states. According to former ESRI researcher Cheng Xiaonong, Soros also funded a trip to Japan; interview, 13 August 2021.

11 '"中国的改革和开放大有希望": 访美国著名金融企业家乔治·索罗斯', *People's Daily*, 29 February 1988, p. 7, archive.today/rWF3K; 陳一諮, 《陳一諮回憶錄》, New Century Press, Hong Kong, 2013, pp. 367–8.

12 Soros, 'Remarks delivered at the World Economic Forum'.

13 '"中国的改革和开放大有希望" …', *People's Daily*.

14 Soros, 'Remarks delivered at the World Economic Forum'; Kaufman, *Soros*, p. 217.

15 Liang & Shapiro, *Son of the Revolution*, pp. 101–2.

16 Kaufman, *Soros*, p. 217.

17 Liang & Shapiro, *Son of the Revolution*, p. 105.

18 Interview, 15 July 2021.

19 梁恒, 《与索罗斯一起走过的日子》, pp. 106–7.

20 Soros, 'Remarks delivered at the World Economic Forum'.

21 梁恒, 《与索罗斯一起走过的日子》, p. 107.

22 梁恒, 《与索罗斯一起走过的日子》, p. 107.

23 '中国改革与开放基金会确定工作重点 资助改革与开放的学术研究 美金融企业家索罗斯宣布每年继续赠款百万美元', *Daily*, 25 August 1988, archive.vn/th38N.

24 梁恒, 《与索罗斯一起走过的日子》, p. 112.

25 George Soros, *Underwriting Democracy*, Public Affairs, New York, 1991, ch. 1, www.georgesoros.com/wp-content/uploads/2017/10/underwriting_democracy-chap-1-2017_10_05.pdf.

26 梁恒, 《与索罗斯一起走过的日子》, pp. 116–17.

27 *CICEC Annual Report 1988*, CICEC, Beijing, no date, p. 33.

28 Liang & Shapiro, *Son of the Revolution*, p. 117; Soros, 'Remarks delivered at the World Economic Forum'.

29 Kaufman, *Soros*, p. 219.

30 Marianne Yen, 'Fund's representatives arrested in China', *Washington Post*, 8 August 1989, www.washingtonpost.com/archive/politics/1989/08/08/funds-representatives-arrested-in-china/24e8b72c-d6fe-4753-a007-51d181239cb6/.

31 Soros, 'Remarks at the World Economic Forum'.

32 Liang & Shapiro, *Son of the Revolution*, pp. 117–20.

33 陸鏗，'陳一諮揭露倒趙大陰謀'，in 沈大為，趙紫陽的崛起與陷落，百姓文化事業有限公司，January 1990, p. 307 sq.; see also Chris Buckley, 'Chen Yizi, a top adviser forced to flee China, dies at 73', *New York Times*, 25 April 2014, www.nytimes.com/2014/04/26/world/asia/chen-yizi-a-top-adviser-forced-to-flee-china-dies-at-73.html.

34 陳一諮，《陳一諮回憶錄》, p. 460.

35 陳一諮，《陳一諮回憶錄》, pp. 459–60; 宗鳳鳴，《趙紫陽軟禁中的談話》，開放出版社，Hong Kong, 2007, p. 67.

36 Chen Yizi's memoirs, published in Hong Kong in 2013, mentioned Yu Enguang and CICEC but did not reveal their positions in the security apparatus. Chen also described *China Economic Daily* Japan correspondent Zhao Wendou (赵文斗) as the ESRI's liaison officer in Japan, when Zhao was in fact an undercover MSS officer. See 陳一諮，《陳一諮回憶錄》, pp. 460, 550.

37 Interview, 15 July 2021.

38 Yu Enguang does not appear on the official list of members of CICEC's first committee (1984–93). See '第一屆理事会名单', CICEC, no date, archive.today/QG7Kp. Keyser's study (p. 78) of the ESRI interpreted CICEC's takeover of the China Fund as a move designed to preserve its independence, although CICEC's status as an MSS front group challenges this idea.

39 梁恒，《与索罗斯一起走过的日子》, p. 107.

40 '于恩光呼吁增强信息网络安全意识', *People's Daily*, 31 October 2001, archive.ph/GVLB4.

41 'Paradise Papers: Everything you need to know about the leak', *BBC*, 10 November 2017, www.bbc.com/news/world-41880153.

42 'YU – Enguang', Offshore Leaks Database, no date, archive.today/feXGu.

43 'YU – Enguang', Offshore Leaks Database.

44 Soros, 'Remarks at the World Economic Forum'.

45 The first published suggestion that CICEC is an MSS front organisation may be Mark Stokes & Russell Hsiao, *The People's Liberation Army General Political Department: Political warfare with Chinese characteristics*, Project 2049 Institute, Arlington, VA, 14 October 2013, p. 39, fn. 259, project2049.net/wp-content/uploads/2018/04/P2049_Stokes_Hsiao_PLA_General_Political_Department_Liaison_101413.pdf.

Chapter 2 Spymaster: Yu Enguang

1 Marian Burros, 'What is to be learned from the great chefs of Canton?', *Washington Post*, 24 July 1980, archive.ph/VL5vX.

2 This is described in the memoirs of a former Central Investigation Department officer. 严廷昌，《洪波细浪》，上海辞书出版社，September 2010, pp. 4–5.

3 Liang claimed that Yu admitted to him that the MSS had no evidence for the accusations against Soros. 梁恒，《与索罗斯一起走过的日子》，Guangdong Economic Press, Guangzhou, 2012, p. 107; '2005中国小姐风

采大赛华中赛区简介(3)', *Sina*, 4 July 2005, archive.fo/Tk0ep; 丁柯, '特工 – 民运 – 法轮功: 一个生命的真实故事(上)', *Minghui*, 12 September 2003, archive.today/JAHz8. In 1993 he was appointed to the National People's Congress Supervisory and Judicial Affairs Committee. In 1998 he was appointed to the National People's Congress Foreign Affairs Committee. '第九届全国人民代表大会外事委员会主任委员、副主任委员、委员名单', National People's Congress, 1 March 2008, archive.today/Cexy5.

4 梁恒, 《与索罗斯一起走过的日子》, pp. 111–14.

5 Yu travelled to Afghanistan for official meetings in 1992. 周刚 & 邓俊秉, 《出使友邻十三载》, 五洲传播出版社, March 2019, p. 91.

6 于恩光, 《白宫内外采访录》, 中国青年出版社, Beijing, 1992, p. 1; 梁恒, 《与索罗斯一起走过的日子》, p. 107.

7 Sirin Phathanothai with James Peck, *The Dragon's Pearl*, Simon & Schuster, New York, 1994, p. 295.

8 于恩光, 《白宫内外采访录》, p. 1.

9 于恩光, 《白宫内外采访录》, p. 1.

10 '余放同志逝世', *People's Daily*, 4 April 2013, archive.vn/LTzSU; 马胜荣 (ed.), 《走向世界 新华社国际报道70年 1931–2001》, 新华出版社, November 2001, p. 548.

11 Roger Faligot, *Chinese Spies: From Chairman Mao to Xi Jinping*, Scribe, Melbourne, 2019, p. 425.

12 Yu Fang (余放) is pictured in '国家安全部原副部长余放因病逝世 享年80岁', 网易, 22 February 2013, archive.vn/ZZ5KC.

13 '余放同志逝世', *People's Daily*.

14 For three examples, see 罗祥意 & 陈尤文, 《国家安全行政管理》, 时事出版社, March 1995, p. 326; 许天民, 《来自'地下战场'的报告》, no publisher, February 1994, p. 309; 杨建英 & 姜春晖, 《一枚迟到的奖章 情报编》, 中国少年儿童出版社, December 1999, p. 163.

15 孟静 & 童亮, '"暗算"背后的女人', 三联生活周刊, 12 April 2010, p. 65.

16 '余放同志逝世', *People's Daily*.

17 梁恒, 《与索罗斯一起走过的日子》, pp. 116–17.

18 George Soros, 'Remarks delivered at the World Economic Forum', *George Soros* [blog], 24 January 2019, www.georgesoros.com/2019/01/24/remarks-delivered-at-the-world-economic-forum-2/; 梁恒, 《与索罗斯一起走过的日子》, pp.106–9.

19 Zhang Liang (compiler), Andrew J. Nathan and Perry Link (eds), *The Tiananmen Papers*, Abacus, London, 2002, pp. 445–59.

20 George Soros, *Underwriting Democracy*, Public Affairs, New York, 1991, ch. 1, www.georgesoros.com/wp-content/uploads/2017/10/underwriting_democracy-chap-1-2017_10_05.pdf.

21 Zhang, *The Tiananmen Papers*, p. 459. Another example of the Party's narrative about the closure of Soros's China Fund is contained in an article published by the Chinese Maoist website Utopia (乌有之乡): 周文琪, '美国基金会与中国改革开放', *Utopia*, 20 January 2008, archive.today/YeJ6G.

22 陸鏗, '陳一諮揭露倒趙大陰謀', in 沈大為, 《趙紫陽的崛起與陷落》, 百姓文化事業有限公司, January 1990, pp. 307 sq.

23 Interview with Cheng Xiaonong, 13 August 2021.

24 Chen Yizi described Zhao Wendou (赵文斗) as ESRI's liaison officer in Japan. At the time, most if not all *China Economic Daily* foreign correspondents were MSS officers, and Zhao later became deputy director of the Development Research Center Asia–Africa Development Research Institute, another entity covertly run by the MSS. 中华日本学会, & 北京日本学研究中心 (eds), 《中国的日本研究》, 社会科学文献出版社, September 1997, p. 282; 陳一諮, 《陳一諮回憶錄》, New Century Press, Hong Kong, 2013, pp. 550.

25 Interview with Cheng Xiaonong, 13 August 2021.

26 梁恒, 《与索罗斯一起走过的日子》, p. 119.

Chapter 3 Nestling spies in the united front

1   George Soros, *Underwriting Democracy*, Public Affairs, New York, 1991, ch. 1, www.georgesoros.com/wp-content/uploads/2017/10/underwriting_democracy-chap-1-2017_10_05.pdf.

2   易凯, '中国国际文化交流中心理事会在京成立', *People's Daily*, 6 July 1984.

3   Xi Zhongxun had been the Central Secretariat member responsible for oversight of the Central Investigation Department. In the late 1980s, Xi spent 70–80% of his effort on united front work matters, according to his colleague, UFWD minister Yan Fumin. Alex Joske, 'The Central United Front Work Leading Small Group: Institutionalising united front work', *Sinopsis*, 23 July 2019, sinopsis.cz/en/joske-united-front-work-lsg/; '习仲勋认为本事的职位是两回事', 新浪历史, 11 October 2013, archive.ph/Xmoh3.

4   '第一届理事会名单', CICEC, no date, web.archive.org/web/20190924114406/http://www.cicec.org.cn/lshhd/427.html.

5   '1985年 中国国际文化交流中心 致英若诚邀请函', 孔夫子旧书网, no date, web.archive.org/web/20200627073806/http://book.kongfz.com/26571/388838842/.

6   Ying Ruocheng & Claire Conceison, *Voices Carry: Behind bars and backstage during China's revolution and reform*, Rowman & Littlefield, Lanham, MD, 2009, pp. xxii, 206, 223. '第一届理事会名单', CICEC.

7   David Lampton with Yeung Sai-cheung, *Paths to Power: Elite mobility in contemporary China*, University of Michigan Center for Chinese Studies, Ann Arbor, MI, 1986, p. 101.

8   The defection of General Li Zongren (李宗仁) was handled by the Central Investigation Department, particularly through one of its officers in Switzerland, Xu Danlu (徐淡庐). See '毛泽东与李宗仁握手', 广西党史网, 23 February 2013, archive.vn/2g2k3; 柳哲, '李宗仁回国往事: 瑞士大使馆原首席参赞徐淡庐的亲历回忆', 文史春秋, no. 9, 2017, pp. 20–2.

9   CICEC members Bai Zhenduo (白振铎), aka Bai Hao (白浩), and Yu Zichen (于自臣) were both deputy bureau chiefs in the MSS. Both had worked in intelligence during the Civil War before joining the Central Ministry of

Public Security after its establishment. Bai formally retired from the MSS in 1986 to become chairman of China Fuli Group (中国富利集团), a major MSS-controlled trading company. Their common history in the MPS is shared with several other early CICEC and Social Investigation Bureau officers, although some such as Ding Wenbin (丁文彬) and Hang Xiongwen (杭雄文) may have had backgrounds in the Central Investigation Department. See 《弘毅守正 笃行日新》, 东北师范大学出版社, November 2014, p. 52; 乳山市党史市志办公室编，天南地北乳山人, 威海市新闻出版局准印, November 2000, p. 3; *CICEC Annual Report 1985*, CICEC, Beijing, no date, pp. 16–17.

10 '于恩光为中心成立二十周年题词' [Yu Enguang's dedication for the twentieth anniversary of CICEC's founding], CICEC, no date, archive.vn/pwWeN.

11 '中国国际文化交流中心介绍' [video], YouTube, 2015, www.youtube.com/watch?v=Pat_81CN1b4.

12 Those whose names were removed include Geng Huichang (耿惠昌), who became MSS minister under Hu Jintao and Xi Jinping; Gao Fengyi (高凤仪), the pseudonym of MSS vice minister Gao Yichen (高以忱); and Wu Shizhong (吴世忠), then head of the MSS's 13th Bureau and the China Information Technology Security Evaluation Center (中国信息安全产品测评认证中心).

13 '江雪 (1948–)', China Writers Association, no date, web.archive.org/web/20200710051734/http://www.chinawriter.com.cn/zxhy/member/1540.shtml.

14 '爱情河', 百度百科, no date, archive.vn/spBnO.

15 'Jiangnan Social University', China Defence Universities Tracker, unitracker.aspi.org.au/universities/jiangnan-social-university/. For a detailed account of the Jiangnan Social University, see a memoir co-authored by the school's founder: 尹光华 & 罗祥意, 《春华秋实集》, 时代文化出版社, Beijing, 2009.

16 The bureau has been referred to as the Social Liaison Bureau (社会联络局) or Social Investigation Bureau (社会调查局). Further details of CICEC's relationship with the 12th Bureau will appear below. Social Investigation Bureau chiefs Mao Guohua (毛国华) and Lin Di (林地) both held positions in CICEC, as did Tao Dawei (陶大卫), bureau chief around 2008, and Wang Yamin (王亚民), who may have been a deputy chief.

17 See 'Hong Kong-related designations; Iran-related designations and designations updates; Global Magnitsky designations; counter terrorism designation update; non-proliferation designations updates', US Department of the Treasury, 15 January 2021, archive.ph/4iCAt.

18 '李保东秘书长会见中国国际文化交流中心副理事长孙文清一行', Bo'ao Forum for Asia, 7 January 2020, web.archive.org/web/20200613182048/English.boaoforum.org/2019ldhj/48391.jhtml; '全国政协第121期地方政协干部 (委员)培训班在北戴河举办', CPPCC, 25 May 2018, archive.ph/OvJt8.

19 See '孙文清的个人简历', *People's Daily Japan Edition*, 5 August 2001, archive.ph/Hhq0C; 孙文清 & 裴军, '胡锦涛提议建立亚太森林恢复与可持续管理网络', 中国青年报, 9 September 2007, archive.ph/5mevM; '河北辛集中学建校六十周年校庆专刊', 四川省青川中学, 9 April 2020, archive.ph/K2GxT.

20 郭瑞華 (ed.), 《中共對台工作組織體系概論》, Ministry of Justice Investigation Bureau, June 1999, p. 161.

21 Peter Mattis & Matthew Brazil, *Chinese Communist Espionage: An intelligence primer*, Naval Institute Press, Annapolis, MD, 2019, p. 56.

22 Interview with a former US intelligence officer.

23 It's unclear how the 12th Bureau's operations relate to those of the 2nd Bureau, responsible for 'open-line' operations through the ministry's network of foreign intelligence officers using official or semi-official cover. Numerous 2nd Bureau officers or alumni, such as Yu Fang (余放), Gao Yichen (高以忱), Guo Changlin (郭长林), Li Zhaodong (李肇东) and Xue Fukang (薛福康), have been affiliated with 12th Bureau fronts including CICEC and China Reform Forum. Given this overlap and the role of Yu Fang as a vice minister, it's highly likely that the same MSS vice minister who oversees the 2nd Bureau is responsible for the 12th Bureau.

24 Interview with a former US intelligence officer.

25 Interview with former US intelligence officers.

26 罗祥意 & 陈尤文 (eds), 《国家安全行政管理》, 时事出版社, 1995, p. 181.

27 Companies and associations connected to the bureau include the China Writers Association (中国作家协会), China Swan International Tours (中国天鹅国际旅游公司), Shinework Media (北京闪亮文化传播有限责任公司 and related companies), International Culture Publishing Corporation (国际文化出版公司), China Friendship Publishing Company (中国友谊出版公司), China International Cultural Exchange Foundation (中国国际文化交流基金会), China International Culture and Arts Company (中国国际文化艺术有限公司), Chia Tai Ice Music Production Ltd (正大国际音乐制作中心), Chinese Culture Exchange and Cooperation Promotion Association (中华文化交流与合作促进会), China Reform Forum (中国改革开放论坛), Songshan Forum (嵩山论坛), Emerging Economies Forum (新兴经济体论坛), Monterey Books and Stationers (美国洛杉矶蒙特利图书文具公司), 香港中华文化出版有限公司, and 星光国际出版有限公司.

28 Gerry Groot, 'The united front in an age of shared destiny', in Geremie Barmé with Linda Jaivin & Jeremy Goldkorn (eds), *Shared Destiny*, ANU Press, Canberra, 2015, pp. 129–34, archive.ph/Ykl7E.

29 This and following paragraphs about the Jian Hua Foundation and CICEC are drawn from information in Miwa Hirono, *Civilizing Missions*, Palgrave Macmillan, New York, 2008, pp. 101–29.

30 '中国国际文化交流中心将在京兴建', 北京日报, 13 January 1982, archive.vn/WsTTv; 'Huang Zhen, 80, Beijing envoy who helped plan Nixon's

visit', *New York Times*, 11 December 1989, www.nytimes.com/1989/12/11/obituaries/huang-zhen-80-beijing-envoy-who-helped-plan-nixon-s-visit.html.

31 易凯, '中国国际文化交流中心大厦奠基典礼在京举行', *People's Daily*, 20 July 1984.

32 Hirono, *Civilizing Missions*, pp. 102–3.

33 中共江苏省委党史工作办公室 (ed.), 《陈丕显年谱 1916–1995》, 中共党出版社, December 2000, p. 272; CICEC, 《我们走过三十年》, CICEC, 2014, p. 8.

34 '彭冲理事长第四届历史大会的讲话', 中国国际文化交流中心, no date, web.archive.org/web/20190412074528/http://www.cicec.org.cn/lshhd/44.html.

35 John Kerry & Hank Brown, *The BCCI Affair*, Committee on Foreign Relations, United States Senate, ch. 14, irp.fas.org/congress/1992_rpt/bcci/14abudhabi.htm; 伍秀珊, '国际商业信贷银行中国部总经理说 中东国家投资者开始把注意力转向中国 强调应同中国合作共同促进第三世界贸易', 人民日报, 25 December 1984, p. 6.

36 In 1982, a foundation established by the bank reportedly awarded a $100,000 'Third World Prize' to Zhao Ziyang. It is unclear if the prize money was accepted. Kerry & Brown, *The BCCI Affair*, ch. 5; William C. Triplett II, 'China's weapons mafia', *Washington Post*, 27 October 1991, www.washingtonpost.com/archive/opinions/1991/10/27/chinas-weapons-mafia/5a0f8884-8953-4bbe-9ae8-fc72fb09442f/; John Pomfret, 'BCCI reportedly moved millions of dollars out of China', *AP*, 8 August 1991, archive.ph/Xye9i.

37 Xiong Xianghui (熊向晖), one of China's most famous spies, was a deputy chief of the CID (covered as a deputy head of the UFWD) immediately before becoming CITIC's party secretary. Kong Dan (孔丹), who headed CITIC from 2000 to 2010, is the son of CID chief and MSS advisor Kong Yuan (孔原) and himself an active member of MSS front groups such as CICEC. See 傅颐, '熊向晖和荣毅仁在中信的交往', *Sina*, 6 November 2005, archive.ph/l3ScP; '孔丹副理事长会见日中国际交流协会会长、日本原民主党党首海江田万里先生一行', CICEC, no date, web.archive.org/web/20170306083702/http://www.cicec.org/yhwl/653.html.

38 '中华人民共和国国家安全部', *People's Daily Online*, 31 July 2012, archive.vn/krUSY.

39 For early research on the overseas presence of united front work, see Clive Hamilton, *Silent Invasion: China's influence in Australia*, Hardie Grant Books, Melbourne, 2018; Gerry Groot, 'The rise and rise of the United Front Work Department under Xi', *China Brief*, April 2018, jamestown.org/program/the-rise-and-rise-of-the-united-front-work-department-under-xi/; John Garnaut, 'How China interferes in Australia', *Foreign Affairs*, March 2018, www.foreignaffairs.com/articles/china/2018-03-09/how-china-interferes-australia; Anne-Marie Brady, 'Magic weapons: China's political

influence activities under Xi Jinping', Wilson Center, September 2017, www.wilsoncenter.org/article/magic-weapons-chinas-political-influence-activities-under-xi-jinping.

40 Peter Mattis & Alex Joske, 'The third magic weapon: Reforming China's united front', *War on the Rocks*, 24 June 2019, archive.ph/53QwD.

41 Joske, 'The Central United Front Work Leading Small Group'.

42 Alex Joske, 'Reorganizing the United Front Work Department: New structures for a new era of diaspora and religious affairs work', *China Brief*, 9 May 2019, jamestown.org/program/reorganizing-the-united-front-work-department-new-structures-for-a-new-era-of-diaspora-and-religious-affairs-work/.

43 毛泽东, '《共产党人》发刊词', Marxists.org, 4 October 1939, www.marxists.org/chinese/maozedong/marxist.org-chinese-mao-19391004.htm.

44 Alex Joske, *The Party Speaks for You: Foreign interference and the Chinese Communist Party's united front system*, ASPI International Cyber Policy Centre, Canberra, June 2020, archive.ph/s4ZMl.

45 See discussion of Huang Xiangmo in Joske, *The Party Speaks for You*.

46 Interview with a former US intelligence officer.

47 薛钰, '周恩来与党的隐蔽战线——试谈民主革命时期周恩来对我党情报保卫工作的贡献', www.people.com.cn, no date, web.archive.org/web/20180309073811/http://www.people.com.cn/GB/shizheng/8198/9405/34150/2544000.html.

48 Central Social Department is arguably the most accurate if less common translation of the agency's name – *zhongyang shehui bu* 中央社会部. 'Social Affairs Department' is more often used. See also Matthew Brazil, *The Darkest Red Corner: Chinese Communist Intelligence and its place in the Party 1926–1945*, PhD thesis, University of Sydney, 4 January 2013, p. 138. Kang Sheng spent time receiving intelligence training in Russia before becoming the first head of the Social Affairs Department. See 郭華倫, 《中共史論》, 國際關係研究所, vol. 4, 1971, p. 250.

49 Brazil, *The Darkest Red Corner*, p. 152.

50 郭華倫, 《中共史論》, p. 251. Similarly, CID officers often used UFWD cover. For example, Xiong Xianghui was concurrently a UFWD vice minister in his last years at the CID. The pattern also extended to provincial investigation departments and the local UFWD counterparts.

51 郭華倫, 《中共史論》, pp. 156, 230–2.

52 郭華倫, 《中共史論》, pp. 156–7. According to the diairies of Yang Shangkun, Li Kenong, a legendary Party intelligence officer and the first head of the CID, initially proposed calling the agency the 'Investigation and Research Department' (调查研究部). 杨尚昆, 《杨尚昆日记》, 中央文献出版社, Beijing, p. 165.

53 Mao Zedong, '中国社会各基层的分析', Marxists.org, 1 December 1925, www.marxists.org/chinese/maozedong/marxist.org-chinese-mao-19251201.htm.

54 郭華倫, 《中共史論》, pp. 157–8.

55 安飞麟 & 李敬尧 (eds), 《冀中对敌隐蔽斗争》, 中共党史出版社, 1994, pp. 10, 234.

56 '嘉华学院与澳洲埃迪斯科文大学签署交流合作协议', Beijing Technology and Business University, 18 February 2009, archive.ph/dH8j3; '燕京理工学院 (原北京化工大学北方学院)2009年大事记', Yanjing Institute of Technology, no date, archive.ph/qwNwJ.

57 '2003国际微电子论坛在京举行', CICEC, no date, archive.vn/OshUX; '2003年高超推进技术国际研讨会在京举行', CICEC, no date, archive.vn/AAXHA.

58 '法国钢琴家理查德·克莱德曼：20年, 变与不变', *People's Daily*, 12 January 2013, archive.ph/xoZUb.

59 *CICEC Annual Report 1988*, CICEC, Beijing, no date, pp. 22–3; William C. Trott, 'To all the Chinese girls I've loved before', *United Press International*, 26 April 1988, archive.today/9pJjb.

60 Wang Shuren (王树仁) had been the Investigation Department handler of Vita Chieu (周德高) in Cambodia, while officially the commercial attaché in the embassy. He later became a head or deputy head of the Guangdong Investigation Department. It is unclear what role he held in the Guangdong State Security Department, and he may have officially retired by that point. His outward-facing positions included vice chairman of the Guangdong branch of CICEC and deputy director of the Guangdong branch of trade body CCPIT. 《中国国际文化交流中心广东分会会刊》, no publisher, 1988, p. 36; 周德高, 《我与中共和柬共——柬埔寨共产党兴亡追记》, 田園书屋, Hong Kong, 2007, ch. 82.

61 See, for example, Lauren Hilgers, 'The mystery of the exiled billionaire whistle-blower', *New York Times*, 10 January 2018, www.nytimes.com/2018/01/10/magazine/the-mystery-of-the-exiled-billionaire-whistleblower.html.

62 Kate O'Keeffe & Christopher M. Matthews, 'UN bribery probe uncovers suspected Chinese agent', *Wall Street Journal*, 19 August 2016, www.wsj.com/articles/u-n-bribery-probe-uncovers-suspected-chinese-agent-1471621609.

63 '太极拳师设局诈骗弟子　百年太极文化蒙羞受辱', 山西新报网, 21 December 2016, archive.ph/wipUQ.

64 Interview with former intelligence officials; 郝汀 & 章钟峨, 《文化大革命中的中央调查部》, no publisher, 2013, p. 477–9.

65 熊真, 《一对外交官夫妇的足迹》, 江苏人民出版社, p. 195; 许家屯, 《许家屯香港回忆录》, pp. 51–4. See also Xuezhi Guo, *China's Security State: Philosophy, evolution and politics*, Cambridge University Press, Cambridge, September 2012, pp. 362–63.

66 熊真, 《一对外交官夫妇的足迹》, p. 195.

67 Overseas bureaus of newspapers like *Guangming Daily*, *China Economic Daily*, *China Youth Daily* and *Wenhui Bao* expanded after 1985 and remain in use by the MSS. See Mattis & Brazil, *Chinese Communist Espionage*, p. 49.

68 Mattis & Brazil, *Chinese Communist Espionage*, p. 91.

69 Vice Minister Zhou Shaozheng may have been the only former Central Investigation Department intelligence officer represented among the MSS's initial leadership (Vice Minister Wang Jun (王珺) was from the CID but had an administrative background). His obituaries did not mention his time in the MSS. See '国务院任免工作人员名单', *People's Daily*, 14 December 1985, p. 4; '政协全国委员会原秘书长周绍铮逝世', 新华网, 4 December 2007, archive.ph/vuDW9; 全国政协研究室 (ed.), 《中国人民政协全书上》,中国文史出版社, 1999, p. 879; 中华人民共和国国务院公报, no. 26, 1983, p. 1195.

70 Interview with a former intelligence official.

71 Interview with a former intelligence official; Roger Faligot, *Chinese Spies: From Chairman Mao to Xi Jinping*, Scribe, Melbourne, 2019, pp. 131–40.

72 Alex Joske, 'Secret police: The Ministry of Public Security's clandestine foreign operations', *Sinopsis*, 25 January 2022, sinopsis.cz/wp-content/uploads/2022/01/mps0.pdf.

73 Taiwanese scholar Guo Ruihua states that the Central Investigation Department (CID) and the Ministry of Public Security's 1st, 2nd, 3rd and 4th bureaus were the primary sources of MSS officers at the agency's creation. While some sources state the entire CID was incorporated into the MSS, Guo claimed that parts of the CID were also absorbed by the Work Committee for Departments Directly Under the CPC Central Committee (中央直属机关工作委员会), which oversees many of the 'all-China' mass organisations. Some intelligence officers from 2PLA and 3PLA were also brought into the MSS. Regarding the MPS, other sources only mention parts of the 1st Bureau – currently called the Political Security Protection Bureau (政治安全保卫局) – being incorporated into the MSS. See 郭瑞華 (ed.), 《中共對台工作組織體系概論》, 法務部調查局2004, pp. 132–3; '资料: 中华人民共和国国家安全部', CNTV, 16 February 2011, archive.vn/OFWdq.

74 In January 2021, an MSS spokesperson described the ministry's creation as being driven by 'the Party Centre's deep analysis of the state security trends faced by the country after reform and opening'; '国家安全部新闻办答记者问：忠诚践行领袖训词, 坚定履行光荣使命', 人民日报, 8 January 2021, archive.ph/qYdbC. See also '为确保国家安全价钱反间谍工作 国务院提请大会批准成立国家安全部', *People's Daily*, 7 June 1983, p. 2.

75 An official history names at least five vice ministers of the Ministry of Public Security who were imprisoned during the Cultural Revolution. '国务院工作机构', The History of the People's Republic of China, no date, web.archive.org/web/20180319084538/http://www.hprc.org.cn/gsw/detail_zzslk.jsp?channelid=75034&record=2892.

76 See Michael Schoenhals, 'The Central Case Examination Group, 1966–79', *China Quarterly*, no. 145, March 1996, pp. 87–111.

77 On the CID's role in elite purges, two former Central Investigation Department officers claimed that Wang Dongxing instructed Luo Qingchang to bring Yang Shungkun back from Shanxi province so he could be subjected

to investigation in Beijing. 郝汀 & 章钟峨，《文化大革命中的中央调查部》, p. 34.

78 The Central Investigation Department has not been studied in depth but the most detailed and accurate pieces of secondary literature on it are Mattis & Brazil, *Chinese Communist Espionage*, pp. 43–50 and 沈迈克 (Michael Schoenhals), '关于中国共产党中央调查部的历史考察', *Contemporary China History Studies*, vol. 17, no. 2, March 2010, pp. 97–105; 蒋華杰, '龍の眼からみた世界—公開情報の研究と中華人民共和国の外交政策決定—' [Spying worldwide: Open-source intelligence estimate and PRC's foreign policy making], 社会システム研究, no. 32, March 2016, pp. 227–43.

79 See, for example, criticism by CID officer Xu Danlu (徐淡庐) of Luo in one of his notebooks: '36开本 民国时期 红色特工 建国后统战部主任 徐淡庐重要笔记', 孔夫子旧书网, no date, archive.ph/20BXP. Former CID officer and entrepreneur Yuan Geng (袁庚) also confronted Luo after he was imprisoned during the Cultural Revolution. 涂俏,《袁庚传: 改革现场》, 作家出版社, 2008, p. 59.

80 Interview with Gao Wenqian, 24 August 2021. Luo was particularly close to Kang Sheng and once thanked him in a speech for teaching him to read and write and 'raising me through shit and piss' ('是康老一把屎一把尿把我拉扯大的'). Hua Guofeng also courted Luo shortly before seizing leadership in 1976. See 郝汀 & 章钟峨,《文化大革命中的中央调查部》, p. 14. 熊蕾, '1976年, 华国锋和叶剑英怎样联手的', 新浪历史, 21 August 2014, archive. ph/yzS8R; Guo, *China's Security State*, pp. 361–3.

81 Interview with Gao Wenqian, 24 August 2021.

82 郝汀 & 章钟峨,《文化大革命中的中央调查部》, pp. 477–9.

83 郝汀 & 章钟峨,《文化大革命中的中央调查部》, pp. 415–24.

84 《伍修权传》, 当代中出版社, January 2016, p. 294.

85 '习仲勋与党的群众路线专题研讨会在京召开', 中国政协网, 26 May 2016, archive.ph/z8yDv; '习仲勋认为本事的职位是两回事', 新浪历史, 11 October 2013, archive.ph/Xmoh3; 吴闻, '扒一扒中共情报头子罗青长的华丽外衣', 新世纪, 16 April 2014, archive.ph/ZFc0v.

86 A 1985 CIA report speculated that Minister of State Security Ling Yun was trusted to look after Deng's interests in the MSS in part because he oversaw security for Deng's 1979 visit to the United States. 'How China makes foreign policy', CIA Directorate of Intelligence, CIA-RDP04T00447R000100530001-5, January 1985, p. 7, web.archive.org/web/20180612121053/https://www.cia.gov/library/readingroom/docs/CIA-RDP04T00447R000100530001-5.pdf. Zhou Shaozheng was described by two former CID officers as Luo's 'trusted aide' and was rapidly promoted by him. Nonetheless, he passed scrutiny of his Cultural Revolution activities before joining the MSS. 郝汀 & 章钟峨,《文化大革命中的中央调查部》, no publisher, 2013, pp. 5, 485; '关于周绍铮同志在‘文化大革命‘中表现的调查报告' in 王一华 (ed.),《中华人民共和国大事日志》, 济南出版社, August 1992, p. 1040.

87 Yang Shangkun was also consulted by Chen Pixian, soon to replace Peng Zhen as secretary of the Central Political-Legal Affairs Commission. Not long after, Chen Pixian, Wu Xiuquan (military intelligence), Luo Qingchang, Liu Fuzhi (on the cusp of becoming head of the MPS) and Ling Yun together authored a key report on the planned creation the MSS that was delivered to Party leaders in March 1983. 中共江苏省委党史工作办公室 (ed.), 《陈丕显年谱 1916–95》, 中共党出版社, December 2000, pp. 269–70.

88 Chen Yun hired Xu Yongyue as his secretary on Luo Qingchang's recommendation. 郭瑞華 (ed.), 《中共對台工作組織體系概論》, 法務部調查局, 2004, p. 319. See also David Ian Chambers, 'Edging in from the cold: The past and present state of Chinese intelligence historiography', *Studies in Intelligence*, vol. 56, no. 3, September 2012, p. 35.

89 Peter Mattis, 'The dragon's eyes and ears: Chinese intelligence at the crossroads', *National Interest*, 20 January 2015, archive.ph/2Gogi.

90 Mattis & Brazil, *Chinese Communist Espionage*, p. 54.

91 Wuxi Xinxing Industry and Trade Joint Company (无锡新兴工贸联合公司) was at the centre of the corruption scandal that brought down Chen Xitong. The company was officially credentialed as a front company for the Beijing State Security Bureau (using its cover name, the Beijing Municipal People's Government External Liaison Office), and Deng Bin, the head of Wuxi Xinxing, was an officer of the bureau on paper. 杨书文, 翁开国 & 李宏敏, 《金融形势法律事务》, 工商出版社, September 1999, pp. 412–16; 'Two executed for corruption', *South China Morning Post*, 30 November 1995, archive.ph/enZBA; Thom Beal, 'Six charged in China pyramid scheme', *United Press International*, 29 July 1995, archive.ph/7dQkm.

92 'Wang may have flown to Beijing after US consulate visit', *Bloomberg*, 10 February 2012, web.archive.org/web/20150211235847/https://www.bloomberg.com/news/articles/2012-02-10/chinese-official-may-have-flown-to-beijing-after-consulate-1-.

93 The Political Legal Commission reportedly proposed creating the MSS in late 1981. In January 1983, the Central Secretariat 'in principle' approved its establishment. In April 1983 the Central Secretariat issued a report approving the MSS's creation, which was read by Deng Xiaoping and received input from Chen Yun, Li Xiannian and Ye Jianying. 《伍修权传》编写组, 《伍修权传》, 当代中国出版社, January 2016, p. 294.

94 This role may have been supplanted by the Central State Security Commission (中央国家安全委员会) established by Xi Jinping in 2013 as he purged the previous secretary of the Political-Legal Commission, Zhou Yongkang. See Samantha Hoffman & Peter Mattis, 'Managing the power within: China's State Security Commission', *War on the Rocks*, 18 July 2016, warontherocks.com/2016/07/managing-the-power-within-chinas-state-security-commission/.

95 Liu Min (刘敏), a grandson of Marshall Zhu De, worked in CICEC. Peng Zhen's daughter Fu Yan (傅彦) reportedly chaired an MSS-controlled company called Beijing Fuli Company (北京富利公司). '郴州市人民

政府大事记', 郴州市人民政府, July 2010, archive.ph/ZMhqj; 肖伟俐, 《家风》, 新华出版社, January 2006, p. 131; interview with a former intelligence official.

96 '情报专家揭秘间谍生活:不会打破伦理道德底线', 中国新闻网 via 鳳凰網, 10 June 2009, archive.vn/UiWk8.

97 罗祥意 & 陈尤文 (eds), 《国家安全行政管理》, 时事出版社, 1995, p. 301.

Chapter 4 A bloodbath marks a new era

1 中国法律年鉴编辑部 (ed.), 《中国法律年鉴 1990》, 中国法律年鉴社, November 1990, p. 57.

2 See a reflection on the massacre by John Pomfret in 'A massacre, erased', *Washington Post*, 30 May 2019, www.washingtonpost.com/graphics/2019/opinions/global-opinions/tiananmen-square-a-massacre-erased/.

3 James Palmer, 'What China didn't learn from the collapse of the Soviet Union', *Foreign Policy*, 24 December 2016, foreignpolicy.com/2016/12/24/what-china-didnt-learn-from-the-collapse-of-the-soviet-union/.

4 George Soros, *Underwriting Democracy*, Public Affairs, New York, 1991, ch. 1, www.georgesoros.com/wp-content/uploads/2017/10/underwriting_democracy-chap-1-2017_10_05.pdf.

5 中国法律年鉴编辑部 (cd.), 《中国法律年鉴 1990》, p. 57. Those recognised included MSS science and technology experts Zhao Hongcai (赵鸿才) and Jin Yi (晋毅), and radio operator Xiong Xuexi (熊学喜). Xiong had served in the CID, which posted him to Vietnam, Syria, Karachi and Poland to handle communications between missions there and Beijing. On Zhao, see 赵良庆主编, 《杨承宗教授九十五华诞纪念文集》, 安徽大学出版社, 2006, p. 111. On Jin, see 吴万锁 (ed.), 中共洪洞县委党史研究室编, 《槐乡骄子 洪洞县中共党史人物资料》, 中共党史出版社, 2004, p. 48. On Xiong, see 孔翔翔, 梁国银 et al. (eds), 《天涯还叫郧阳人》, vol. 2, pp. 572–7.

6 王骏 et al. (eds), 中国人民解放军联络工作史 (上), 中国人民解放军总政治部联络部, May 1998, p. 174.

7 罗青长, '罗青长同志在苏鲁皖地区有关情侦人员落实政策回报小型座谈会上的讲话', 22 October 1990, in 许天民, 《回忆录：来自地下战场的报告》, no publisher, July 1997, pp. 416-7.

8 David Ian Chambers, 'Edging in from the cold: The past and present state of Chinese intelligence historiography', *Studies in Intelligence*, vol. 56, no. 3, September 2012, pp. 33–7, web.archive.org/web/20201212173738/https://www.cia.gov/library/center-for-the-study-of-intelligence/csi-publications/csi-studies/studies/vol.-56-no.-3/pdfs/Chambers-Chinese%20Intel%20Historiography.pdf.

9 Shen Anna (沈安娜), a famous CCP spy who worked as a stenographer for the Kuomintang leadership in the 1940s, was among those awarded that day. 华克放, '我的母亲沈安娜', in 海南省文化交流促进会 (ed.), 《红色记忆：不爱红装爱武装》, 南海出版公司, June 2013, p. 141.

10 奉化市人事局 & 奉化日报 (eds), 《奉籍英才》, 奉化日报, p. 261.

11 Mao, alongside fellow MSS officer Cao Dapeng, was included in the Beijing Foreign Studies University School of English and International Studies' list of students commencing in 1950. See '1950级校友名录', BFSU School of English and International Studies, no date, archive.vn/rK3Ij.

12 The school was the predecessor to Beijing Foreign Studies University. Since retiring, Mao has been active in BFSU alumni events. See 杨宏伟, '从延安走来的北京外国语大学, *PLA Daily*, 7 July 2019, p. 8, archive.vn/PrrN3.

13 After retiring, Mao gave a gift to Crook at a commemoration of the sixtieth anniversary of the Korean War military academies at BFSU. See '追忆无悔人生 感悟爱国情怀——我校举行参加抗美援朝军事干部学校校友60周年纪念会', BFSU, 26 October 2010, archive.vn/iWHbP; '伊莎白教授纪录片首映式暨103岁生日庆祝会举行', BFSU, 17 December 2018, archive.vn/uEOTL.

14 奉化市档案局 & 奉化市科学技术局 (eds), 《奉化在外知名人士录》, 2004, pp. 14–15; 奉化市人事局 & 奉化日报 (eds), 《奉籍英才》, p. 261; Australia–China Council, *Third Annual Report 1981*, Australian Government Publishing Service, Canberra, 1982, p. 17, www.dfat.gov.au/sites/default/files/australia-china-council-third-annual-report-1981.pdf.

15 奉化市档案局，奉化市科学技术局 (eds), 《奉化在外知名人士录》, pp. 14–15.

16 Forrest J. Boyd, 'The church in China', *Christianity Today*, 17 March 1972, archive.vn/LviNJ.

17 See an interview with NBC's Barbara Walters: 'Assignment: China – "The week that changed the world"' [video], USC US-China Institute via YouTube, 25 January 2012, 14:26, www.youtube.com/watch?v=uyCZDvec5sY.

18 Richard Pearson, 'Political journalist Theodore H. White dies at 71', *Washington Post*, 17 May 1986, www.washingtonpost.com/archive/local/1986/05/17/political-journalist-theodore-h-white-dies-at-71/5dad84a2-a9e9-489e-affa-1c6dfce8ded9/.

19 The statement is commonly known as the 'Shanghai communiqué'. See 'Joint statement following discussions with leaders of the People's Republic of China', US Department of State, 27 February 1972, history.state.gov/historicaldocuments/frus1969-76v17/d203.

20 USC US-China Institute, 'Assignment: China', 56:25.

21 I. C. Smith & Nigel West, *Historical dictionary of Chinese intelligence*, Scarecrow Press, Lanham, MD, 2012, p. 110.

22 David Wise, *Tiger Trap: America's secret spy war with China*, Houghton Mifflin Harcourt, Boston, 2011, p. 34.

23 Office of the Inspector General, *A Review of the FBI's Handling and Oversight of FBI Asset Katrina Leung: Unclassified executive summary*, US Department of Justice, May 2006, archive.ph/qi1jO.

24 Bill Gertz, *Enemies*, Crown Forum, New York, 2006, pp. 31–2.

25 Wise, *Tiger Trap*, p. 210; National Association of Chinese-Americans, 'An early history of NACA (1978–1980)', Yellow River by George Leung

[website], 1 January 1981, sites.google.com/site/yellowriverbackupsite/ chinese/other/naca/naca1a; 'Katrina Leung', Yellow River by George Leung [website], no date, archive.ph/sTMA0.

26 陈元等 (ed.), 《中国统一战线辞典》, 中共党史出版社, 1992, p. 201.

27 See, for example, the role of Han Yangshan (韩仰山), a CID officer in Shanghai, in the 1971 visit: 邓伟志, 《邓伟志全集 续集 2》, 上海大学出版社, December 2017, p. 128. For more information on the Shanghai branch of the Central Investigation Department, see '1962.4.29中共上海市委调查部的编制机构情况和意见 (绝密)', 中共国史料, 29 April 2015, archive.ph/ngl6M.

    CID head Luo Qingchang and deputy head Xiong Xianghui also met Yang on several occasions. 熊向晖, 《我的情报与外交生涯》, 北京: 中共党史出版社, 1999, p. 455; "华主席, 邓副主席会见并宴请杨振宁博士", Xinhua, 27 August 1977; 徐达深, 《中华人民共和国实录 第3卷 内乱与抗争-"文化大革命"的十年 1972–1976》, 吉林人民出版社, June 1994, p. 1099.

    Wang Zhesheng 汪哲生, who is described as meeting Yang in 1974, was probably a CID officer and later appeared in an MSS role. See '常务理事名单', 中国企业投资协会, 3 July 2012, web.archive.org/web/20180119070941/ www.ceia.cn/show.php?contentid=38960; 鄭宇欽, 《中共國家安全部組織與運作模式之研究》, master's thesis, Tamkang University, June 2005, p. 28.

28 Wise, *Tiger Trap*, p. 32.

29 Office of the Inspector General, *A Review of the FBI's Handling*.

30 Office of the Inspector General, *A Review of the FBI's Handling*.

31 Gertz, *Enemies*, p. 27.

32 Wise, *Tiger Trap*, pp. 35–6. Leung and her husband were also accused of false tax returns and mortage deductions, failing to declare income from business activities in Hong Kong and China, and orchestrating a scheme involving a shell company they controlled in Hong Kong to claim mortgage interest deductions when they had actually already paid off their mortgage. See Randall Thomas, 'Affidavit for Katrina Leung', 2003, via FAS, fas.org/irp/ops/ci/leung.html

33 Wise, *Tiger Trap*, p. 26.

34 Office of the Inspector General, *A Review of the FBI's Handling*; Wise, *Tiger Trap*, p. 37.

35 Office of the Inspector General, *A Review of the FBI's Handling*.

36 Only part of the FBI's bugging of the Los Angeles consulate was exposed. Bugs in its photocopiers were only removed in 1999, according to Wise, *Tiger Trap*, p. 27.

37 Office of the Inspector General, *A Review of the FBI's Handling*; Wise, *Tiger Trap*, p. 27. Wise suggests that Leung may have learnt about the program from documents pilfered from Smith's briefcase. However, Smith's claim that he never knew about the program does not appear to have been questioned.

38 Wise, *Tiger Trap*, p. 41.

39 I. C. Smith, 'Female spy Katrina Leung' [video], *C-SPAN*, 7 September 2009, www.c-span.org/video/?284892-3/female-spy-katrina-leung.

40 Office of the Inspector General, *A Review of the FBI's Handling*; Randall Thomas, 'Affidavit for James J. Smith', Federation of American Scientists, 2003, via FAS, irp.fas.org/ops/ci/smith.html.

41 John Pomfret, 'China finds bugs on jet equipped in US', *Washington Post*, 19 January 2002, www.washingtonpost.com/archive/politics/2002/01/19/china-finds-bugs-on-jet-equipped-in-us/65089140-2afe-42e0-a377-ec8d4e5034ef/.

42 Wise, *Tiger Trap*, p. 106.

43 David Rosenzweig, 'Spying case tossed out', *Los Angeles Times*, 7 January 2005, www.latimes.com/archives/la-xpm-2005-jan-07-me-katrina7-story.html.

44 Wise, *Tiger Trap*, p. 177.

45 晨鸟之歌, '唐树备：海峡两岸的摆渡人', 微信, 2 February 2021, archive.today/S9uxd; 晨鸟之歌, '美梦成真--史无前例的中国一刊', 微信, 22 January 2021, archive.ph/dLwCV.

46 '孟加拉国总统诗集在我国出版', *People's Daily*, 7 March 1987, p. 3; 晨鸟之歌, '急流勇退--大结局后的抉择', 微信, 14 February 2021, archive.ph/WcwHR.

47 '孟加拉国总统诗集在我国出版', *People's Daily*, 7 March 1987, p. 3.

48 Xie worked at the Aviation Industry Department's 628 Research Institute, which was responsible for aviation science and technology intelligence research. It is unclear exactly when he joined the MSS, and whether he was already an officer prior to joining the International Culture Publishing Corporation in January 1988. His WeChat posts do not mention his nor the publishing house's relationship with the MSS. See 晨鸟之歌, '破冰留美之旅', 微信, 4 March 2021, archive.ph/DoQ2h; '讲"一千零一夜"故事的文人--谢善骁', 视联浙江, 3 January 2019, archive.ph/9llcg; '六院身边办公的四所—航空科技情报研究所', *CAN News*, 12 July 2019, archive.ph/e1mgq.

49 晨鸟之歌, '北京人在洛杉矶', 微信, 25 December 2020, archive.today/sT9wL.

50 谢善骁, '《科技导报》与"保钓"运动', 科技导报, 2011, vol. 30, no. 8, p. 82.

51 Mathematical Sciences Research Institute, 'About the film', Taking the Long View [website], 2011, archive.ph/tR9TK.

52 Wise, *Tiger Trap*, p. 40.

53 At the time *Science and Technology Review* (科技导报) was set up, the MSS did not yet exist and any alleged intelligence agency backing for it may have come from the Central Investigation Department, which had chaperoned Yang Chen-ning on his trips to China. See Wise, *Tiger Trap*, p. 42.

54 周德高, 《我与中共和柬共——柬埔寨共产党兴亡追记》, 田園书屋, 2007, p. 216.

55 谢善骁, '蓦然回首', in 宋南平 (ed.), 《第二届我与科协征文优秀作品集》, vol. 1, 科学普及出版社, December 2008, pp. 85–7.

56 Wise, *Tiger Trap*, pp. 40–1.

57 Several PRC publications, including Xie's WeChat posts, describe her as such.

58 I was unable to independently confirm Leung's membership of the All-China Federation of Returned Overseas Chinese (中华全国归国华侨联合会), supervised by the Overseas Chinese Affairs Office and United Front Work Department. See '陈文英中国各项"荣衔"维持不变?', *Boxun*, 28 June 2003, archive.ph/40NUc; '陈文瑛间谍案引发侨界"线民"之争', 看中国, 8 May 2003, archive.ph/axE8R.

59 晨鸟之歌, '"书"中岂无两岸情', 微信, 28 January 2021, archive.ph/Ujeb0.

60 '杨尚昆会见美籍华人', *People's Daily*, 12 July 1989, p. 1.

61 晨鸟之歌, '北京人在洛杉矶'.

62 晨鸟之歌, '"书"于余澜 (一) -- 一个"裁缝"的喜和乐', 微信, 1 November 2020, archive.ph/RK0m1.

63 'Chronology', *Frontline*, PBS, January 2004, www.pbs.org/wgbh/pages/frontline/shows/spy/leung/cron.html.

64 Wise, *Tiger Trap*, pp. 86–8.

65 陈文英, '"双面间谍案"主角陈文英12年来首度公开发声', 侨胞网 via 微信, 18 December 2015, archive.ph/UTgpt.

66 Interview with a former foreign intelligence official.

67 Xie described meeting David Fon Lee and Peter Chow in Beijing in July 1989, while Lee was also one of J. J. Smith's contacts according to both Lee and Katrina Leung. See 晨鸟之歌, '北京人在洛杉矶'; Michael Kirk, 'From China with love', *Frontline*, PBS, 2003, archive.ph/1PUdU; 陈文英, '"双面间谍案"主角陈文英12年来首度公开发声'.

68 陈文英, '"双面间谍案"主角陈文英12年来首度公开发声', 侨胞网 via 微信, 18 December 2015, archive.ph/UTgpt; K. Connie Kang and Megan Garvey, 'Two decades of deception revealed', *Los Angeles Times*, 12 May 2003, archive.ph/SPsAD.

69 Interview with a former foreign intelligence official.

70 Wise, *Tiger Trap*, p. 28.

71 Charles Burton, 'Recent PRC influence operations to counter public demands for a more effective response to the Chinese régime's political interference in Canada', *Sinopsis*, 31 July 2019, sinopsis.cz/en/burton_influence_operations_canada/.

72 '吉林省某政法单位招生简章 (一)', 南开大学, 21 February 2021, archive.ph/WS8QS; '【就业信息】中央某政法单位 (山东, 公务员编制)招生简章', 东南大学, 30 October 2020, archive.ph/ecFir.

73 李尚志, '外籍华人在中国国际文化交流中心举行的座谈会上表示 振兴中华是每个炎黄子孙的责任', *People's Daily*, 2 October 1984.

74 李尚志, '外籍华人在中国国际文化交流中心', *People's Daily*.

75 'Wan-go H. C. Weng Collection', Museum of Fine Arts Boston, no date, archive.ph/iWZ0P.

76 Russell Lowe (罗绍汉) was an editor for the English edition of Huang Yunji's *San Francisco Journal* (时代报) newspaper. Huang was also known as Maurice H. Chuck. See 黄运基, 《唐人街》, 花城出版社, November 2004, p. 44; Xiong Guohua (Diana Hong trans.), 'Maurice H. Chuck and the *San Francisco Journal*: Promoting US-China friendship and Asian American issues', *Chinese America: History & Perspectives*, 2009, p. 137.

77 Interview with a former US intelligence officer.

78 Zach Dorfman, 'How Silicon Valley became a den of spies', *Politico*, 27 July 2018, www.politico.com/magazine/story/2018/07/27/silicon-valley-spies-china-russia-219071/.

79 '旧金山中国和平统一促进会要求美政府彻查江南命案并依法惩处罪犯', 参考消息, 6 February 1985, archive.ph/qGPXF/. Weng once spoke at an event organised by the Red Guard group I Wor Kuen (义和拳). '翁绍裘: 美国华人新闻工作者', 中国侨网, no date, archive.ph/zbB1I; FBI file on Asian American Political Alliance, December 1969, archive. ph/LXVIB; 何慧, '冷战期间美国华人左翼青年团体的变迁', *Wuhan University Journal* (Humanity Sciences), vol. 67, no. 4, July 2014, pp. 43–8.

80 Hong Kong Companies Register filings from the 1990s show that Liu Bing (刘冰), along with another of Xie's contacts and International Culture Publishing Corporation overseas advisor Tsang Shau Hung (曾守雄), was an owner of China Culture Publishing Company (中华文化出版公司) in Hong Kong. Xie has been described as head of Hong Kong China Culture Publishing Company (香港中华文化出版公司), which is probably the same company. See '讲"一千零一夜"故事的文人--谢善骁', 视联浙江.

81 晨鸟之歌, '美梦成真--史无前例的中国一刊', WeChat, 22 January 2021, archive.ph/dLwCV.

82 '胡仙：许家屯统战《星岛日报》', *Radio France Internationale*, 5 February 2018, archive.ph/saHQl; Mei Duzhe, 'How China's government is attempting to control Chinese media in America', *China Brief*, 21 November 2001, web.archive.org/web/20160206174939if_/http://www.jamestown. org/programs/chinabrief/single/?tx_ttnews%5Btt_news%5D=28481&tx_ ttnews%5BbackPid%5D=191&no_cache=1#.VrYyNyiTKbi.

83 Lachlan Markay, 'DOJ brands Chinese-owned US newspaper a foreign agent', *Axios*, 25 August 2021, archive.ph/gIWUi.

84 晨鸟之歌, '美梦成真--史无前例的中国一刊'.

Chapter 5 Chinagate: The plot to buy the White House

1 Bethany Allen-Ebrahimian & Zach Dorfman, 'Suspected Chinese spy targeted California politicians', *Axios*, 8 December 2020, archive.ph/77D4h.

2 The paper is not dated but appears to have been written in 1998, because Gao refers to Jiang Zemin's 1997 visit to America as happening 'last year'. 高以忱, '关于加强对美国国会工作的几点思考', in 现实问题的理论思考 编委会 (eds), 《现实问题的理论思考：中央党校97级中青年干部培训班 学员论文集》(vol. 2), 中共中央党校出版社, June 1999, pp. 1433–40.

3 For a recent example indicating that the 2nd Bureau manages open-line officers, see Li Zhenhuan (李振环), a former *Guangming Daily* correspondent in Turkey around 2015 who has the same name as an officer of the 2nd Bureau as reported in 2018: '关于2018年中央和国家机关脱贫攻坚先进 集体、优秀个人候选名单的公示', 旗帜网, 13 September 2018, archive. ph/lYvRi; 李振环, '伊斯坦布尔, 拥堵并快乐着', *Guangming Daily*, 9 April 2015, archive.ph/IGxLV. See also Ding Ke's account of working in that MSS

bureau: 丁柯，'特工——民运——法轮功：一个生命的真实故事（上）'，Minghui, 12 September 2003, archive.ph/JAHz8.

4 '第三届理事会理事名单', CICEC, no date, web.archive.org/web/20190717022707/cicec.org.cn/lshhd/425.html. Gao reportedly left active service in the MSS around 2012. Malcolm Moore, 'Chinese official found spying for the CIA', *Telegraph*, 1 June 2012, www.telegraph.co.uk/news/worldnews/asia/china/9306134/Chinese-official-found-spying-for-the-CIA.html.

5 Gao also claims to be fluent in French and Russian and worked as the *Guangming Daily*'s Moscow correspondent prior to his DC posting. He entered Heilongjiang University as a Russian-language student in 1972. See '精通多种语言的国务院防范办副主任高以忱部长莅临我院视察指导工作', 河北外国语学院, 5 September 2011, archive.fo/1qNTi; 胡婷，李倩钰 et al., '高以忱：做客校友讲坛解读优秀传统文化 对话黑大俄语人指导对俄办学工作', 黑龙江大学, 22 November 2018, archive.fo/gfQfV.

6 Interview with a former intelligence official.

7 高凤仪 & 石湘秋，《美利坚合众国传真》, Jilin People's Publishing House, Changchun, January 1998, p. 3.

8 Lena H. Sun & John Pomfret, 'The curious cast of Asian donors', *Washington Post*, 27 January 1997, archive.ph/wQbEr.

9 David Jackson & Lena H. Sun, 'Liu's deals with Chung: An intercontinental puzzle', *Washington Post*, 24 May 1998, archive.ph/XRxZ6.

10 Jackson & Sun, 'Liu's deals with Chung'.

11 Jackson & Sun, 'Liu's deals with Chung'.

12 'Charlie Trie pleads guilty to federal campaign finance violations', US Department of Justice, 21 May 1999, archive.ph/SlBUm.

13 Ng's Mandarin name is Wu Lisheng (吴立胜). He appeared at the ninth Chinese People's Political Consultative Conference (CPPCC) as one of 176 'specially invited' representatives. '第九届中国人民政治协商会议全国委员会组成人员名单', CPPCC, 20 November 2019, archive.ph/Mit3I.

14 Office of Public Affairs, 'Chairman of Macau real estate development company sentenced to prison for role in scheme to bribe United Nations ambassadors to build a multi-billion dollar conference center', US Department of Justice, 11 May 2018, archive.ph/BAogX.

15 Kate O'Keeffe, 'China tycoon back under US scrutiny', *Wall Street Journal*, 16 October 2015, archive.ph/lsCCH.

16 Kate O'Keeffe & Christopher M. Matthews, 'UN bribery probe uncovers suspected Chinese agent', *Wall Street Journal*, 19 August 2016, archive.ph/jwKRW; Office of Public Affairs, 'Former manager for international airline pleads guilty to acting as an agent of the Chinese government', US Department of Justice, 17 April 2019, archive.ph/OjrFd; Christopher M. Matthews, 'Former manager for international airline pleads guilty to acting as an agent of the Chinese government', *Wall Street Journal*, 31 August 2016, archive.ph/cwomj.

17 Jackson & Sun, 'Liu's deals with Chung'; David Johnston, 'Committee told of Beijing cash for Democrats', *New York Times*, 12 May 1999, archive.ph/yu4pU.

18 Francis X. Clines, 'US inquiry opens window on the military elite of China', *New York Times*, 16 May 1998, archive.ph/VZHT5. The recent story of Wang Liqiang and Xiang Xin provides a similar case, mixing Hong Kong–based arms deals, espionage and political interference operations. See Alex Joske, 'Analysing Wang Liqiang's claims about China's military networks', *The Strategist*, 12 December 2019, www.aspistrategist.org.au/analysing-wang-liqiangs-claims-about-chinas-military-networks/.

19 Johnston, 'Committee told of Beijing cash for Democrats'.

20 Robert L. Jackson, 'Clinton donor Riady pleads guilty to conspiracy charge', *Los Angeles Times*, 12 January 2001, archive.ph/97iRj.

21 Bob Woodward, 'Findings link Clinton allies to Chinese intelligence', *Washington Post*, 10 February 1998, archive.ph/DzhiY.

22 Brian Duffy & Bob Woodward, 'Senate panel is briefed on China probe figure', *Washington Post*, 12 September 1997, archive.ph/NgxT7.

23 *Investigation of Illegal or Improper Activities in Connection with 1996 Federal Election Campaigns*, Senate Committee on Governmental Affairs, 10 March 1998, ch. 17, archive.ph/hdeUh.

24 'They let her clean the China', *Economist*, 17 May 2003, archive.ph/AhSa7.

25 Neil A. Lewis, 'Thai donor to Democrats pleads guilty', *New York Times*, 22 June 2000, archive.ph/K1dmp.

26 David Corn & Dan Moldea, 'Influence peddling, Bush style', *Nation*, 5 October 2000, archive.ph/96jQW.

27 In 2019, Chearavanont was seated next to General Secretary Xi Jinping at a major meeting of overseas united front figures. '习近平会见世界华侨华人代表，谢国民、陈文雄等多位潮籍华人参加会议', 天下潮商传媒 via Sohu, 29 May 2019, archive.ph/Hidxc.

28 Chia Tai Ice Music Production (正大国际音乐出版中心) was managed by CICEC's Jiang Ling (江凌), a former PLA cadre who oversaw CICEC's efforts in the entertainment industry. 新闻出版署办公室 (ed.), 《新闻出版工作文件选编 (1992年)》, no publisher, June 1995, p. 385. On Jiang Ling, see 张宣, 《明星是怎样制造的》, 现代出版社, August 2008, p. 3.

29 Corn & Moldea, 'Influence peddling, Bush style'.

30 Josh Rogin, 'Congress shines light on Georgetown's CCP-linked foreign funding', *Washington Post*, 9 December 2020, www.washingtonpost.com/opinions/2020/12/09/congress-shines-light-georgetowns-ccp-linked-foreign-funding/.

31 Michael Morell (host), 'China expert Chris Johnson on the future of the US-China relationship' [podcast], *Intelligence Matters*, 3 October 2018, www.stitcher.com/show/intelligence-matters/episode/china-expert-chris-johnson-on-the-future-of-the-u-s-china-relationship-56542015.

32 Morell, 'China expert Chris Johnson'.

33 Interview with a former US foreign intelligence official.

34 Interview with a former US intelligence official.

35 Jackson & Sun, 'Liu's deals with Chung'.

36 Interview with a former US intelligence official.

37 John F. Harris, 'White House unswayed by China allegations', *Washington Post*, 20 July 1997, www.washingtonpost.com/wp-srv/politics/special/campfin/stories/cf072097.htm.

38 Richard Baker, Philip Dorling & Nick McKenzie, 'ALP donor Helen Liu had close ties with a senior Chinese military intelligence operative', *Sydney Morning Herald*, 4 June 2017, www.smh.com.au/national/alp-donor-helen-liu-had-close-ties-with-a-senior-chinese-military-intelligence-operative-20170602-gwjazb.html.

39 Richard Baker, Philip Dorling & Nick McKenzie, 'The go-betweens', *Sydney Morning Herald*, 2017, www.smh.com.au/interactive/2017/chinas-operation-australia/the-go-betweens.html.

40 Dan Sabbagh, 'MI5 accuses lawyer of trying to influence politicians on behalf of China', *Guardian*, 13 January 2022, archive.ph/WwHZE; 'US designates 2 Salvadorans for helping China, corruption', *AP News*, 3 July 2021, archive.ph/rkqQ9; Sam Cooper, 'How China made Canada a global node for narcos and cyber-criminals', *Sunday Guardian Live*, 15 May 2021, archive.ph/wZEfc; Martin Hála, 'CEFC: Economic diplomacy with Chinese characteristics', *Sinopsis*, 8 February 2018, archive.ph/lLUkU.

41 William Rempel & Allan Miller, 'First Lady's aide solicited check to DNC, donor says', *Los Angeles Tmes*, 27 July 1997, www.latimes.com/archives/la-xpm-1997-jul-27-mn-16814-story.html.

42 Nicholas D. Kristof, 'China worried by Clinton's linking of trade to human rights', *New York Times*, 9 October 1992, archive.ph/BEVwG.

43 James Mann, *The China Fantasy: How our leaders explain away Chinese repression*, Viking, New York, 2007, p. 69.

44 Mann, *The China Fantasy*, pp. 69–71.

45 高以忱, '关于加强对美国国会工作的几点思考', p. 1434.

46 高以忱, '关于加强对美国国会工作的几点思考', p. 1434.

47 This and quotes in following paragraphs from 高以忱, '关于加强对美国国会工作的几点思考'.

48 Office of Public Affairs, 'Chinese national arrested for allegedly acting within the United States as an illegal agent of the People's Republic of China', US Department of Justice, 25 September 2018, archive.ph/d2IBk.

49 'United States of America v. Ji Chaoqun criminal complaint', United States District Court Northern District of Illinois Eastern Division, 21 September 2018, www.justice.gov/opa/press-release/file/1096411/download.

50 Interview with a former foreign intelligence official.

51 Interview with a former foreign intelligence official.

52 Interview with a former US intelligence officer.

53 Jonas Parello-Plesner, 'China's LinkedIn honey traps', *Hudson Institute*, 23 October 2018, archive.ph/z9n98. On the geographical priorities of different parts of the MSS, see Nigel Inkster, *China's Cyber Power*, Routledge, London, 2016, p. 55.

54 'German spy agency warns of Chinese LinkedIn espionage', *BBC News*, 10 December 2017, www.bbc.com/news/world-europe-42304297.

55 Peter Mattis, 'Contrasting China's and Russia's influence operations', *War on the Rocks*, 16 January 2018, warontherocks.com/2018/01/contrasting-chinas-russias-influence-operations/.

56 *CICEC Annual Report 1998–1999*, CICEC, Beijing, December 2000, p. 56. For commentary on Li's appointment as vice president, see Benjamin Kang Lim & John Rutwich, 'China's Xi flexes muscle, chooses reformist VP – sources', Reuters, 12 March 2013, www.reuters.com/article/uk-china-parliament-li-idUKBRE92B09720130312; Lily Kuo, 'China's new vice president is a hopeful sign for reformers', *Quartz*, 15 March 2013, qz.com/62883/chinas-new-vice-president-is-a-hopeful-sign-for-reformers/.

57 高以忱,'关于加强对美国国会工作的几点思考'.

58 Squire Patton Boggs, 'Re: Engagement of Squire Patton Boggs (US) LLP', United States Department of Justice, 26 August 2021, efile.fara.gov/docs/2165-Exhibit-AB-20210826-81.pdf.

59 Interview with a former US intelligence officer; Tim Reid & Susan Cornwell, 'Exclusive: China launches lobbying push on currency bill', *Reuters*, 12 October 2011, archive.ph/nYghz.

60 Interview with a former US intelligence officer.

61 Tanner Greer, 'Xi Jinping in translation: China's guiding ideology', *Palladium*, 31 May 2019, archive.ph/xNkM0.

Chapter 6 Playing the long game

1   Interview with a former foreign intelligence official. The bureau may have lost some of this role with the establishment of an 18th Bureau focused on US operations around 2010. Nonetheless, the Social Investigation Bureau's networks are still active across the globe. See also Peter Mattis & Matthew Brazil, *Chinese Communist Espionage: An intelligence primer*, Naval Institute Press, Annapolis, MD, 2019, p. 56.

2   His PLA uncle Gao Tianhui (高天辉) had been involved in Chinese Communist Youth League work with future general secretary Hu Yaobang, who attended his funeral in 1976. See '高文谦, '高天辉及其子文谦', China Red Travel, 2 February 2012, web.archive.org/web/20180908141925/http://www.crt.com.cn/news2007/News/jryw/122294350K339JB99KDE7A941AK7F.html; Gao Wenqian (高文谦), '心底的怀念', *Beijing Spring*, December 2005, web.archive.org/web/20200903024729/http://webcache.googleusercontent.com/search?q=cache%3AFzPYql-Xx4QJ%3Abeijingspring.com%2Fbj2%2F2005%2F120%2F20051129151649.htm+&cd=1&hl=en&ct=clnk&gl=au. See also 《烈火真金》, 群众出版社, Beijing, 1979, p. 36.

3   《烈火真金》, p. 72. See also Michael Schoenhals, *Spying for the People: Mao's secret agents, 1949–1967*, Cambridge University Press, Cambridge, 2013, p. 31.

4 陈弘毅, '李良：无私无畏 严守机密', *People's Daily*, 19 September 2019, p. 16, archive.today/M9QMj.

5 《烈火真金》, pp. 65–6.

6 Larry Wu-tai Chin (金無怠) was a mole in the CIA's Foreign Broadcast Information Service who was primarily handled by the Ministry of Public Security. Likewise, Ministry of Public Security officer Xu Tianmin (许天民), later a Guangdong State Security Department officer, was sent to Hong Kong to handle a double agent working for Taiwanese intelligence there. 许天民, 《回忆录：来自地下战场的报告》, no publisher, July 1997, pp. 363–84.

7 Lu Zhongwei (陆忠伟) and Dong Haizhou (董海舟) both headed the Tianjin State Security Bureau before becoming vice ministers responsible for foreign intelligence.

8 《烈火真金》, p. 55.

9 《烈火真金》, p. 26.

10 '优秀公安干部李良在同林彪、"四人帮"斗争中英勇献身 公安部号召广大公安干警向李良烈士学习', *People's Daily*, 22 July 1978.

11 《烈火真金》, p. 60.

12 《烈火真金》, pp. 27, 64.

13 《烈火真金》, p. 75.

14 According to Jeremy J. Stone, who met with Lin on several occasions, Lin was fifty in 2004. Jeremy J. Stone, *Catalytic Diplomacy: Russia, China, North Korea and Iran*, Catalytic Diplomacy, Carlsbad, CA, 2010, p. 201, archive.ph/9I77h.

15 Contradicting his earlier paper, Lin Di's online biography claims he worked in the countryside until 1979. This discrepancy, combined with his claim that the Tianjin Public Security Bureau moved him to Tianjin in 1977, ostensibly to look after his mother, indicates that he probably entered the security services around then. '林地', China Institute for Innovation and Development Strategy, no date, web.archive.org/web/20130907043056/http://www.ciids.cn/home/leaderinfo/34e0f0b9-5080-47ae-88be-de9769c53995.

16 '林地', China Institute for Innovation and Development Strategy.

17 Cao Dapeng (曹大鹏), who was probably also an MSS officer, worked with Lin in the CASS Foreign Affairs Bureau. Cao had been in the same class as Mao Guohua at the Beijing Foreign Languages School in 1950 and later worked in CICEC. See '1950级校友名录', BFSU School of English and International Studies, no date, archive.vn/rK3Ij.

18 郭瑞華 (eds), 《中共對台工作組織體系概論》, Ministry of Justice Investigation Bureau, December 2004, p. 135; Mattis & Brazil, *Chinese Communist Espionage*, p. 56.

19 Peter Mattis, 'China's misunderstood spies', *The Diplomat*, 31 October 2011, thediplomat.com/2011/10/chinas-misunderstood-spies/; 'Russia claims China spy arrest', *AsiaOne*, 5 October 2011, www.asiaone.com/print/News/AsiaOne%2BNews/World/Story/A1Story20111005-303422.html.

20 *Annual Report: 1983–84*, Academy of the Social Sciences in Australia, Canberra, 1984, p. 13, socialsciences.org.au/publications/annual-report-1983-84/.

21 See Lena H. Sun, 'Students exposed to Iacocca capitalism training center for jobs in US-China relations opens in Nanjing', *Washington Post*, 13 September 1986, archive.ph/p9qJW.

22 In a 2001 speech, Lin said he studied under A. Doak Barnett, a leading American China scholar who headed Hopkins Nanjing's faculty committee. See 'The beginning of new relations' [video], *C-SPAN*, 23 April 2001, www.c-span.org/video/?163854-2/beginning-relations&event=163854&playEvent.

23 Xu Meihong & Larry Engelmann, *Daughter of China: A true story of love and betrayal*, Wiley, New York, 1999.

24 *Association for Communication of Transcultural Study*, Association for Communication of Transcultural Study, Tokyo, no date, p. 5, www.act-f.or.jp/Disclosure/PDF/Brochure.pdf.

25 赵克斌, '海峡两岸及海外华人现代化研究讨论会在台湾举行', 《社会学研究》, 1993, vol. 6, p. 92. In 1994 he attended an international conference on Tibet as a translator. See 马大正, 王嵘 & 杨镰 (eds), 《西域探险考察大系: 西域考察与研究》, 新疆人民出版社, 1994, p. 546.

26 Arthur Hummel Jr (ambassador to China, 1981–85) and Ambassador John H. Holdridge (deputy head of mission in Beijing, 1973–75, and national intelligence officer for East Asia/Pacific, 1978–81) were also founding members of the foundation.

27 Freeman described the trip in a 2011 article: Chas Freeman, 'With Nixon in China', *ChinaFile*, 30 September 2011, www.chinafile.com/nixon-china.

28 'Honorary advisors', US–China Policy Foundation, no date, uscpf.org/html/advisors.html. For Hagel's views on China at the time, see Robert Nolan, 'Chuck Hagel, in his own words, on US foreign policy challenges', US News, 3 January 2013, archive.ph/X3J72.

29 'Honorary advisors', US–China Policy Foundation.

30 'Founders and board members', US–China Policy Foundation, no date, archive.today/pmFZ0.

31 Steve Mufson, 'A benefactor flexes his wallet', *Washington Post*, 11 May 2000, www.washingtonpost.com/archive/politics/2000/05/11/a-benefactor-flexes-his-wallet/e04e4ddf-a4b8-4a68-8093-79e3c3cebe33/; Brody Mullins, 'Greenberg has invested a lot in politics', *Wall Street Journal*, 25 March 2005, archive.ph/Q8RmW.

32 'Honorary advisors', US–China Policy Foundation; 《美国工商年鉴》编辑部 (eds), 《美国工商年鉴》, 国际文化出版公司, 1990, p. 24.

33 Ken Silverstein, 'Alexander Haig's last years', *Mother Jones*, September/October 1999, motherjones.com/politics/1999/09/alexander-haig-still-in-control/.

34 《我们走过三十年》, CICEC, 2014, p. 30.

35 The delegation also met with military intelligence chief Xiong Guangkai, who was a friend of MSS Vice Minister Yu Fang. See '专业考察团', CICEC, no date, web.archive.org/web/20040309222900/http://www.cicec.org.cn/huodong.96/9647.htm; 'October 14–18, Beijing', US–China Policy Foundation, no date, web.archive.org/web/20041011024340/http://www.uscpf.org/html/events/1996/10141996.html; 熊光楷, 《藏书 记事 忆人》, 新华出版社, 2008.

36 '第四届理事会理事名单', CICEC, no date, archive.ph/TseK8.

37 'USCPF events', US–China Policy Foundation, no date, archive.ph/QVzMN.

38 See '全国人大代表团访问美国情况的书面报告', National People's Congress, no date, archive.ph/Y6dFQ; 钱彤, '朱镕基会见美国国会议员就中美关系和共同关心的问题交换了意见', *People's Daily*, 1 April 1999, archive.ph/v0VU2; '交流与交锋——曾建徽忆中美首次建立议会间正式交流机制', 中国人大, 10 January 2013, archive.ph/uYgUl; '温家宝会见美国众议院美中议员交流代表团', *Sina*, 15 January 2003, archive.ph/rQhSg; 曾建徽, 《议会外交》, 五洲传播出版社, 2006, pp. 28, 49, 82, 114.

39 See 'The beginning of new relations', *C-SPAN*.

40 'The beginning of new relations', *C-SPAN*.

41 'The beginning of new relations', *C-SPAN*.

42 The earliest possible date for Lin assuming leadership of the bureau is 1996, when Mao Guohua retired as chief of the bureau. 奉化市人事局 & 奉化日报 (eds), 《奉籍英才》, p. 262. Lin may have also headed the 5th Bureau at some stage. Some sources describe it as an intelligence analysis bureau, others as a coordination and tasking body for the MSS's many provincial and municipal branches. The lack of open-source information about it supports it having such an internally focused role. See Mattis & Brazil, *Chinese Communist Espionage*, p. 56.

43 Jeffrey D. Sachs & William Schabas, 'The Xinjiang genocide allegations are unjustified', *Project Syndicate*, 20 April 2021, archive.today/TJOId; '中国经济代表团访问美国', CICEC, no date, web.archive.org/web/20040620160533/http://www.cicec.org.cn/huodong/96/9665.htm; Jichang Lulu & Martin Hála, 'The CCP's model of social control goes global', *Sinopsis*, 20 December 2018, sinopsis.cz/en/the-ccps-model-of-social-control-goes-global. Fan Gang, a leading Chinese economist, was part of the delegation and has been a member of two other MSS front groups: China Reform Forum and China Enterprise Investment Association. Lin also met with Massachusetts governor Bill Weld.

44 '第四届理事会理事名单', CICEC '第七届国际文化交流赛克勒杯中国书法竞赛', CICEC, no date, web.archive.org/web/20190717022813/http://www.cicec.org.cn/whys/2015/0302/314.html.

45 '美国国会议员助手代表团', CICEC, no date, web.archive.org/web/20041026230221/http://www.cicec.org.cn/huodong/98/9862.htm; '第二批美国国会议员助手代表团访华', CICEC, no date, web.archive.org/web/20041026141628/http://www.cicec.org.cn/huodong/2000/00082.htm; '第三批美国国会议员助手代表团访华', CICEC, no date, web.archive.org/web/20041105121019/http://www.cicec.org.cn/huodong/2001/010812.htm; Tan Yingzi, 'Congressional leaders still ignorant about China, Sino-US expert says', *China Daily*, 12 November 2010, archive.ph/wGBB4.

46 '授予彭冲理事长、程思远总顾问"美国联邦肯塔基克罗最高荣誉奖"', CICEC, no date, web.archive.org/web/20041026225741/http://www.cicec.org.cn/huodong/98/9860.htm.

47 '文化中心代表赴美进行工作访问', CICEC, no date, web.archive.org/ web/20040224060357/http://www.cicec.org.cn/huodong/2001/010422. htm; 'Chi Wang', Committee of 100, no date, archive.ph/C6OWX.

48 全国政协港澳台侨委员会, 中国文化教育基金会编撰, 《荣誉与责任： 列席全国政协大会的海外侨胞画传》, 暨南大学出版社, December 2005, p. 160. The association worked with the Overseas Chinese History Society of China (中国华侨历史学会) and All-China Federation of Returned Overseas Chinese to produce the bimonthly *Overseas Chinese Resources* (华侨华人资料) journal.

49 Its address in 1996 was recorded as 21 Daxing Hutong, the same as the MSS's *National Security Information* (国家安全通讯) magazine. A 2006 broadcast industry yearbook records its address as the CICEC building on Dongtucheng Road. See 《中国通信信息大全》编委会 (ed.), 《中国通信 信息大全》, 人民邮电出版社, March 1996, vol. 1, p. 3; 中国广播电影电视 总局, 《中国广播电视年鉴》编委会 (eds), 《中国广播电视年鉴 2006》, 中国官博电视年鉴社, 2006, p. 443.

50 Gao Qi (高崎) is the wife of Liu Min (刘敏) who studied in France and became a PLA linguist before working in CICEC. '学校举办"红色基因代 代传, 革命后代话初心"主题教育党课', Luzhou Vocational and Technical College, 21 October 2019, archive.ph/S0PjA; 吴江辉, '中华文化交流与合 作促进会来校访问', Huaqiao University, 29 March 2021, archive.ph/z2w5B.

51 For example, the think tank network partnered with the Social Investigation Bureau's Chinese Association for the Promotion of Cultural Exchange and Cooperation to run a 2017 academic conference in Beijing that was attended by numerous Central and Eastern European academics, government officials and business representatives. Participants in the conference attended an MSS-organised cultural event in Beijing where they learnt about tai chi, flower arrangement and traditional Chinese medicine. See '2017年中东欧 国家学者研讨班开班仪式在京成功举办', *People's Daily*, 27 June 2017, archive.today/l5UsW; '华彩绽放: "一带一路"倡议背景下的中华传统文化 "走出去"系列讲座及观摩活动在京成功举办', China-CEEC Think Tanks Network, 30 June 2017, archive.ph/jykV0.

The Chinese Association for the Promotion of Cultural Exchange and Cooperation and its secretary-general have themselves been members of the network. See '16+1智库网络理事会理事名单 (2018)', China-CEEC Think Tanks Network, 9 May 2019, archive.ph/DSVUj; '中国中东欧国际智库交 流与合作网络理事单位(2017增选)', China-CEEC Think Tanks Network, 20 December 2017, archive.ph/vBZOX.

52 Lukáš Valášek, 'Vedení Akademie věd odvolalo manažera kvůli vazbám na čínskou komunistickou stranu', Aktuálně.cz, 16 November 2021, archive.ph/ nYUbL.

53 *Annual Report 2019*, China-CEE Institute, 2020, china-cee.eu/wp-content/ uploads/2020/01/2019-annual-report-China-CEE-Institute_12Jan2020. pdf; '中国中东欧国际智库交流与合作网络简介 (2019)', China-CEEC Think Tanks Network, 1 January 2019, https://archive.today/rrlMb. See also Lukáš Valášek, 'Odsouzeného antisemitu platí Čína. Na Akademii věd se

podílí na akcích o Číně i Rusku', Aktuálně.cz, 4 November 2021, zpravy. aktualne.cz/domaci/v-akademii-ved-pracuje-odsouzeny-antisemita-porada-konferenc/r~d5e89e2a359611ec8fa20cc47ab5f122/.

54 吴江辉, '中华文化交流与合作促进会来校访问'.

55 'Founders and board members', US–China Policy Foundation, no date, web. archive.org/web/20071001025004/http://www.uscpf.org/html/founders.html.

56 Laura Rozen, 'Chas Freeman to chair NIC?', *Foreign Policy*, 19 February 2009, foreignpolicy.com/2009/02/19/chas-freeman-to-chair-nic/.

57 Chas Freeman, 'Withdrawal from appointment to chair the National Intelligence Council', *Chas W. Freeman, Jr.* [blog], 10 March 2009, web. archive.org/web/20171024021558/https://chasfreeman.net/withdrawal-of-appointment-to-chair-the-national-intelligence-council/.

58 'National Intelligence Council – what we do', Office of the Director of National Intelligence, no date, www.dni.gov/index.php/who-we-are/organizations/mission-integration/nic/nic-what-we-do.

59 Michael Goldfarb, 'The realist Chas Freeman', *The Nation*, 24 February 2009, web.archive.org/web/20120113011008/http://www.weeklystandard.com/weblogs/TWSFP/2009/02/the_realist_chas_freeman.asp.

60 Eli Binder, 'Chas Freeman on picking fights the US can win', *The Wire China*, 28 June 2020, thewirechina.com/2020/06/28/chas-freeman-on-picking-fights-the-us-can-win/.

61 Wu Po-hsuan & William Hetherington, 'Record number identify as "Taiwanese," poll finds', *Taipei Times*, 5 July 2020, www.taipeitimes.com/News/front/archives/2020/07/05/2003739375.

62 Laura Rozen, 'The controversy over Chas Freeman', *Foreign Policy*, 26 February 2009, foreignpolicy.com/2009/02/26/the-controversy-over-chas-freeman/.

63 David Rothkopf, 'The right choice to be analyst-in-chief', *Foreign Policy*, 25 February 2009, foreignpolicy.com/2009/02/25/the-right-choice-to-be-analyst-in-chief/.

64 Freeman, 'Withdrawal from appointment to chair the National Intelligence Council'.

Chapter 7 Zheng Bijian and China Reform Forum

1 Zheng Bijian, *China's Peaceful Rise: Speeches of Zheng Bijian 1997–2005*, Brookings Institution Press, Washington, DC, 2005, p. 18.

2 The core principle of the drafting process was to 'establish Comrade Mao Zedong's place in history; uphold and develop Mao Zedong Thought'. See 黄黎, '《关于建国以来党的若干历史问题的决议》起草的台前幕后', 近现代史论, archive.ph/VUvRP.

3 Zheng was involved in composing the 'two whatevers' theory under Hua Guofeng; interview with a former Party journalist, 9 July 2021. See 'Resolution on certain questions in the history of our party since the founding of the People's Republic of China', Marxists.org, 27 June 1981, archive.ph/RiA8; 韩刚, '还原华国锋——关于华国锋的若干史实', *Aisixiang*, 18 November 2008, www.aisixiang.com/data/22330.html.

4 For a detailed and insightful discussion of the resolution, from which most of my analysis is drawn, see Robert Suettinger, *Negotiating History: The Chinese Communist Party's 1981*, Project 2049 Institute, Arlington, VA, 17 July 2017, project2049.net/wp-content/uploads/2017/07/P2049_Suettinger_ Negotiating-History-CCP_071717.pdf.

5 Interview with a former Party journalist, 9 July 2021.

6 Zheng, *China's Peaceful Rise*, p. 5.

7 Zheng, *China's Peaceful Rise*, p. 15.

8 Bonnie Glaser & Evan Medeiros, 'The changing ecology of foreign policy-making in China: The ascension and demise of the theory of "peaceful rise"', *China Quarterly*, no. 190, June 2007, pp. 291–310; Satoshi Amako, 'China as a 'Great Power' and East Asian integration', *East Asia Forum*, www.eastasiaforum. org/2010/04/04/china-as-a-great-power-and-east-asian-integration/.

9 Interview with a former Party journalist, 9 July 2021.

10 Interview with an American China scholar, 25 August 2021.

11 Henry Kissinger, *On China*, Penguin Books, New York, 2011, p. 449.

12 Interview with a former Party journalist, 9 July 2021.

13 Jonathan Mirsky, 'Still not the China that two heroes hoped for', *New York Times*, 16 January 2002, archive.ph/iIfX1.

14 Jeremy J. Stone, *Catalytic Diplomacy: Russia, China, North Korea and Iran*, Catalytic Diplomacy, Carlsbad, CA, 2010, p. 201, archive.ph/9I77h.

15 Interview with a former US intelligence officer.

16 Interview with a former US intelligence officer.

17 Interview with a former US intelligence officer.

18 Interview with a former US intelligence officer.

19 Information on the legal entity behind China Reform Forum, Beijing Reform Forum (北京改革开放论坛), accessed on 25 May 2021 from the China national social organisation database at www.chinanpo.gov.cn.

20 The society's name is officially translated as China Society of Economic Reform.

21 For information on Wang Guiwu (王桂五), see 'Wang Guiwu', Asian Affairs, 1998, archive.ph/YJDea; '记离休干部王桂五通知', National Development and Reform Commission, 25 November 2008, archive.ph/dah1S.

22 肖连兵, '改革开放论坛举行迎春联谊', 光明日报, 27 January 1995, p. 3.

23 '第四届理事会第二次理事长会议', CICEC, no date, archive.ph/5Yfml.

24 'Prof. Lin Rong', Asia Society, no date, archive.ph/eNVka.

25 Information on the legal entity behind China Reform Forum, Beijing Reform Forum (北京改革开放论坛), accessed on 25 May 2021 from the China national social organisation database at www.chinanpo.gov.cn. *Baogao wenxue* (报告文学), *Overseas Digest* (海外文摘), China International Public Relations Association (中国国际公共关系协会) and the Chinese Association for the Promotion of Cultural Exchange and Cooperation (中华文化交流与合作促进会 or 中华文化交流促进会) have all used 35 Baofang Hutong as an address in the past and all can be tied to the MSS Social Investigation Bureau. See 陈冬东 (ed.), 《中国社会团体组织大全》,

专利文献出版社, October 1998, p. 811; 飞物公共事务所 (ed.), 《新编信息咨询公关广告服务中介企业名录》, 中国友谊出版公司, February 1994, p. 82; 傅溪鹏, '中国报告文学学会"难产"简录与《报告文学》杂志简史', 中国作家网, 9 May 2008, archive.ph/tC8Uo.

26 '改革开放论坛第二届理事会理事, 顾问名单', China Reform Forum, no date, web.archive.org/web/20000511141834/http://www.crf.org.cn/introduction/introduction.htm.

27 Peng Puzhang (彭普彰 or 彭普璋). '改革开放论坛第二届理事会理事, 顾问名单', China Reform Forum, no date, web.archive.org/web/20000511141834/http://www.crf.org.cn/introduction/INTRODUCTION.htm.

28 李国庆, '市场经济与税制改革国际研讨会在京举行', 光明日报, 11 October 1996, p. 3; 肖连兵, '"欧元启动对中国经济的影响国际研讨会" 在京召开', 光明日报, 18 July 1998, p. 3; 江山, '《东亚经济白皮书》发行式在京举行', 光明日报, 2 November 1996, p. 3.

29 Peter Mattis & Matthew Brazil, *Chinese Communist Espionage: An intelligence primer*, Naval Institute Press, Annapolis, MD, 2019, p. 101.

30 吴震, '改革开放论坛举行第二届理事会', 光明日报, 16 February 2000.

31 David Shambaugh, 'Training China's political elite: The Party School system', *China Quarterly*, no. 196, December 2008, pp. 827–44.

32 Interview with an American scholar who works on China policy, 18 August 2021.

33 China Reform Forum [website homepage], archived 11 October 2000, web.archive.org/web/20000101180427/http://www.crf.org.cn/index.htm.

34 Embassy Beijing, 'Tiananmen: June 4 memories remain fresh for twenty-something youth, dissidents, and the Party, despite censorship', WikiLeaks, cable 09BEIJING1387_a, 22 May 2009, wikileaks.org/plusd/cables/09BEIJING1387_a.html.

35 郭瑞華 (ed.), 《中共對台工作組織體系概論》, Ministry of Justice Investigation Bureau, December 2001, p. 320.

36 郭瑞華 (ed.), 《中共對台工作組織體系概論》, p. 320.

37 Mattis & Brazil, *Chinese Communist Espionage*, p. 102; '许永跃, '社会治安综合治理要齐抓公关', 人民日报, 27 January 1997, p. 11.

38 Michael S. Chase & James C. Mulvenon, 'The decommercialization of China's Ministry of State Security', *International Journal of Intelligence and CounterIntelligence*, no. 15, 2002, pp. 481–95. The MSS's business management bureau (企业局 or 企业司) may have been reformed and downgraded or disbanded during this period and a new bureau established for stability maintenance (维稳) work, including counterterrorism. Some sources also suggest that the MSS largely converted its geographically organised bureaus into functional bureaus (such as the open-line operations bureau) during this period, with the exception of bureaus for Hong Kong, Macau and Taiwan work.

39 '大事记档案', 改革开放论坛, no date, web.archive.org/web/20010405011451/http://www.crf.org.cn/about/home.htm.

40 Interview with a former intelligence officer.

Chapter 8 The concoction of China's peaceful rise

1   Shirley A. Kan et al., *China–US Aircraft Collision Incident of April 2001: Assessments and policy implications*, Congressional Research Service via FAS, 10 October 2001, fas.org/sgp/crs/row/RL30946.pdf.

2   Kim Zetter, 'Burn after reading: Snowden documents reveal scope of secrets exposed to China in 2001 spy plane incident', *The Intercept*, 10 April 2017, theintercept.com/2017/04/10/snowden-documents-reveal-scope-of-secrets-exposed-to-china-in-2001-spy-plane-incident/.

3   Ray Cheung, 'Knives being sharpened behind Sino-US smiles', *South China Morning Post*, 26 October 2003, www.scmp.com/article/432380/knives-being-sharpened-behind-sino-us-smiles.

4   Condoleezza Rice, 'Campaign 2000: Promoting the national interest', *Foreign Affairs*, January/February 2000, archive.ph/v5cun.

5   David M. Lampton, 'The stealth normalization of US-China relations', *National Interest*, no. 73, 2003, p. 39.

6   Interview with a former Western intelligence official.

7   Michael Clarke, 'Counterterrorism yearbook 2019: China', *Strategist*, 27 March 2019, www.aspistrategist.org.au/counterterrorism-yearbook-2019-china/; Sean Roberts, *Imaginary terrorism? The global war on terror and the narrative of the Uyghur terrorist threat*, PONARS Eurasia Working Paper, March 2012, web.archive.org/web/20180814105827/http://www.ponarseurasia.org/sites/default/files/Roberts_WorkingPaper_March2012.pdf.

8   Robin Wright, 'Chinese detainees are men without a country', *Washington Post*, 24 August 2005, www.washingtonpost.com/wp-dyn/content/article/2005/08/23/AR2005082301362.html; Leyland Cecco, '"It breaks my heart": Uighurs wrongfully held at Guantánamo plead to be with families', *Guardian*, 7 October 2020, www.theguardian.com/us-news/2020/oct/07/uighur-men-guantanamo.

9   [Author name redacted], *US-China Counterterrorism Cooperation: Issues for US policy*, Congressional Research Service, 15 July 2010, www.everycrsreport.com/files/20100715_RL33001_b6a3bc61b40d5ae265bdd06c57f36b5991d8f715.pdf.

10 Lampton, 'The stealth normalization of US-China relations', p. 39.

11 'Public wants proof of Iraqi weapons program: Majority says Bush has yet to make the case', Pew Research Center, 16 January 2003, www.pewresearch.org/wp-content/uploads/sites/4/legacy-pdf/170.pdf.

12 '中国式公关', 环球杂志 via *Sina*, 16 October 2007, archive.ph/1B3Y1.

13 Iris Brest, *Condoleezza Rice: Oral history*, Stanford University, 2017, stacks.stanford.edu/file/vd234gk9851/vd234gk9851.pdf.

14 John W. Lewis & Hua Di, 'China's ballistic missile programs: Technologies, strategies, goals', *International Security*, vol. 17, no. 2, 1992, pp. 5–40.

15 Kathleen O'Toole, 'Hua Di arrested in China', *Stanford Report*, 28 October 1998, archive.ph/uAdsz.

16 Kathleen O'Toole, 'Hua Di arrested in China'.

17 '中国式公关', 环球杂志.

18 The Foreign Ministry's Li Zhaoxing and General Wang Zaixi of the Taiwan Affairs Office were also named as members of the group, although apparently with lower status. James Kynge, 'Apparatchik who may raise the party's clout', *Financial Times*, 15 March 2002.

19 Richard H. Haass, 'China and the future of US-China relations', US Department of State, 5 December 2002, web.archive.org/web/20090205172433/https://2001-2009.state.gov/s/p/rem/15687.htm.

20 China Reform Forum [website homepage], archived 8 June 2003, web.archive.org/web/20030608230032/www.crf.org.cn/index.htm.

21 '中国式公关', 环球杂志.

22 See reference to Zheng's report to Hu Jintao in Bonnie Glaser & Evan Medeiros, 'The changing ecology of foreign policy-making in China: The ascension and demise of the theory of "peaceful rise"', *China Quarterly*, no. 190, June 2007, p. 294.

23 郑必坚, '建议就"中国和平崛起发展道路"展开研究' in 郑必坚, 《改革的历程》, 中共中央党校出版社, December 2006, p. 137.

24 Robert B. Zoellick, 'Whither China: From membership to responsibility?', US Department of State, 21 September 2005, 2001-2009.state.gov/s/d/former/zoellick/rem/53682.htm.

25 Two years later, Zoellick, now an executive at Goldman Sachs, again reiterated the responsible stakeholder policy in a *Financial Times* article. Robert Zoellick, 'China and America need a new Shanghai agreement', *Financial Times*, 26 April 2007, www.ft.com/content/50e89462-ec33-11db-a12e-000b5df10621.

26 陈先奎 & 辛向阳, '中国和平崛起是否可能？', 中国政治学, 2 September 2004, web.archive.org/web/20040922003955/http://www.cp.org.cn/2233/ReadNews.asp?NewsID=3119.

27 陈先奎 & 辛向阳, '中国和平崛起是否可能？'.

28 Zheng Bijian, *China's Peaceful Rise: Speeches of Zheng Bijian 1997–2004*, Brookings Institution Press, Washington, DC, 2005, pp. 28–9, www.brookings.edu/wp-content/uploads/2012/04/20050616bijianlunch.pdf.

29 Zheng, *China's Peaceful Rise*, p. vi.

30 Zheng, *China's Peaceful Rise*, p. 16.

31 Interview with an American scholar of China policy.

32 Robert Suettinger, 'The rise and descent of "peaceful rise"', *China Leadership Monitor*, no. 12, p. 7, www.hoover.org/sites/default/files/uploads/documents/clm12_rs.pdf.

33 Suettinger, 'The rise and descent', pp. 3–4.

34 金民卿, '习近平关于和平发展的大智慧', *People's Daily*, 8 August 2017, archive.ph/46H7W; '王毅：中国的历史智慧是"国霸必衰", 而不是"国强必霸"', Xinhua, 24 April 2021, archive.ph/D6ear.

35 Suettinger, 'The rise and descent', p. 8. See also Shanghai Consulate, 'East China views on peaceful rise and harmonious world', WikiLeaks, cable 06SHANGHAI6459_a, 12 October 2006, wikileaks.org/plusd/cables/06SHANGHAI6459_a.html.

36 '郑必坚："和平崛起"同"和平发展"是一回事', 中国新闻网, 21 September 2007, archive.ph/VIMvh.

37 John J. Tkacik Jr, 'China's "peaceful" rise at stake in power struggle', *Heritage Foundation*, 8 September 2004, www.heritage.org/asia/commentary/chinas-peaceful-rise-stake-power-struggle. Though more cautious than Tkacik regarding the concrete consequences of the term, Evan Medeiros's analysis of the debate over peaceful rise is more aligned with the idea that it represented a genuine policy debate. See Evan Medeiros, 'China debates its "peaceful rise" strategy', *YaleGlobal*, 22 June 2004, web.archive.org/web/20040706175149/ http://yaleglobal.yale.edu/display.article?id=4118.

38 Rice, 'Campaign 2000: Promoting the national interest', *Foreign Affairs*, January/February 2000, www.foreignaffairs.com/articles/2000-01-01/ campaign-2000-promoting-national-interest.

39 Henry Kissinger, *On China*, Penguin Books, New York, 2011, p. 449.

40 Bonnie Glaser & Evan Medeiros, 'The changing ecology of foreign policy-making in China: The ascension and demise of the theory of "peaceful rise"', *China Quarterly*, no. 190, June 2007, p. 300.

41 Charles Huztler, 'China promotes "peaceful rise" to quell US fears', *Wall Street Journal*, 13 September 2005, www.wsj.com/articles/SB112655405658338346. See also Richard McGregor, 'Hu at pains to keep China from peasants' revolt', *Financial Times*, 8 September 2005, www.ft.com/content/75793a7e-1fd0-11da-853a-00000e2511c8.

42 Shanghai Consulate, 'East China views on peaceful rise and harmonious world'.

43 Bonnie Glaser, 'Chinese foreign policy research institutes and the practice of influence', in Gilbert Rozman (ed.), *China's Foreign Policy: Who makes it, and how is it made?*, Palgrave Macmillan, New York, 2013, p. 120; '论坛理事会', China Reform Forum, no date, web.archive.org/web/20050205014701/ http://www.crf.org.cn/about/home.htm.

44 Shi Zhihong (施芝鸿) was an advisor to China Reform Forum. '"中国和平崛起与亚洲的新角色"圆桌会议：参会人员名单', China Reform Forum, no date, web.archive.org/web/20070622133609/http:// www.crf.org.cn/2005roundtable/participants.htm; [Untitled], China Reform Forum, no date, web.archive.org/web/20070814172500/http://www.crf.org. cn/exchange/more.htm; '中国改革开放论坛天大研究院出席韩国济州岛和平论坛研讨会', 天大研究院, 29 March 2011, archive.ph/62xzz.

45 Jeremy J. Stone, *Catalytic Diplomacy: Russia, China, North Korea and Iran*, Catalytic Diplomacy, Carlsbad, CA, 2010, p. 201, archive.ph/9I77h.

Chapter 9 WikiLeaks reveals the MSS

1 Interview with an American China scholar.

2 Christopher Andrew & Vasili Mitrokhin, *The Sword and the Shield: The Mitrokhin Archive and the secret history of the KGB*, Basic Books, New York, 1999, pp. 33–5.

3 Christopher Andrew & Vasili Mitrokhin, *The Mitrokhin Archive: The KGB in Europe and the West*, Allen Lane, London, 1999, p. 328.

4   '139. Memorandum of conversation' in Steven E. Phillips (ed.), *Foreign Relations of the United States, 1969–1976*, vol. XVII, China, 1969–1972, Government Printing Office, Washington, DC, 2006, archive.ph/5wSnj.

5   Kate O'Keeffe, Aruna Viswanatha & Cezary Podkul, 'China's pursuit of fugitive businessman Guo Wengui kicks off Manhattan caper worthy of spy thriller', *Wall Street Journal*, 22 October 2017, archive.ph/r6TTK.

6   Tania Branigan, 'Chinese news sites steer clear of China-related WikiLeaks cables', *Guardian*, 6 December 2010, www.theguardian.com/world/2010/dec/05/china-news-sites-wikileaks-cables.

7   Copies of various lists can still be found online. 刘刚, '共匪无间道：维基解密公布为美国工作的中国公知名单', 独立评论, 4 September 2012, archive.ph/7H3jf.

8   See also Peter Ford, 'WikiLeaks outing of Chinese sources fails to spark retribution – so far', *Christian Science Monitor*, 13 September 2011, www.csmonitor.com/World/Asia-Pacific/2011/0913/WikiLeaks-outing-of-Chinese-sources-fails-to-spark-retribution-so-far.

9   'Exclusive: Arrested spy compromised China's US espionage network: sources', Reuters, 15 June 2012, www.reuters.com/article/us-china-usa-espionage-idUSBRE85E06G20120615.

10 Zach Dorfman, 'Botched CIA communications system helped blow cover of Chinese agents', *Foreign Policy*, 15 August 2018, web.archive.org/web/20180816011636/https://foreignpolicy.com/2018/08/15/botched-cia-communications-system-helped-blow-cover-chinese-agents-intelligence/.

11 Embassy Beijing, 'CICIR, Party School scholars assess top leaders approved ASAT test but were unaware of details, timing', WikiLeaks, cable 07BEIJING2903_a, 30 April 2007, archive.ph/1fxIS.

12 Interview with an American China scholar, 25 August 2021.

13 Interview with a former US intelligence officer.

14 '丁奎松副理事长', China Reform Forum, no date, web.archive.org/web/20050306141621/http://www.crf.org.cn/about/bio/dingkuisong.htm; interview with an American China scholar, 25 August 2021.

15 See biography of Ding Kuisong in 'Contributors', *Cambridge Review of International Affairs*, vol. 9, no. 1, 1995, p. 5. On CICIR's relationship to the MSS, see Peter Mattis & Matthew Brazil, *Chinese Communist Espionage: An intelligence primer*, Naval Institute Press, Annapolis, MD, 2019, p. 56.

16 The Centre for World Personage Studies (aka Division for World Personage Studies, 世界人物研究室 or 世界人物研究中心) was reportedly headed by Ke Yongzhen (possibly 可永真) in 1992; *China Exchange News*, vol. 20, no. 3–4, 1992, p. 7. The unit is probably the same as that referred to by Roger Faligot as the 'Institute for the Study of Major International Figures'; Roger Faligot, *Chinese Spies: From Chairman Mao to Xi Jinping*, Scribe, Melbourne, 2019, p. 419.

17 See 中国现代国际关系研究所世界人物研究室, 海外文摘杂志社, 《世界人物大辞典》, 国际文化出版公司, 1990; 现代国际关系研究所世界人物研究室,《东南亚南亚名人录》, 时事出版社, 1990; 中国现代国际关系研究院世界人物研究中心,《影响当今世界的重要思想人物》, 时事出版社, January 2013.

18 '丁奎松副理事长', China Reform Forum.

19 '丁奎松副理事长', China Reform Forum. Lu Zhongwei (陆忠伟), a Japan expert, became head of the Tianjin State Security Bureau under the pseudonym Zhong Wei (钟卫). See Peter Mattis, 'The dragon's eyes and ears: Chinese intelligence at the crossroads', *National Interest*, 20 January 2015, web.archive.org/web/20170704085737/https://nationalinterest.org/feature/the-dragons-eyes-ears-chinese-intelligence-the-crossroads-12062.

20 The assistant head of an MSS bureau such as CICIR would probably be a division-level (处级) post in preparation for promotion to deputy bureau chief. Indicating how such roles are a promotion track, MSS vice ministers often receive the title after spending time as an assistant minister (部长助理).

21 Interview with an American China scholar, 25 August 2021.

22 The delegation of thirteen from the China Universities Alumni Association (高校校友海外联谊会) reportedly visited Taiwan in May 2001 at the invitation of Taiwan's Chinese Youth Exchange Association (中华青年交流协会). '两岸关系大事记2001年5月', 华夏经纬网, 12 June 2003, archive.ph/6n6Tg. The group has visited Taiwan on at least two other occasions, as well as Harvard University. Its current secretary-general, Li Peisong (李培松), was previously a deputy secretary-general of China Reform Forum and a visiting scholar at Harvard University. See 'Fairbank Center welcomes postdocs, scholars', *Harvard Gazette*, 26 October 2006, archive.ph/mNOVO.

23 '明德师范教育奖励基金捐赠仪式在我校隆重举行', 北京师范大学教育基金会 via www.DaxueCN.com, 18 June 2011, archive.ph/GWKjp.

24 Embassy Beijing, 'The Fourth CCP Plenum: Reform with no change', WikiLeaks, cable 09BEIJING2533_a, 3 September 2009, archive.ph/IJlgr.

25 Embassy Beijing, 'Tiananmen: June 4 memories remain fresh for twenty-something youth, dissidents, and the Party, despite censorship', WikiLeaks, cable 09BEIJING1387_a, 22 May 2009, archive.ph/Ddi8C.

26 ibid n 25. In Chinese politics, 'left' generally refers to the orthodox Maoist and Marxist side of the political spectrum.

27 David Ownby, 'Maps – New Left', Reading the China Dream [website], no date, www.readingthechinadream.com/new-left.html.

28 Embassy Beijing, 'Tiananmen: June 4 memories remain fresh'.

29 Edward Wong, 'Arms sales to Taiwan will proceed, US says', *New York Times*, 15 December 2009, www.nytimes.com/2009/12/16/world/asia/16taiwan.html.

30 Interview with a former foreign intelligence officer.

31 张智 & 燕则春, '薛福康: 国关人要有崇高情怀', 10 January 2016, archive.ph/Mrm0v. Xue's first known report from Canberra was published on 21 June 1989: 骆以清 & 薛福康, '贯彻保护战略 制止土地剥蚀: 澳大利亚环保官员谈环境问题', 光明日报, 21 June 1989, p. 4. For testimony from a former MSS officer about the relationship between the *Guangming Daily*

(光明日报) and the MSS, see 丁柯, '特工——民运——法轮功：一个生命的真实故事 (上)', *Minghui*, 12 September 2003, archive.today/JAHz8.

32 Cao Huayin (曹化银) attended a 1998 conference in Hawaii as a researcher and interpreter at CICEC. Christopher B. Johnstone, 'Conference report: US-China Security Cooperation in Northeast Asia, May 26–28, 1998, Honolulu, Hawaii', Asia-Pacific Center for Security Studies, no date, archive.today/7ewI5.

33 里彻尔森 (曹化银, 周遵友 & 张帆 trans.), 《兰利奇才----美国中央情报局科技分局内幕》, CITIC Press, Beijing, 2002.

34 Embassy Beijing, 'Taiwan: Chinese continue to express concern over Chen Shui-bian's UN referendum', WikiLeaks, cable 07BEIJING5326_a, 14 August 2007, wikileaks.org/plusd/cables/07BEIJING5326_a.html/.

35 Embassy Beijing, 'Annual legislative session concludes with passage of property law', WikiLeaks, cable 07BEIJING1790_a, 16 March 2007, archive.ph/e3QBW.

36 Cao also gave a speech at Princeton University during this period: 'Nassau notes', *Princeton Weekly Bulletin*, 1 March 2004, archive.ph/mMj2o.

37 'Fairbank Center welcomes postdocs, scholars', *Harvard Gazette*.

38 Embassy Beijing, 'DPRK nuclear test threat: Views of Chinese academic and media observers', WikiLeaks, cable 06BEIJING21220_a, 7 October 2006, archive.ph/f6vCD.

39 Embassy Beijing, 'Taiwan: Chinese continue to express concern'.

40 Michael Schoenhals, *Spying for the People: Mao's secret agents, 1949–1967*, Cambridge University Press, Cambridge, 2013, pp. 150–1.

41 Mattis & Brazil, *Chinese Communist Espionage*, p. 67.

42 《我们走过三十年》, CICEC, no date, p. 11.

43 '中国国际公共关系协会领导机构名单', China International Public Relations Association, no date, web.archive.org/web/20030603215915/http://www.cipra.org.cn:80/organization/organization.asp.

44 '中国改革开放论坛介绍', China Reform Forum, no date, archived 3 May 2010, web.archive.org/web/20100503062355/http://www.crf.org.cn:80/about/index.htm.

45 'Executive vice chairman', China Reform Forum, no date, archive.ph/dxZHw.

46 '第四届理事会理事名单', CICEC, no date, archive.ph/wip/0VyMm.

47 '中国国际公共关系协会领导机构名单', CIPRA, no date, archived 9 June 2002, web.archive.org/web/20020609183043/http://cipra.org.cn/organization/organization.asp.

48 '陶大为', Chinese People's Political Consultative Conference, no date, archive.today/hYVUR.

49 '孙永海', Chinese People's Political Consultative Conference, no date, archive.ph/Y8HfE.

50 Mattis, 'The dragon's eyes and ears'.

51 The current iteration of this bureau may use the name Overseas Security Protection Bureau (海外安全保卫局) and includes a state-owned

Enterprises Division (国企处). The 10th Bureau also appears to have maintained relationships with universities in China, perhaps indicating that it recruits Chinese students before they go abroad. Mattis & Brazil, *Chinese Communist Espionage*, p. 56; 中国高等教育教育学会保卫学专业委员会 (ed.), 《中国高等教育学会保卫学专业委员会会志 1991–2010年》, 武汉大学出版社, 2011, p. 135.

52 Tao was appointed a deputy head of the Shaanxi State Security Department in March 1998. In 2002–05 he was head of the Henan State Security Department. It's common for headquarters officers to spend a few years running provincial departments to gain experience and then return to Beijing in senior leadership roles; '陕西省政府人事任免通知', 中国网, 1 November 2011, archive.vn/DJGg5; 河南年鉴编辑部 (ed.), 《河南年鉴2002》, 河南年鉴社, September 2002, p. 59; '省十届人大常委会第十三次会议任免名单', 河南人大, 19 January 2005, archive.fo/k6UWW.

53 '中国改革开放论坛介绍', China Reform Forum.

54 On Lu Zhongwei's time in Tianjin, see '天津市国家安全局局长来我校作报告', Tianjin Party School, no date, web.archive.org/web/20070102025850/ http://www.tjdx.gov.cn/xyxw/system/2006/10/27/000045377.shtml; '天津市人大常委会决定任免名单', 北方网, 25 February 2005, archive.today/ U8dvq.

55 '中国改革开放论坛介绍', China Reform Forum.

Chapter 10 The revolving door: Scholars and the MSS

1 This section is based on an interview with an American scholar of China policy. Some details have been removed or adjusted in the interests of the interviewee's anonymity.

2 Officers of 2PLA, the PLA General Political Department's Liaison Department (now the Political Work Department's Liaison Bureau), and the MSS have completed stints at DC think tanks such as the Atlantic Council as visiting scholars. See description of 2PLA's Chen Xiaogong in Peter Mattis & Matthew Brazil, *Chinese Communist Espionage: An intelligence primer*, Naval Institute Press, Annapolis, MD, 2019, p. 62, and of former MSS officer Yang Hengjun (aka Yang Jun) in Echo Hui & Dylan Welch, 'A spy and a democracy pedlar: The complicated truths in the life of Australian citizen Yang Hengjun', *ABC News*, 3 March 2020, www.abc.net. au/news/2020–03–23/writer-yang-hengjun-held-in-china-was-in-chinese-spy-agency/12077720.

Zhang Yuwen (张毓文) was a senior PLA Navy Liaison Department officer who was sent to Washington, DC in 1989, covered as a researcher with the China Association for International Friendly Contact, to cultivate the head of a think tank. An abridged report by Zhang on his time in the United States can be found in 《海军联络工作史》, 总政治部联络部, October 1999, pp. 747–50.

3 吴天佑, 傅曦, '为里根出谋划策的思想库', 现代国际关系, 1981, no. 1, pp. 55–64; 吴天佑, 傅曦, '为里根出谋划策的思想库(继)', 现代国际关系,

1982, no. 2, pp. 62–64; 吴天佑, 傅曦, '为里根出谋划策的思想库(续完)', 现代国际关系, 1983, no. 3, pp. 59–64.

4　于恩光, '美国的思想库', 战略与管理, 1994, no. 1.

5　In 2005, China Reform Forum held meetings and workshops in France, the Netherlands, the United Kingdom and Spain in cooperation with the French Institute of International Relations. 'The Forum on China's peaceful rise & Sino-European relations', Tianda Institute, 16 December 2005, archive.ph/kQuMd.

6　Zhou Qiyuan (周琪媛) was press attaché in the PRC embassy in France circa 2016. She was listed as China Reform Forum's head of European exchange programs in 2001. '在法中资企业聚焦"一带一路"与媒体对话', 中国侨网, 24 May 2016, archive.ph/uCBTE; '工作机构主要成员', China Reform Forum, 2001, web.archive.org/web/20010421203645/http://www.crf.org.cn/about/standing.htm.

7　See 'Major researchers and staff', Carnegie Endowment for International Peace, 2004, web.archive.org/web/20090610120213/http://www.carnegieendowment.org/programs/china/chinese/about/Staff.cfm.

8　'China's peaceful rise?', Carnegie Endowment for International Peace, 20 September 2004, web.archive.org/web/20060111212843/http://www.carnegieendowment.org/events/index.cfm?fa=eventDetail&id=714&&prog=zch.

9　Minxin Pei, 'Concluding remarks', Carnegie Endowment, 21 September 2004, web.archive.org/web/20060111212903/http://www.carnegieendowment.org/pdf/pei.pdf.

10　Pei, 'Concluding remarks'.

11　Minxin Pei, 'A fresh approach on China', *International Herald Tribune* via Carnegie Endowment, 9 September 2005, web.archive.org/web/20051020222559/http://www.carnegieendowment.org/publications/index.cfm?fa=view&id=17435.

12　Jonathan Fanton, 'Commentary from Jonathan Fanton on Carnegie Endowment's New Vision launch', MacArthur Foundation, 7 February 2007, archive.ph/H9Oul.

13　See C. Raja Mohan, *India's New Foreign Policy Strategy*, Carnegie Endowment, 26 May 2006, web.archive.org/web/20210803053044/https://carnegieendowment.org/files/Mohan.pdf; 'Rising India: Opportunities and lessons for China', Carnegie Endowment, 26 May 2006, archive.ph/3lqfw.

14　MSS officers affiliated with China Reform Forum, the CASS Taiwan Studies Institute and CICIR attended this meeting. 'Preventing and resolving conflict across the Taiwan Strait', Carnegie Endowment, 6 April 2005, archive.ph/Zhuxh.

15　'China's development direction after three decades of reform', Carnegie Endowment, 13 April 2009, archive.ph/tAcNA.

16　'A new beginning: American foreign policy under a new administration', Carnegie Endowment, 10 November 2008, archive.ph/lc9eW.

17　'Carnegie Corporation awards $3 million for Carnegie Endowment's China program', *Philanthropy News Digest*, 11 January 2008, archive.ph/Aj3x5.

18 Zhang Ye (张烨), who appears on a 2007 membership list and was also affiliated with the Chinese Academy of Social Sciences, and Freda Wang (王一讯), who is also a member of the Center for China and Globalization's council. 'Members', China Reform Forum, no date, web.archive.org/web/20070821001210/http://www.crf.org.cn/about/members/htm; 'Wang Yixun', CCG, no date, archive.vn/0OdhX.

19 '2002年1月动态', China Reform Forum, no date, web.archive.org/web/20020812000652/http://crf.org.cn/about/news/200201.htm; '三月动态', China Reform Forum, no date, web.archive.org/web/200212212856/http://crf.org.cn/about/news/200203.htm.

20 See 'Re: China – Chinese banks' illusory earnings (excellent math)', WikiLeaks, Global Intelligence Files 1233762, 7 April 2011, wikileaks.org/gifiles/docs/12/1233762_re-china-chinese-banks-illusory-earnings-excellent-math-.html; 'China insight list', WikiLeaks, Global Intelligence Files 1238650, 1 September 2011, wikileaks.org/gifiles/attach/107/107823_China%20Insight%20list%20Jen.xls.

21 'Frequently asked questions', RAND Corporation, no date, archive.ph/a3S4M.

22 Bijian Zheng & Charles Wolf Jr (eds), *Proceedings of the 6th Annual RAND-China Reform Forum Conference, August 28–29, 2003*, RAND Corporation, Santa Monica, CA, 2004, www.rand.org/pubs/conf_proceedings/CF195.html.

23 See '中国改革开放论坛—美国兰德公司第七届年会', China Reform Forum, no date, web.archive.org/web/20070925121608/www.crf.org.cn/annualconference/chineseparticipant.htm. Yin Ruxin (殷汝新) was a senior 2PLA officer, possibly a head or deputy head of the agency in the early 2000s, who had experience working in Japan. China Reform Forum's RAND conference agenda describes him as a senior fellow at China Reform Forum, but he doesn't appear on the group's otherwise extensive membership lists. For a reference to him leading 2PLA in 2002, see 《广东核电大事记 第二集 1995–2002》, 原子能出版社, December 2006, p. 266.

24 This and following Mulvenon quotes from interview with James Mulvenon, 22 September 2021.

25 Zheng & Wolf Jr (eds), *Proceedings of the 6th Annual RAND-China Reform Forum Conference*, p. xiii.

26 This and following information about the planned task forces come from confidential documents.

27 Confidential document.

28 Zach Dorfman & Jenna McLaughlin, 'The CIA's communications suffered a catastrophic compromise. It started in Iran', *Yahoo News*, 2 November 2018, news.yahoo.com/cias-communications-suffered-catastrophic-compromise-started-iran-090018710.html.

29 Jane Perlez, 'FBI bars some China scholars from visiting US over spying fears', *New York Times*, 14 April 2019, www.nytimes.com/2019/04/14/world/asia/china-academics-fbi-visa-bans.html.

30 Edward Wong, 'Important story by @JanePerlez on FBI …', Twitter, 15 April 2019, mobile.twitter.com/ewong/status/1117578643956432896.

31 Perlez, 'FBI bars some China scholars'.

32 '中国国际友好联络会第五届理事会理事', China Association for International Friendly Contact, no date, archive.ph/tXv0Y.

33 '南海中心举办"中美海洋安全高级对话"', Collaborative Innovation Center of South China Sea Studies, 8 December 2017, archive.ph/GcKRv.

34 '关于我们', 亚太安全与海洋研究, no date, archive.ph/6EX4D.

35 Wu Baiyi (吴白), who was in Atlanta for an event organised by the Carter Center before the visa cancellation, is affiliated with the China Foundation for International Strategic Studies (中国国际战略研究基金会), which intelligence experts Peter Mattis and Matthew Brazil describe as an operational front for the Intelligence Bureau of the PLA Joint Staff Department. See Mattis & Brazil, *Chinese Communist Espionage*, p, 52; '吴白乙', 北京大学中外人文交流研究基地, 20 April 2020, archive.ph/S1p4b.

36 Author correspondence with Peter Mattis.

37 Perlez, 'FBI bars some China scholars'.

38 Nick DiUlio, 'Four new Global Scholars set to visit campus', Princeton University, 16 September 2010, archive.ph/dxtKE; 'Crisis Group's board of trustees', International Crisis Group, no date, archived 3 April 2015, web.archive.org/web/20150403054159/https://www.crisisgroup.org/en/about/board.aspx; 'Wang Jisi', Asia Society Policy Institute, 2021, archive.ph/P6NvD.

39 '第二届理事会理事名单', CICEC, no date, web.archive.org/web/20190924114302/www.cicec.org.cn/lshhd/426.html.

40 Wu Xuewen (吴学文) was covered as an employee of *Xinhua*, the All-China Journalists Association International Liaison Department and the China Institute of Contemporary International Relations. He was among the MSS's foremost Japan experts, having grown up in Japanese-occupied northern China and studied in a Japanese military academy. A colleague, Sun Dongmin (孙东民), recalled how he and Wu were responsible for ensuring Premier Zhou Enlai's security when he met a delegation of Japanese journalists in 1972. 《长春文史资料》编辑部, 《艰辛的历程, 伪满军官学校的学生们》, 1994, p. 422; Roger Faligot, *Chinese Spies: From Chairman Mao to Xi Jinping*, Scribe, Melbourne, 2019, p. 120; '访人民日报高级编辑, 原驻日首席记者孙东民先生', 客觀日本, 24 March 2012, archive.ph/dm2Z5.

41 'International joint research "Japan-US-China cooperation and the future of the Asia Pacific" Washington workshop', Japan Center for International Exchange, no date, web.archive.org/web/20071112235320/https://www.jcie.or.jp/japan/nenji98/g04.htm; 'Exchange', China Reform Forum, no date, web.archive.org/web/20010302085948/http://www.crf.org.cn/english/exchange.htm; Zheng & Wolf Jr (eds), *Proceedings of the 6th Annual RAND-China Reform Forum Conference*.

42 '改革开放论坛第二届理事会理事、顾问名单', China Reform Forum, no date, web.archive.org/web/20000511141834/http://www.crf.org.cn/introduction/introduction.htm; '第三届理事会理事名单', CICEC, no date, web.archive.org/web/20190717022707/cicec.org.cn/lshhd/425.html.

43 Melinda Liu, 'Donald Trump and China's Year of the Hawk', 18 January 2017, *Politico*, www.politico.com/magazine/story/2017/01/donald-trump-and-chinas-year-of-the-hawk-214656/.

44 Fan Lingzhi, 'Visa cancellations absurd', *Global Times*, 19 April 2019, archive.ph/xHRS0.

45 'Members', China Reform Forum; '中国国际公共关系协会第四届理事会第二次会议名单', China International Public Relations Association, 6 September 2011, web.archive.org/web/20111107143042/http://www.cipra.org.cn/show.php?contentid=267.

Chapter 11 'China never forgets its friends': Elite capture

1 Zheng Bijian, 'China's peaceful rise and opportunities for the Asia-Pacific region', China Reform Forum, 24 April 2004, web.archive.org/web/20040623114957/http://www.crf.org.cn/peacefulrise/zbjspeech4.htm.

2 'George Bush: China's peaceful rise "very important"', *Xinhua* via 中国网, 24 April 2004, archive.ph/MaiSz.

3 'China's Peaceful Rise and Economic Globalization, April 24–25, 2004: Agenda', China Reform Forum, 2004, web.archive.org/web/20040603201555/http://www.crf.org.cn/peacefulrise/agenda2.htm.

4 [Untitled], China Reform Forum, no date, archived 3 February 2007, web.archive.org/web/2007014212410/http://www.crf.org.cn/exchange/more.htm.

5 'China's Peaceful Rise and Economic Globalization', China Reform Forum.

6 '"中国和平崛起与亚洲的新角色"圆桌会议参会人员名单', China Reform Forum, no date, web.archive.org/web/20070622133609/http://www.crf.org.cn/2005roundtable/participants.htm; '中国和平崛起与亚洲的新角色"圆桌会议在博鳌举行', 人民网, 23 April 2005, web.archive.org/web/2012027142910/http://finance.people.com.cn/GB/8215/46676/46937/3343694.html.

7 'Exchange', China Reform Forum, no date, web.archive.org/web/20070203100913/http://www.crf.org.cn/exchange/more.htm.

8 Bob Hawke, 'The Hon Bob Hawke in conversation with Geraldine Doogue', ACRI, 4 June 2015, web.archive.org/web/20210322073355/https://www.australiachinarelations.org/sites/default/files/150604%20Australia-China%20Relations%20Institute%20Prime%20Ministers%20Series%20-%20Hawke%20and%20China%20-%20Transcript.pdf.

9 Geremie Barmé, 'Supping with a long spoon – dinner with Premier Li, November 1988', *China Heritage*, no date, archive.ph/YrgZP.

10 Matt Bevan & Scott Mitchell, 'Previously classified diplomatic cable reveals what PM Bob Hawke thought he knew about the Tiananmen massacre', *ABC News*, 3 June 2021, www.abc.net.au/news/2021-06-03/bob-hawke-tiananman-classified-cable/100184916.

11 Bevan & Mitchell, 'Previously classified diplomatic cable'.

12 Gabrielle Chan, 'Cabinet papers 1988–89: Bob Hawke acted alone in offering asylum to Chinese students', *Guardian*, 1 January 2015, www.theguardian.com/australia-news/2015/jan/01/cabinet-papers-1988-89-bob-hawke-acted-alone-in-offering-asylum-to-chinese-students.

13 Hawke, 'The Hon Bob Hawke in conversation'.

14 Hawke, 'The Hon Bob Hawke in conversation'.

15 Hawke, 'The Hon Bob Hawke in conversation'.

16 Hawke, 'The Hon Bob Hawke in conversation'.

17 Eric Ellis, 'In the mood with Waltzing Matilda at the Shangri-La', *Australian Financial Review*, 22 June 1993, archive.ph/bnKEf.

18 '江泽民分别会见霍克和差猜 感谢他们为发展中澳, 中泰友好做出努力', 人民日报, 4 July 1993, p. 1.

19 Hawke, 'The Hon Bob Hawke in conversation'.

20 Jiang's speech was delivered at the National State Security Work Conference, 9 October 1993. 殷捷 & 王亚民 (eds), 《国家安全机关工作人员读本》, 时事出版社 (内部读物), December 1998, pp. 167–9.

21 David Shambaugh, 'China's international relations think tanks: Evolving structure and process', *China Quarterly*, vol. 171, September 2002, pp. 589–90.

22 '江泽民分别会见霍克和差猜 感谢他们为发展中澳, 中泰友好做出努力', 人民日报, 4 July 1993, p. 1.

23 霍克, '未来世界应给东亚一个机会', 战略与管, no. 1, November 1993, pp. 1–4.

24 Barmé, 'Supping with a long spoon'.

25 吴江, '秦川谈习仲勋二三事', 炎黄春秋, 5 September 2003, archive.vn/kZT3F.

26 '改革开放论坛第二届理事会理事、顾问名单', China Reform Forum, no date, web.archive.org/web/20000511141834/http://www.crf.org.cn/introduction/introduction.htm.

27 谢善骁, '我的董事长秦川', 晨鸟之歌 via WeChat, 26 November 2020, archive.ph/LrTli. MSS Social Investigation Bureau chief Mao Guohua (毛国华) was executive chairman of the company. '毛国华: 梦魂萦绕翠竹情', 奉化新闻网, no date, web.archive.org/web/20071127127121634/http://www1.fhnews.com.cn/gb/node2/node6/node86/node97/userobject1ai835.html.

28 Fang Guoquan (方国全). '四画', 武汉地方志办公室, no date, archive.ph/nmb8X.

29 See Shambaugh, 'China's international relations think tanks'. Gu's son, Major General Liu Nianyuan (刘念远), was a defence attaché and later became a member of the General Staff Department Intelligence Department's Party Committee.

30 赵力 (ed.), 《满族姓氏寻根辞典》, 辽宁民族出版社, March 2012, p. 147.

31 '中国战略与管理研究会大事记', CSSM, no date, web.archive.org/web/20070918030206/http://www.cssm.org.cn/html/index_dsj.html.

32 Correspondence with a former Japanese counterintelligence official.

33 Lucy Macken, 'Bob Hawke to sell Northbridge home for $14m to downsize to CBD pad', Domain, 13 March 2019, www.domain.com.au/news/bob-hawke-sells-northbridge-home-for-14m-downsizes-to-cbd-pad-808969/.

34 Title Tattle, 'Bob Hawke's Northbridge home sells at $9.2 million, not $15 million', Urban.com.au, 11 December 2019, web.archive.org/web/20220316162904/https://www.urban.com.au/news/107881-bob-hawke-sells-northbridge-home-2.

35 Bob Hawke, 'Looking back on China's relations with Australia', East Asia Forum, 27 September 2009, archive.ph/Srzrd.

36 'Sam Dastyari wasn't the first to take Chinese money, just ask Howard', Crikey, 19 December 2017, archive.ph/fZzPb.

37 Blanche d'Alpuget, Hawke: The prime minister, Melbourne University Publishing, Melbourne, 2011, p. 362.

38 'Asia forum ready to begin on Hainan', China Daily via 中国网, 27 February 2001, archive.ph/Xxlra.

39 Janet Hawley, 'From the archive, 1998: The bliss of being Bob and Blanche … and how it all began', Sydney Morning Herald, 17 May 2019, archive.ph/uezYl.

40 朱福东, '我的小回忆录 (10)--兰盟寻梦', Sina Blog, 23 November 2011.

41 孙尚清 (ed.), 《中国咨询研究机构大全》, 中国经济出版社, July 1996, p. 92; 朱福东, '我的小回忆录 (10)'.

42 Qin Chaoying's (秦朝英) 'second-in-command' Liang Weina (梁维娜) had been a military officer specialising in science and technology intelligence. See 南京图书馆 (ed.), 《图书馆学情报学论文素引 1981–1989》, 书目文献出版社, January 1993, p. 747; 朱福东, '我的小回忆录 (10)'.

43 朱福东, '我的小回忆录 (10)'.

44 Hawley, 'From the archive, 1998'.

45 Peter Mattis & Matthew Brazil, Chinese Communist Espionage: An intelligence primer, Naval Institute Press, Annapolis, MD, 2019, pp. 51–2.

46 Hawke, 'The Hon Bob Hawke in conversation'.

47 朱福东, '我的小回忆录 (10)'.

48 Stephen Hutcheon, 'Hawke backs China's horse', Age, 4 May 1996, p. 10.

49 Annual Report 2008, Fortescue Metals Group via ASX, no date, p. 12, www.asx.com.au/asxpdf/20081020/pdf/31czv4tbxph3cw.pdf.

50 Hawley, 'From the archive, 1998'.

51 Hawke, 'The Hon Bob Hawke in conversation'.

52 Jason Clare, 'Transcript of press conference: Sydney: 29 November 2020: changes to HomeBuilder; China; stranded Australians; JobSeeker', Jason Clare MP [website], 29 November 2020, archive.ph/TjG2d.

Chapter 12 The Party you can't leave: Trump, Biden and beyond

1   Zach Dorfman, 'China used stolen data to expose CIA operatives in Africa and Europe', Foreign Policy, 21 December 2020, foreignpolicy.com/2020/12/21/china-stolen-us-data-exposed-cia-operatives-spy-networks/.

2   Chua Chin Hon, 'Beijing replaces top policy thinker', Straits Times, 24 August 2007; Bonnie S Glaser, 'Chinese foreign policy research institutes

and the practice of influence', in Gilbert Rozman (ed.), *China's Foreign Policy: Who makes it, and how is it made?*, Palgrave Macmillan, New York, September 2013, p. 108.

3   '中国战略与管理研究会 简介', China Institute of Strategy and Management, no date, web.archive.org/web/20081204111431/http://www.cssm.org.cn/html/index_gyzzh.html.

4   '中国21实际城镇化发展战略论坛', 中国网, February 2006, archive.ph/Yrz8N.

5   '论坛成员', China Reform Forum, no date, web.archive.org/web/20010803180542/http://www.crf.org.cn/about/home.htm.

6   'Obama more popular abroad than at home, global image of US continues to benefit', Pew Research, 17 June 2010, ch. 5, archive.ph/0Wfc2.

7   'Event agenda: The Strategic Forum for US-China Clean Energy Cooperation', Brookings Institution, no date, archive.ph/PGmMk.

8   'Event agenda: The Strategic Forum for US-China Clean Energy Cooperation', Brookings Institution.

9   Peter Mattis, 'China's digital authoritarianism: Surveillance, influence, and political control', prepared statement for hearing before the House Permanent Select Committee on Intelligence, 16 May 2019, www.congress.gov/116/meeting/house/109462/witnesses/HHRG-116-IG00-Wstate-MattisP-20190516.pdf. See also Alexander Bowe, *China's Overseas United Front Work*, US-China Economic Security and Review Commission, 24 August 2018, pp. 15–6, web.archive.org/web/20180909101348/https://www.uscc.gov/sites/default/files/Research/China's%20Overseas%20United%20Front%20Work%20-%20Background%20and%20Implications%20for%20US_final_0.pdf.

10 Rachelle Younglai, 'The man with the key to China: Barrick Gold's quest to open new doors', *Globe and Mail*, 6 December 2013, www.theglobeandmail.com/report-on-business/industry-news/energy-and-resources/the-man-with-the-key-to-china-barrick-golds-quest-to-open-new-doors/article15814739/.

11 Landon Thomas Jr & Joseph Kahn, 'Co-president at Goldman announces his retirement', *New York Times*, 25 March 2003, www.nytimes.com/2003/03/25/business/co-president-at-goldman-announces-his-retirement.html.

12 *The Brookings Institution: Annual report 2006*, Brookings Institution, 2006, www.brookings.edu/wp-content/uploads/2016/07/2006-Annual-Report.pdf.

13 'John Thornton to succeed James A. Johnson as chairman of the Brookings board', Brookings Institution, 11 June 2003, archive.ph/648h4.

14 'Exchange', China Reform Forum, no date, web.archive.org/web/20070203100913/http://www.crf.org.cn/exchange/more.htm.

15 'China's Peaceful Rise and Economic Globalization, April 24–25, 2004: Agenda', China Reform Forum, 2004, web.archive.org/web/20040603201555/http://www.crf.org.cn/peacefulrise/agenda2.htm.

16 Josh Rogin, *Chaos Under Heaven: Trump, Xi, and the battle for the twenty-first century*, Mariner Books, Boston, p. 65.

17 '2nd US-China Strategic Forum on Clean Energy Cooperation', Brookings Institution, no date, web.archive.org/web/20190115132420/brookings. edu/wp-content/uploads/2012/04/cef_program_en.pdf; 'List of CRF International Advisory Committee', China Reform Forum, no date, web. archive.org/web/20060616070317/http://www.crf.org.cn/council.htm.

18 '约翰桑顿', 中国国际经济交流中心, 10 May 2017, archive.today/amJui.

19 Rogin, *Chaos Under Heaven*, pp. 65–6.

20 Rogin, *Chaos Under Heaven*, p. 66; Benjamin Haas, 'Steve Bannon compares China to 1930s Germany and says US must confront Beijing', *Guardian*, 11 September 2017, www.theguardian.com/us-news/2017/sep/11/steve-bannon-compares-china-to-1930s-germany-and-says-us-must-confront-beijing.

21 Michael Kranish & Renae Merle, 'Stephen K. Bannon, architect of anti-globalist policies, got rich as a global capitalist', *Washington Post*, 31 March 2017, www.washingtonpost.com/politics/stephen-k-bannon-architect-of-antiglobalist-policies-got-rich-as-a-global-capitalist/2017/03/31/47382082-0a8b-11e7-a15f-a58d4a988474_story.html.

22 According to journalist Josh Rogin, Thornton met Trump in his Trump Tower office in December 2016. Rogin, *Chaos Under Heaven*, pp. 66–7.

23 Interview with a former White House official, 21 October 2021.

24 John L. Thornton, 'Long time coming: The prospects for democracy in China', *Foreign Affairs*, January/February 2008, www.foreignaffairs.com/articles/asia/2008-01-01/long-time-coming/.

25 Jeremy J. Stone, *Catalytic Diplomacy: Russia, China, North Korea and Iran*, Catalytic Diplomacy, Carlsbad, CA, 2010, p. 197, archive.ph/9I77h.

26 Embassy Beijing, 'Tiananmen: June 4 memories remain fresh for twenty-something youth, dissidents, and the Party, despite censorship', WikiLeaks, Cable 09BEIJING1387_a, 22 May 2009, wikileaks.org/plusd/cables/09BEIJING1387_a.html.

27 Zheng Bijian, *China's Peaceful Rise: Speeches of Zheng Bijian 1997–2004*, Brookings Institution Press, Washington, DC, 2005, www.brookings.edu/wp-content/uploads/2012/04/20050616bijianlunch.pdf.

28 John L. Thornton, remarks in 'US-China relations in the next decade' [video], *C-SPAN*, 18 January 2011, 31:40, www.c-span.org/video/?297572-1/us-china-relations-decade.

29 John L. Thornton, 'Foreword' in Zheng, *China's Peaceful Rise*, p. vi.

30 See 'The beginning of new relations' [video], *C-SPAN*, 23 April 2001, www.c-span.org/video/?163854-2/beginning-relations&event=163854&playEvent.

31 Thornton, 'Long time coming'.

32 Rogin, *Chaos Under Heaven*, pp. 67–8.

33 Rogin, *Chaos Under Heaven*, p. 68.

34 Rogin, *Chaos Under Heaven*, p. 67; interview with a former White House official, 21 October 2021.

35 Emily Rauhala, 'Bannon's views on China depend on whom he is talking to', *Washington Post*, 12 September 2017, www.washingtonpost.com/news/worldviews/wp/2017/09/12/stephen-k-bannons-views-on-china-depend-on-whom-he-is-talking-to/.

36 Rogin, *Chaos Under Heaven*, p. 68.

37 Interview with a former White House official, 21 October 2021.

38 Interview with a former White House official, 21 October 2021.

39 Catherine Wong, 'Kissinger's "secret" China trip recalled as Wall Street veteran meets key Chinese leaders, visits Xinjiang', *South China Morning Post*, 27 September 2021, web.archive.org/web/20210926210542/https://www.scmp.com/news/china/diplomacy/article/3150003/kissingers-secret-china-trip-recalled-wall-street-veteran.

40 Chris Buckley & Steven Lee Myers, 'Biden's China strategy meets resistance at the negotiating table', *New York Times*, 26 July 2021, www.nytimes.com/2021/07/26/world/asia/china-us-wendy-sherman.html; 'Special Presidential Envoy for Climate John Kerry's visit to Japan and the People's Republic of China', US Department of State, 3 September 2021, www.state.gov/special-presidential-envoy-for-climate-john-kerrys-visit-to-japan-and-the-peoples-republic-of-china/.

41 Dean Cheng, 'Sherman's China visit was a quiet disaster', *Foreign Policy*, 3 August 2021, web.archive.org/web/20210811120625/https://foreignpolicy.com/2021/08/03/sherman-china-visit-quiet-disaster/.

42 'Chairman Zheng Bijian met with Mr. John L. Thornton, chair emeritus of the Board of Trustees of the Brookings Institution', China Institute for Innovation and Development Strategy, 31 August 2021, archive.ph/2tynI.

43 Wong, 'Kissinger's "secret" China trip recalled'.

44 Wong, 'Kissinger's "secret" China trip recalled'; Catherine Wong, 'What Chinese vice-president told old friend from US about Communist Party's legitimacy', *South China Morning Post*, 28 September 2021, archive.ph/Wt5qC.

45 Rogin, *Chaos Under Heaven*, pp. 21, 48.

46 'Chinese government invites top Wall Street bankers to Beijing', *Financial Times* via *Irish Times*, 9 September 2018, archive.ph/qlNpt.

47 Rogin, *Chaos Under Heaven*, p. 51.

48 Norihiko Shirouzu, 'US-China group seeking to bolster financial ties to meet in autumn – source', Reuters, 25 August 2021, archive.today/tGa75; Cathy Chan, 'Wall Street chiefs meet China officials amid market turmoil', *Bloomberg*, 14 September 2021, archive.today/Yd5wy.

49 Maxim Tucker, 'China accused of hacking Ukraine days before Russian invasion', *Times*, 1 April 2022, archive.ph/LKwfZ; Edward Wong & Julian E. Barnes, 'China asked Russia to delay Ukraine war until after Olympics, US officials say', *New York Times*, 2 March 2022, archive.ph/WGEiP; Demetri Sevastopulo, 'America's lopsided China strategy: All guns and no butter', *Financial Times*, 26 April 2022, archive.ph/lgKZO.

50 Meng Changlin (孟长林) was listed as a CIIDS deputy secretary-general in 2019 and was concurrently listed as China Reform Forum's office director.

Meng was also a contributor to a CICIR dictionary of important international figures published in 1990, suggesting he was working for the MSS then. See '秘书处', CIIDS, no date, web.archive.org/20190131025123/http://www.ciids.cn/content/2016-05/18/content_17423638.htm; '秘书处', China Reform Forum, no date, web.archive.org/web/20070821001227/http://www.crf.org.cn/about/standing.htm; '办公室', CRF, no date, web.archive.org/web/20200327174619/http://www.crf.org.cn/msc.asp?cid=010003; 《世界人物大辞典》编委会 (ed.), 《世界人物大辞典》, 国际文化出版公司, Beijing, front matter.

Zheng Bijian's personal secretary during his China Reform Forum years, Wang Boyong (王博永), is now a vice president and secretary-general of CIIDS, but his public biography does not indicate any other connections to the MSS. See '한중관계와 동아시아 번영', KEAF, no date, p. 31, archive.ph/UXQbE; '秘书处', CIIDS, no date, archive.ph/GfRHp; '王博永', CIIDS, no date, archive.ph/vF8qZ.

51 In particular, there is extensive overlap between China Reform Forum's membership and CIIDS's through individuals such as CASS's Zhou Hong (周弘), the Central Party School's Li Junru (李君如), Yang Jiemian (杨洁勉) of the Shanghai Institute for International Studies, Peking University's Wang Jisi (王缉思), the MSS's Lin Di (林地), former Zeng Qinghong secretary Shi Zhihong (施芝鸿), Wang Yuanlong (王元龙), and MSS 11th Bureau chief and CICIR director Yuan Peng (袁鹏). '学术委员会', CIIDS, no date, archive.ph/D3Plu; '理事会', CIIDS, no date, archive.ph/LxT7v; '高级顾问', CIIDS, no date, archive.ph/re98O.

52 This front group was the China International Culture Exchange Foundation. Its director, Wang Xuejun (王学珺), was a deputy secretary-general of China Reform Forum under the homophonous name Wang Xuejun (王学军). '王博永会见中国国际文化交流基金会理事长王学珺', CIIDS, 21 March 2019, archive.vn/120fq.

53 The Chinese People's Association for Friendship with Foreign Countries (中国人民对外友好协会), an organisation subordinate to the Ministry of Foreign Affairs, was also a co-organiser of the event. 'Australia Friendship Forum on Economy and Trade celebrated its grand opening at the Imperial Springs Convention Center', Imperial Springs International Forum, 31 August 2011, archive.ph/BNLU4. On the association's status within the Party-state, see Jichang Lulu, 'Repurposing democracy: The European Parliament China friendship cluster', *Sinopsis*, 26 November 2019, pp. 21–3, sinopsis.cz/wp-content/uploads/2019/11/ep.pdf.

54 邓圩 & 梁秀梅, '"中澳经贸友好交流"从都国际峰会隆重揭幕', *People's Daily*, 31 August 2011, archive.ph/A2kaY.

55 John Garnaut, Deborah Snow & Nic Christensen, 'Behind the mysterious Dr Chau', *Sydney Morning Herald*, 4 July 2009, archive.ph/wp1F9.

56 Deborah Snow, Nic Christensen & John Garnaut, 'Man of property donates millions', *Sydney Morning Herald*, 4 July 2009, archive.ph/9Fq70.

57 Clive Hamilton, *Silent Invasion: China's influence in Australia*, Hardie Grant Books, Melbourne, 2018, pp. 75–9.

58 Amy Greenbank & Andrew Greene, 'Chinese-born billionaire Chau Chak Wing donating millions to Australian veterans', *ABC News*, 13 December 2019, www.abc.net.au/news/2019–12–14/digger-donations-billionaire-chau-chak-wing-donating-veterans/11797700.

59 Nick McKenzie & Angus Grigg, 'Kevin Rudd quietly met Chau Chak Wing in China', *Sydney Morning Herald*, 24 May 2018, www.smh.com.au/politics/federal/kevin-rudd-quietly-met-chau-chak-wing-in-china-20180524-p4zh99.html. During the same weekend trip, Rudd met with provincial officials and spoke at a local university. See '招玉芳副省长会见并宴请澳大利亚外交部长陆克文', 广东省人民政府外事办公室, 21 May 2011, archive.ph/ibws6.

60 Brad Norington, 'ALP branch accepts Shorten edict on donations from Chinese businessmen', *Australian*, 21 July 2017, www.theaustralian.com.au/nation/politics/alp-branch-accepts-shorten-edict-on-donations-from-chinese-businessmen/news-story/1fb8315ed1c6d52906ea6a797a4d1c8e.

61 Nick McKenzie & Richard Baker, 'Political donor Chau Chak Wing behind UN bribe scandal, Parliament told', *Sydney Morning Herald*, 22 May 2018, archive.ph/teOc1.

62 Anthony Galloway, 'Labor senator names businessman as "puppeteer" behind foreign interference plot', *Sydney Morning Herald*, 14 February 2022, archive.ph/6bAaF.

63 Jamie McKinnell, 'Businessman Chau Chak Wing awarded $590,000 in defamation case against ABC', *ABC News*, 2 February 2021, www.abc.net.au/news/2021-02-02/chau-chak-wing-wins-defamation-case-against-abc/13111934.

64 '郑必坚会见澳大利亚前总理陆克文', CIIDS, 9 May 2019, archive.ph/4G6i4.

65 'Chak Wing, Chau', Club de Madrid, no date, archive.ph/LNhKr; *2018 Annual Report*, World Leadership Alliance – Club de Madrid, April 2019, archive.ph/KwQwP.

66 Devin Leonard, 'Deep thoughts with the homeless billionaire', *Bloomberg*, 28 September 2012, archive.ph/TtaZG.

67 Leonard, 'Deep thoughts with the homeless billionaire'.

68 Laura Schreffler, 'Nicolas Berggruen: International man of democracy (and mystery)', *Haute Living*, 11 September 2019, web.archive.org/web/20210126201448/https://hauteliving.com/2019/09/nicolas-berggruen-renovating-democracy/673090/.

69 'History', Berggruen Institute, 2018, web.archive.org/web/20220226084747/https://www.berggruen.org/history/.

70 Clive Hamilton & Marieke Ohlberg, *Hidden Hand: Exposing how the Chinese Communist Party is reshaping the world*, Hardie Grant Books, Melbourne, 2020, p. 209.

71 'Authors say Western-style democracy won't work in Hong Kong' [video], CGTN America via YouTube, 18 October 2014, www.youtube.com/watch?v=nrhANAmPOxg; Hamilton & Ohlberg, *Hidden Hand*, p. 208.

72 Nicolas Berggruen, 'China', Thoughts by Nicolas Berggruen [website], no date, archive.ph/CqkP2.

73 See Zheng Bijian, 'China's "One Belt, One Road" plan marks the next phase of globalization', *HuffPost*, 18 May 2017, archive.ph/URj1S; Zheng Bijian, 'The three globalizations and China', *HuffPost*, 27 January 2014, archive.ph/JqZpT; 'The WorldPost: Monthly archives: January 2018', *Washington Post*, 2018, archive.ph/bMRsr.

74 Nathan Gardels, '21st Century Council meets with Chinese leadership at Understanding China conference', Berggruen Institute, 4 November 2013, archive.ph/JIPdM.

75 Bethany Allen-Ebrahimian & Zach Dorfman, 'Suspected Chinese spy targeted California politicians', *Axios*, 8 December 2020, archive.ph/77D4h.

76 Allen-Ebrahimian & Dorfman, 'Suspected Chinese spy targeted California politicians'.

77 Allen-Ebrahimian & Dorfman, 'Suspected Chinese spy targeted California politicians'.

78 '除方芳外 美民主党众议院委员再曝与他有关系？', 阿波罗新闻网, 15 December 2020, archive.ph/ZSQnK; Zach Dorfman, 'How Silicon Valley became a den of spies', *Politico*, 27 July 2018, archive.ph/SmYoN.

79 Allen-Ebrahimian & Dorfman, 'Suspected Chinese spy targeted California politicians'.

80 Allen-Ebrahimian & Dorfman, 'Suspected Chinese spy targeted California politicians'.

81 Allen-Ebrahimian & Dorfman, 'Suspected Chinese spy targeted California politicians'.

Chapter 13 The Goddess of Mercy: Buddhism as a tool of influence

1 '两岸四地高僧大德集聚海南三亚', 七塔禅寺, 25 April 2005, archive.ph/RHhz8.

2 '世界上最大的观音像原来在三亚 南海上的一个传奇', 纳兰小鱼 via *Sina*, no date, archive.ph/1VKao.

3 '南山海上观音工程总指挥季素福访谈录', Sohu Travel, 21 April 2005, web.archive.org/web/20070131023119/http://travel.sohu.com/20050421/n225283727.shtml.

4 Justin McCurry, 'Japan says diplomat's suicide followed blackmail by China', *Guardian*, 30 December 2005, www.theguardian.com/world/2005/dec/29/japan.china; Hiroko Nakata, 'China slammed over cryptographer honey trap suicide', *Japan Times*, 1 April 2006, www.japantimes.co.jp/news/2006/04/01/national/china-slammed-over-cryptographer-honey-trap-suicide/.

5 Peter Mattis, 'Shriver case highlights traditional Chinese espionage', *China Brief*, 5 November 2010, jamestown.org/program/shriver-case-highlights-traditional-chinese-espionage/.

6 Mara Hvistendahl, 'The friendly Mr Wu', *1843 Magazine*, 25 February 2020, www.economist.com/1843/2020/02/25/the-friendly-mr-wu; 'Ron Rockwell Hanson felony complaint', US Department of Justice, 2 June 2018,

www.justice.gov/opa/press-release/file/1068176/download; Office of Public Affairs, 'Former State Department employee sentenced for conspiring with Chinese agents', US Department of Justice, 9 July 2019, www.justice.gov/opa/pr/former-state-department-employee-sentenced-conspiring-chinese-agents; Nate Thayer, 'How the Chinese recruit American journalists as spies', Nate Thayer [blog], 1 July 2017, web.archive.org/web/20170703131210/http://www.nate-thayer.com/how-the-chinese-recruit-american-journalists-as-spies/; interview with an American scholar.

7   Ji Sufu (季素福) worked in what is now known as the Shanghai Aerospace Control Technology Research Institute (上海航天控制技术研究所) or the 803rd Research Institute of the China Aerospace Science and Technology Corporation's 8th Academy. See 'Shenzhou Space Park Group Limited', HKEX, 1 August 2018, web.archive.org/web/20210824112735/http://webcache.googleusercontent.com/search?q=cache:2wSOYcGnTtIJ:www.hkexnews.hk/listedco/listconews/sehk/2018/0802/LTN20180802038_C.pdf+&cd=1&hl=en&ct=clnk&gl=au; 凌翔, '专访上海航天控制技术研究所所长', 兵器知识, vol. 2, 2016, archive.ph/iQPnW.

8   CCP espionage cases exposed by Taiwan often reveal some of these administrative cover organisations. Mark Stokes & Russell Hsiao, *The People's Liberation Army General Political Department: Political warfare with Chinese characteristics*, Project 2049 Institute, Arlington, VA, 14 October 2013, p. 60, fn. 125, project2049.net/wp-content/uploads/2018/04/P2049_Stokes_Hsiao_PLA_General_Political_Department_Liaison_101413.pdf.

9   '刘际民：孝老爱亲模范', 温州新闻网, 9 July 2019, web.archive.org/web/20210824123353/http://webcache.googleusercontent.com/search?q=cache%3A_L7oM7XO5YkJ%3Azhihui.66wz.com%2Fsystem%2F2019%2F07%2F09%2F105176630.shtml+&cd=1&hl=en&ct=clnk&gl=au.

10 The official study specifically refers to 'double-ised companies' (两化企业) of the Fourth Office. As this terminology is normally reserved for covert state security or public security companies, I have translated it as 'cover companies'. 谢玲丽 (ed.), 《上海发展研究：国有资产管理论》, 上海远东出版社, December 1995, p. 80.

11 An online biography of Feng Shujun (冯叔君) states that he worked in the Fourth Office from 1990 to 2006 and also served as deputy secretary-general of the Shanghai International Culture Association (上海市对外文化交流协会), CICEC's Shanghainese counterpart organisation. '冯叔君', 上海市社会科学界联合会, no date, archive.ph/mGtPH.

12 Shanghai Guanglian, a deregistered company owned by the Fourth Office, was registered to the Anting Villa (20 or 46 Anting Road). '上海广联(集团)控股有限公司', 爱企查, no date, archive.ph/4946L. The villa was owned by General Jiang Baili (蒋百里), father-in-law of Chinese missile scientist Qian Xuesen (钱学森). '安亭路上历史建筑', 高参88的博客, 6 January 2017, archive.ph/ckf7O; '国民政府要员寓局表', 上海市地方志办公室, 10 July 2003, archive.ph/yFkux.

13 上海民政局, '准予上海新世纪社会发展基金会基金会变更登记决定书', 上海社会团体管理局, 26 November 2012, archive.today/kjlKf.

14 See records on 上海社会组织信息公开平台.

15 上海新世纪社会发展基金会, '上海市基金会年度工作报告书 2017', 上海社会组织信息公开平台, 26 March 2018.

16 Thank you to Nathan Ruser for helping estimate the building's floor space.

17 '上海瑞宁路1号', 百度知道, archive.ph/D9hle.

18 The bureau has several major office facilities across the city, but Ruining Road appears to be the largest.

19 上海新世纪社会发展基金会, '上海市基金会年度检查报告书 2016', 上海社会组织信息公开平台, 3 March 2017.

20 The SSSB's Shanghai International Culture Association (上海对外文化交流协会) is also an organiser of the event. 曹崔秀, '第二届澜沧江-湄公河青年创新创业训练营崇明闭营', 中国青年报, 23 July 2018, archive.ph/NgZFK; '上海新世纪社会发展基金会成功协办第四届澜沧江-湄公河流域治理与发展青年创新设计大赛', 上海尚医医务工作者奖励基金会, 24 January 2019, archive.vn/xpj52.

21 While the charity's current head is retired officer Jiang Youmin (蒋佑民), the rest of its staff appear to be active SSSB employees, several of whom are relatively senior division-level (处级) officers.

22 Curiously, an unidentified Mr/Ms Li (黎) was one of the largest donors to the Shanghai New Century Social Development Foundation in recent years, giving RMB8 million at once.

23 '海南108米南山海上观音工程建造纪实', 海南日报 via *Sina*, 24 April 2005, archive.ph/mpbGD.

24 Yuan Wanzhen (袁婉贞), a financial manager from the Shanghai Fourth Office, was concurrently the Nanshan project's chief financial officer. '上海交大 创新与金融DBA课程 | 管理者的财务视野：透视企业资本及其经营的管理 – – 袁婉贞 导师', 活动行, 2016, www.huodongxing.com/event/1330419630400.

25 上海新世纪社会发展基金会, '上海市基金会年度工作报告书 2017', 上海社会组织信息公开平台, 26 March 2018. On Xu Yuesheng (徐越胜) being the company's Party secretary, see '上海宁国山寺隆重举行"现代宋制寺院与传统营造技艺"专题研讨会', 上海宁国禅寺, 19 April 2021, archive.md/CJGX6.

26 上海新世纪社会发展基金会, '上海市基金会年度检查报告书 2016', 上海社会组织信息公开平台, 3 March 2017. On Shanghai Tianhua's address, see www.mapbar.com, archive.md/338Oh. Shanghai Tianhua (上海天华信息发展公司) is owned by two other SSSB companies (also donors to the bureau's charity), Shanghai Kaixiang Investment Management Co Ltd (上海开祥投资管理有限公司) and Shanghai Huaxing International Shipping Co (上海华兴国际货运公司).

27 Feng Fumin (冯馥敏) was appointed to the SSSB Political Department role in 2002 and first headed its charity in 2012. '大事记 2002年8月', 《上海党史与党建》, October 2002, www.doc88.com/p-2844358531556.html;

上海民政局, '准予上海新世纪社会发展基金会基金会变更登记决定书', 上海社会团体管理局, 26 November 2012, archive.today/kjlKf. State security organs' political departments, among other things, may oversee domestic propaganda efforts designed to improve the image of state security work and encourage cooperation from the general public.

28 Shanghai Shangke Enterprises (上海上科实业总公司) was originally a branch of China National Sci-Tech Information Import and Export Corporation (中国科技资料进出口总公司), which is still covertly owned by the MSS. The company ultimately owns nearly 54% of Sanya Nanshan Pumen Tourism Development (三亚南山普门旅游发展有限公司). In the late 1990s, Wu Feifei (吴菲菲) was the chairwoman of China National Sci-Tech Information Import and Export Corporation, which was registered to an address in Shanghai at the time. For unclear reasons, its address has moved between cities, including Tianjin, several times. '中国科技资料进出口总公司', Kanzhun, no date, archive.ph/loAdf; 中国工商企业咨询服务中心 (ed.), 《中国企业登记年鉴: 全国性公司特辑 1993》, 中国经济出版社, January 1994, p. 306; '三亚南山普门旅游发展有限公司', QCC, no date, archive.ph/jQquY.

29 Hong Kong's A.P. Plaza Investments Limited (亞太投資有限公司) ultimately owns 39.80% of Sanya Nanshan Pumen Tourism Development (三亚南山普门旅游发展有限公司). It includes Li Kam Fu aka Li Jinfu (李锦富) and Xu Yuesheng (徐越胜) as shareholders. Several other individuals with ties to Shanghai have been involved in the company, but their backgrounds are unclear. *A.P. Plaza Investments Limited Annual Return*, Hong Kong Companies Registry, 24 September 2014; '三亚南山普门旅游发展有限公司', QCC, no date, archive.ph/jQquY.

30 '海南三亚南山功德基金会2019年度工作报告', 民政部, 22 June 2020.

31 '【立此存照】颂歌新赛季 宗教编(一)佛教徒要把十九大报告当成佛经来学习', 中国数字时代, 12 December 2017, archive.ph/J7GT1.

32 '中国佛教协会副会长印顺简历', 中国佛教文化信息中心, 2 February 2010, archive.ph/lAeq6.

33 '大道不孤 初心不改 – 专访全国政协委员, 中国佛教协会副会长印顺', 人民政协报, 28 January 2021, archive.ph/xmeC5.

34 张薇 & 阮建华, '大山里的"虔诚之心"', 建筑新网, 26 September 2017, archive.ph/r5Wl2; Ma Zhiping & Liu Xiaoli, 'Nanhai Buddhism Academy opens in Sanya', *China Daily*, 24 September 2017, archive.ph/gjIrT.

35 The Hainan Sanya Nanshan Gongde Foundation's 2019 annual report states that over 80% of its charitable spending – RMB35 million – went towards the Nanhai Buddhist Academy that year. In 2020 it gave RMB31 million to the academy. '海南三亚南山功德基金会2019年度工作报告', 民政部, 22 June 2020; 海南三亚南山功德基金会2020年度工作报告', 民政部, 23 March 2021.

36 '中国那烂陀！南海佛学院2019年秋季开学典礼隆重举行', 南海佛学院, 24 September 2019, archive.ph/WMF5Z.

37 Santosh Singh, 'Nalanda University starts today, from a convention centre, with 15 students lodged in a hotel', *Indian Express*, 1 September 2014, archive. ph/5r2TF; Yatish Yadav, 'Soft power: China gets its own Nalanda university, shames India', *New Indian Express*, 5 June 2017, archive.ph/r2KXH.

38 张薇 & 阮建华, '大山里的"虔诚之心"'.

39 Anne Wisman, 'China to open its own Nalanda University in Hainan province in September', *Buddhistdoor Global*, 6 June 2017, archive.ph/NE7kZ.

40 See Jichang Lulu, 'PRC religious policy and relations with Buddhism in Mongolia under Xi Jinping', draft presentation, Mongolia and the Mongol: Past and Present Conference, Warsaw, 6–9 May 2018, p. 6.

41 Lulu, 'PRC religious policy and relations with Buddhism', p. 6. See Miguel Martin, 'Global religion and the United Front: The case of Mongolia', *China Brief*, 10 July 2018, jamestown.org/program/global-religion-and-the-united-front-the-case-of-mongolia/.

42 See also Gregory V. Raymond, 'Religion as a tool of influence: Buddhism and China's Belt and Road Initiative in mainland Southeast Asia', *Contemporary Southeast Asia*, vol. 42, no. 3, 2020, pp. 346–71.

43 Alex Joske, 'Reorganizing the United Front Work Department: New structures for a new era of diaspora and religious affairs work', *China Brief*, 9 May 2019, jamestown.org/program/reorganizing-the-united-front-work-department-new-structures-for-a-new-era-of-diaspora-and-religious-affairs-work/.

44 Zhou Hua, 'New crackdowns on foreign churches in China exposed', *Bitter Winter*, 31 August 2019, bitterwinter.org/new-crackdowns-on-foreign-churches-in-china-exposed/; Chen Jinsheng, 'Three-Self clergy warn congregations to beware of fake believers', *Bitter Winter*, 7 June 2019, bitterwinter.org/clergy-warn-to-beware-of-fake-believers/; Piao Junying, 'China's provinces intensify persecution of South Korean Christianity', *Bitter Winter*, 9 June 2018, bitterwinter.org/chinas-provinces-intensify-persecution-of-south-korean-christianity/.

45 Zhao Puxuan (照普选) has a background in a range of roles, including as a PLA propaganda official, Sanya discipline inspection official and in 2016 Party secretary of the Sanya People's Political Consultative Conference. '陕西省政协副主席王卫华赴南山寺及南海佛学院调研', 中国新闻网, 23 March 2021, archive.ph/inQgc; '赵普选当选政协三亚市第六届委员会主席', 海南网, 15 January 2012, archive.ph/WXj61. Jichang Lulu notes that the head of the Hainan UFWD visited the academy shortly before its inauguration as evidence of its significance for united front work; Lulu, 'PRC religious policy and relations with Buddhism', p. 6.

46 Raymond, 'Religion as a tool of influence'.

47 Note that 'sinicise' (中国化) refers to the state of China and suggests transforming Buddhism through contemporary nationalism and Party ideology, as Buddhism in China already underwent waves of sinicisation in centuries past. See Lulu, 'PRC religious policy and relations with Buddhism'; '印顺: 男孩佛学院致力打造中国化的佛学体系', 新华网, 5 September

2017, web.archive.org/web/20180728225904/http://www.hq.xinhuanet. com/news/2017-09/05/c_1121608478.htm.

48 顿诚, '发乳同源 和合共生 – – 从佛教观点探讨中国传统文化的智慧', 尼泊尔中华寺, no date, archive.ph/eBOMD.

49 Raymond, 'Religion as a tool of influence', p. 363.

50 印顺, '构建南海命运共同体, 开创南海佛教新时代', Hainan Committee of the Chinese People's Political Consultative Conference, 2018, archive.ph/ AArrD.

51 Martin, 'Global religion and the United Front'.

52 '2019年南海佛教深圳圆桌会开幕, 中新社 via Sohu, 20 October 2019, archive.ph/XXOek.

53 '高僧大德齐聚2017南海佛教深圳圆桌会隆重举行', 佛教在线, 27 January 2018, archive.ph/uuFRv.

54 Nadège Rolland, 'Beijing's vision for a reshaped international order', *China Brief*, 26 February 2018, jamestown.org/program/beijings-vision-reshaped-international-order/. See also Liza Tobin, 'Xi's vision for transforming global governance: A strategic challenge for Washington and its allies', *Texas National Security Review*, vol. 2, no. 1, 2018, tnsr.org/2018/11/ xis-vision-for-transforming-global-governance-a-strategic-challenge-for-washington-and-its-allies/.

55 '大道不孤 初心不改 – 专访全国政协委员, 中国佛教协会副会长印顺', 人民政协报, 28 January 2021, archive.ph/xmeC5.

56 '印顺: 南海是中国的', *Caijing*, 10 December 2017, web.archive.org/ web/20171211130751/http://economy.caijing.com.cn/20171210/4374867. shtml. Delegates reportedly signed a memorandum, but the text includes no endorsement of China's claims in the South China Sea; it simply advocates for a system of peaceful and fair relations in the region. '南海佛教圆桌会备忘录: 佛教领袖共同守护南海和平', 凤凰佛教, 26 November 2017, archive.ph/4fxLA. See Martin, 'Global religion and the United Front'.

57 '高僧大德齐聚2017南海佛教深圳圆桌会隆重举行', 佛教在线; '"南海佛教深圳圆桌会"新闻发布会: 守护南海和平', 凤凰佛教, 25 November 2017, archive.ph/PEhBS.

58 Raymond, 'Religion as a tool of influence', pp. 358–60. See also Milton Osborne, 'Buddhist monks and political activism in Cambodia', *Interpreter*, 29 September 2014, www.lowyinstitute.org/the-interpreter/buddhist-monks-and-political-activism-cambodia.

59 As Tibetan Buddhism is predominant in Mongolia, some of Nergüi's monks study at the Tibetan Academy of Buddhism in Beijing. Lulu, 'PRC religious policy and relations with Buddhism', pp. 20–3.

60 Martin, 'Global religion and the United Front'; '蒙古善妙寺方丈: 希望印顺大和尚将世界佛教团体团结起来', 南海佛教网, 30 November 2017, web.archive.org/web/20180731080849/https://mp.weixin.qq.com/s/ gkwQux4Bqaz0xagziPW-bQ.

61 Martin, 'Global religion and the United Front'.

62 Lulu, 'PRC religious policy and relations with Buddhism', pp. 20–3; 'Wang Yi meets with Mongolian Deputy Prime Minister Sainbuyan Amarsaikhan', Ministry of Foreign Affairs of the People's Republic of China, 16 September 2021, archive.ph/mGoQA; 'Mongolia's new PM forms cabinet', *Xinhua*, 29 January 2021, archive.ph/lDJPT.

63 Javier C. Hernández, 'Chinese spiritual leader is accused of harassing female followers', *New York Times*, 2 August 2018, archive.ph/98su3.

    Australia's Wang Xinde (王信得) is a well-documented example of an overseas Buddhist leader engaged in promoting political positions aligned with the CCP. See Clive Hamilton & Marieke Ohlberg, *Hidden Hand: Exposing how the Chinese Communist Party is reshaping the world*, Hardie Grant Books, Melbourne, 2020, pp. 202–3.

64 '2020男孩佛教深圳圆桌会开幕：以人文交流力量凝聚人心助力抗疫', 深圳特区报, 31 December 2020, archive.ph/CMP2m.

65 '专访印顺大和尚：到伦敦取经的中国僧侣', 26 October 2015, archive.ph/Vvp2H.

66 The research institute's official English name is the 'Cambridge Research Institute for Silk Road Studies', but the Chinese name should be translated as 'Cambridge Research Institute for Belt and Road Studies'. Zilan Wang (王子兰), a Cambridge Museum of Archaeology and Anthropology researcher who is involved in the Digital Museum of Global Buddhist Heritage, was present at the unveiling of Yinshun's Cambridge institute. '南海佛学院与中国剑桥基金会 就建立"剑桥一带一路研究院"达成', 南海佛教网, no date, archive.ph/ZeRdu; 'Digital Museum of Global Buddhist Cultural Heritage', Museum of Archaeology and Anthropology, no date, archive.ph/7DkHn.

67 '印顺大和尚率中佛协代表团参访澳洲 促进文化交流', 凤凰佛教, 11 June 2014, archive.ph/NuM2e; Su-Lin Tan, Angus Grigg & Andrew Tillett, 'Huang Xiangmo told Australian residency was cancelled after moving to Hong Kong', *Australian Financial Review*, 6 February 2019, www.afr.com/politics/federal/huang-xiangmo-told-australian-residency-was-cancelled-after-moving-to-hong-kong-20190206-h1axd9.

68 'CAIFC receives a delegation of Agon Shu from Japan', China Association for International Friendly Contact, 9 July 2015, archive.ph/EKiHE; '行动，让世界更加美好 – 印顺大和尚出席亚洲文明对话大会并发言', 禅风网, no date, archive.ph/MeXcj. For a thorough and authoritative discussion of the China Association for International Friendly Contact (中国国际友好联络会), see Stokes & Hsiao, *The People's Liberation Army General Political Department*.

69 Russell Hsiao, 'A preliminary survey of CCP influence operations in Japan', *China Brief*, 26 June 2019, jamestown.org/program/a-preliminary-survey-of-ccp-influence-operations-in-japan/.

Conclusion: Facing up to the MSS

1 '园区导视标牌-国家安全部冷泉基地项目', 北京方向标标牌有限公司, no date, archive.ph/xYqLR.

2 '中控员', BOSS直聘, 17 January 2022, archive.ph/BYPxU. Beijing Jinjiang Beifang Property Management (北京锦江北方物业管理有限公司) may also provide services to MSS facilities at 5 Wanshou Road (万寿路5号院). '物业管家', www.hc1230.com, 19 January 2021, archive.ph/eziXz.
3 One Chinese psychologist reportedly presented on communication and persuasion techniques at an unspecified MSS training base. '郑日昌讲座 郑日昌教授最近讲座信息', 无锡文化网', 28 October 2019, archive.ph/hw2IV.
4 钱江, '最强间谍墓碑惊现北京！', 《世纪》 via Sohu, 26 January 2019, archive.ph/NEDn9.
5 'Jiangnan Social University', China Defence Universities Tracker, 14 November 2019, archive.ph/mlqmi.
6 'NCNA kicked out', *Taiwan Today*, 1 September 1960, archive.ph/vqEob; '肯尼亚当局采取不友好行动无理要求我记者离境 新华社记者王德铭回京受到欢迎 我驻肯使馆和新华社负责人分别指出，肯政府对我记者的指责是没有根据的，我们不能不深表遗憾', 人民日报, 5 August 1965, p. 5, archive.ph/UJuf5.
7 Interview with a former US intelligence officer.
8 Vernon Loeb & Walter Pincus, 'Beijing prefers the sand to the moles', *Washington Post*, 12 December 1999, www.washingtonpost.com/wp-srv/WPcap/1999-12/12/097r-121299-idx.html; David Wise, 'America's other espionage challenge', *New York Times*, 5 March 2018, web.archive.org/web/20180305174938/https://www.nytimes.com/2018/03/05/opinion/china-espionage.html.
9 Peter Mattis, 'The analytic challenge of understanding Chinese intelligence services', *Studies in Intelligence*, vol. 56, no. 3, 2012, pp. 48–9, www.cia.gov/static/6ba6d7cb6151971fda8a14600cd86fbe/Beyond-Spy-vs-Spy.pdf.
10 Samantha Hoffman & Peter Mattis, 'Managing the power within: China's State Security Commission', *War on the Rocks*, 18 July 2016, warontherocks.com/2016/07/managing-the-power-within-chinas-state-security-commission/.
11 Interview with a former US intelligence officer.
12 Alex Joske, Lin Li, Alexandra Pascoe & Nathan Attrill, *The Influence Environment*, Australian Strategic Policy Institute, Canberra, 17 December 2020, www.aspi.org.au/report/influence-environment.
13 Interview with a former US intelligence officer.
14 See Christopher Andrew, 'Intelligence, international relations and under-theorisation', *Intelligence and National Security*, vol. 19, no. 2, 2004, p. 177.
15 Paul Charon & Jean-Baptiste Jeangène Vilmer, *Les opérations d'influence chinoises*, IRSEM, 2021, pp. 81–2, www.irsem.fr/rapport.html.
16 Some exceptions relate to Russian records and Swiss archives. Ariane Knüsel, 'Swiss counterintelligence and Chinese espionage during the Cold War', *Journal of Cold War Studies*, vol. 22, no. 3, 2020, pp. 4–31, direct.mit.edu/jcws/article-abstract/22/3/4/95292/Swiss-Counterintelligence-and-Chinese-Espionage?redirectedFrom=fulltext; Filip Kovacevic, 'The Soviet-Chinese spy wars in the 1970s: What KGB counterintelligence knew, part II', Sources

and Methods [blog], 22 April 2021, www.wilsoncenter.org/blog-post/soviet-chinese-spy-wars-1970s-what-kgb-counterintelligence-knew-part-ii.

17 See, for example, the use of sources by Chinese journalist Wu Xuewen (吴学文) by scholars, not realising he was an undercover intelligence officer. Casper Wits, 'Foreign correspondents in the East Asian Cold War: The Sino-Japanese journalist exchange of 1964', *Modern Asian Studies*, vol. 54, no. 5, 2020, pp. 1446–82, www.cambridge.org/core/journals/modern-asian-studies/article/foreign-correspondents-in-the-east-asian-cold-war-the-sinojapanese-journalist-exchange-of-1964/31E861B45E3EC B3A2A5396FA3284236C. On Wu Xuewen, see ch. 10, note 40.

18 A July 2020 US indictment of alleged Guangdong State Security Department hackers included the address and cover name of a major MSS facility in Guangzhou, but those leads did not appear to attract any attention. 'United States of America v. Li Xiaoyu (a/k/a "Oro0lxy") and Dong Jiazhi Indictment', US Department of Justice, 7 July 2020, web.archive.org/web/20220417115140/https://www.justice.gov/opa/press-release/file/1295981/download.

19 Isaac Stone Fish, 'The other political correctness', *New Republic*, 4 September 2018, newrepublic.com/article/150476/american-elite-universities-selfcensorship-china.

20 Jonas Parello-Plesner, 'China's LinkedIn honey traps', *The American Interest* via Hudson Institute, 23 October 2018, www.hudson.org/research/14637-china-s-linked-in-honey-traps.

21 To a lesser degree, the MSS's University of International Relations is involved in similar influence efforts. For example, in 2019 an Australian think tank took a group of Australian politicians and business figures to meet with a UIR scholar. 'Second China Matters study tour', China Matters, no date, web.archive.org/web/20191001215623/http://chinamatters.org.au/wp-content/uploads/2019/09/Biographies-of-Second-Study-Tour-participants.pdf; Daniel Golden, *Spy Schools*, Henry Holt, New York, 2017, pp. 85–110.

22 Peter Mattis & Matthew Brazil, *Chinese Communist Espionage: An intelligence primer*, Naval Institute Press, Annapolis, MD, 2019, p. 56.

23 郝汀 & 章钟峨，《文化大革命中的中央调查部》, no publisher, 2013, p. 486.

24 'Department of International Exchanges', CICIR, no date, archive.ph/PEC16.

25 Tobias Feakin, *Enter the Cyber Dragon*, Australian Strategic Policy Institute, Canberra, June 2013, s3-ap-southeast-2.amazonaws.com/ad-aspi/import/10_42_31_AM_SR50_chinese_cyber.pdf; Jessica Woodall, 'Cyber wrap,' *Strategist*, 10 February 2016, www.aspistrategist.org.au/cyber-wrap-106/.

26 Australian Centre on China in the World & CICIR, *Australia and China: A joint report on the bilateral relationship*, Australian National University, February 2012, ciw-dev.anu.edu.au/joint_report/CIWCICIRJointReport-Australia_and_China-Feb2012.pdf.

27 Office of Public Affairs, 'Jury convicts Chinese intelligence officer of espionage crimes, attempting to steal trade secrets', US Department of Justice, 5 November 2021, www.justice.gov/opa/pr/jury-convicts-chinese-intelligence-officer-espionage-crimes-attempting-steal-trade-secrets; Gorden Corera, 'Looking for China's spies', *BBC*, 19 December 2018, www.bbc.co.uk/news/resources/idt-sh/Looking_for_Chinas_spies.

28 One exception to this may be the arrest of Tang Yuhua (唐宇华) by the FBI in 2011 on charges relating to commercial bribery. Tang was the New York correspondent of Shanghai's *Wenhui Bao* newspaper. According to former MSS officer and *Guangming Daily* correspondent Ding Ke, all *Wenhui Bao* foreign correspondents are MSS officers, a claim that is supported by my own research on the newspaper. 'Three men charged in federal indictment alleging commercial bribery', US Attorney's Office via FBI, 5 December 2011, archive.ph/r63fV; 丁柯, '丁柯：唐宇华到底是不是中共国安特工？', 中国茉莉花行动部落, 28 December 2011, archive.ph/CxFmR.

29 Rory Medcalf (ed.), 'Chinese money and Australia's security', National Security College, Australian National University, March 2017, archive.ph/LP15k.

30 Stephen Dziedzic, 'Australia-China extradition treaty pulled by Federal Government after backbench rebellion', *ABC News*, 27 March 2017, archive.ph/bwNX7.

31 Nick McKenzie, *Power and Influence: The hard edge of China's soft power* [documentary], *Four Corners*, ABC, 5 June 2017, web.archive.org/web/20170927035228/https://www.abc.net.au/4corners/power-and-influence-promo/8579844.

32 Chris Uhlmann, 'Top-secret report uncovers high-level Chinese interference in Australian politics', *Nine News*, 28 May 2018, archive.ph/kkrHX; Malcolm Turnbull, 'Speech introducing the National Security Legislation Amendment (Espionage and Foreign Interference) Bill 2017', Malcolm Turnbull [website], 7 December 2017, archive.ph/mXfxl.

33 Peter Hartcher, 'Huawei? No way! Why Australia banned the world's biggest telecoms firm', *Sydney Morning Herald*, 21 May 2021, web.archive.org/web/20210521020450/https://www.smh.com.au/national/huawei-no-way-why-australia-banned-the-world-s-biggest-telecoms-firm-20210503-p57oc9.html.

34 John Garnaut, 'Engineers of the soul: What Australians need to know about ideology in Xi Jinping's China' [speech transcript], Asian Strategic and Economic Seminar Series, August 2017, via *Sinocism*, 17 January 2019, archive.ph/wb6UV.

35 Kirsty Needham, 'Australia says Yang Hengjun under "arbitrary detention" in China after espionage verdict postponed', Reuters, 28 May 2021, archive.ph/YIeec.

36 John Garnaut, 'Australia's China reset', *Monthly*, August 2018, web.archive.org/web/20180807180411/https://www.themonthly.com.au/issue/2018/august/1533045600/john-garnaut-australia-s-china-reset.

37 John Garnaut, 'Australia's China reset'.

38 Peter Martin, 'CIA zeros in on Beijing by creating China-focused mission center', *Bloomberg*, 7 October 2021, archive.ph/de7DV; Peter Martin, Jennifer Jacobs & Nick Wadhams, 'China is evading US spies – and the White House is worried', *Bloomberg*, 10 November 2021, archive.ph/U2ckp. See also Zachary Dorfman, 'China used stolen data to expose CIA operatives in Africa and Europe', *Foreign Policy*, 21 December 2020, web.archive.org/web/20201221112115/https://foreignpolicy.com/2020/12/21/china-stolen-us-data-exposed-cia-operatives-spy-networks/.

39 See US Attorney's Office 'Former CIA officer arrested and charged with espionage', US Department of Justice, 17 August 2020, archive.ph/CWQQa.

40 David Wise, *Tiger Trap: America's secret spy war with China*, Houghton Mifflin Harcourt, Boston, 2011, p. 88.

41 Office of Public Affairs 'New York City Police Department officer charged with acting as an illegal agent of the People's Republic of China', US Department of Justice, 21 September 2020, archive.ph/AYlJF.

42 US Attorney's Office, 'Former CIA officer arrested and charged with espionage'; Office of Public Affairs, 'Two Chinese hackers associated with the Ministry of State Security charged with global computer intrusion campaigns targeting intellectual property and confidential business information', US Department of Justice, 20 December 2018, archive.ph/vHBM0; Office of Public Affairs, 'US charges three Chinese hackers who work at internet security firm for hacking three corporations for commercial advantage', US Department of Justice, 27 November 2017, archive.ph/Ir07g; see also National Security Division, 'Information about the Department of Justice's China Initiative and a compilation of China-related prosecutions since 2018', US Department of Justice, 14 June 2021, archive.ph/UJvNu.

43 Zolan Kanno-Youngs & David E. Sanger, 'US accuses China of hacking Microsoft', 19 July 2021, archive.ph/2Ztzq. This came after an earlier coordinated attribution of cyber attacks to the Chinese government: Marise Payne, 'Attribution of Chinese cyber-enabled commercial intellectual property theft', Minister for Foreign Affairs, 21 December 2018, archive.ph/EP97J.

44 Daniel Hurst, 'China "propped the doors open" for criminals in Microsoft hack, Australian spy agency boss says', *Guardian*, 29 July 2021, archive.ph/PgMeF.

45 In Australia, these include Liu Haha, Huang Xiangmo, and Chinese academics Chen Hong and Li Jianjun. Sean Rubinsztein-Dunlop & Echo Hui, 'Liberal Party donor Huifeng "Haha" Liu "engaged in acts of foreign interference": ASIO', *ABC News*, 12 March 2021, archive.ph/XhCPF; Byron Kaye, 'Australia revokes visas of two Chinese scholars', Reuters, 9 September 2020, archive.ph/1bgeh; Su-Lin Tan, Angus Grigg & Andrew Tillett, 'Huang Xiangmo told Australian residency was cancelled after moving to Hong Kong', *Australian Financial Review*, 6 February 2019, archive.ph/AEOZf.

46 Dan Sabbagh & Patrick Wintour, 'UK quietly expelled Chinese spies who posed as journalists', *Guardian*, 5 February 2021, archive.ph/rPHLK.

47 Laura Hughes & Helen Warrell, 'MI5 warns UK MPs against "political interference" by Chinese agent', *Financial Times*, 14 January 2022, archive.ph/5q1oV.

48 'Germany charges man with spying for China', *Deutsche Welle*, no date, archive.ph/tAZvz.

49 Yuichi Sakaguchi, 'Japan lashes out against alleged Chinese military cyberattacks', *Nikkei Asia*, 16 May 2021, archive.ph/JfRlj; Yusuke Takeuchi, 'Japan to establish intel unit to counter economic espionage', *Nikkei Asia*, 27 August 2020, archive.ph/pClPH; Tomohiro Osaki, 'Japan boosts checks on Chinese students amid fears of campus spying', *Japan Times*, 15 October 2020, archive.ph/Nzr9u.

50 'Court sentences Estonian marine scientist to prison for spying for China', *ERR*, 19 March 2021, archive.ph/PcTKC.

51 林俊宏 & 劉榮, '與共諜組織多次餐敍　前國防部副部長張哲平遭國安調查', *Mirror Media*, 27 July 2021, archive.ph/Nf3wR; Thomas Grove, 'A spy case exposes China's power play in Central Asia', *Wall Street Journal*, 10 July 2019, archive.ph/WO3se; 'Nepali security authorities identify a Chinese intelligence agency official involved in anti-MCC propaganda', *Khabarhub*, 12 November 2021, archive.ph/ZLZFb; Ezzatullah Mehrdad, 'Did China build a spy network in Kabul?', *Diplomat*, 17 February 2021, archive.ph/fQ7Hz; Lynne O'Donnell, 'Afghanistan wanted Chinese mining investment. It got a Chinese spy ring instead.', *Foreign Policy*, 27 January 2021, archive.ph/nbUMt; Richard C. Paddock, 'Singapore orders expulsion of American academic', *New York Times*, 5 August 2017, archive.ph/4503b; Barbara Moens, 'Belgium probes top EU think-tanker for links to China', *Politico*, 18 September 2020, archive.ph/m5SBq; Alicja Ptak & Justyna Pawlak, 'Polish trial begins in Huawei-linked China espionage case', Reuters, 1 June 2021, archive.ph/2zX3M; Gillian Bonnett, 'Couple denied NZ residence due to Chinese intelligence links', *Stuff*, 30 October 2021, archive.ph/3AnHp; Nayanima Basu, 'Sri Lanka ex-military intelligence head a "Chinese spy" who was "blocking" bombings probe', *Print*, 6 May 2019, archive.ph/xZOif; 'Deux anciens espions condamnés à 8 et 12 ans de prison pour trahison au profit de la Chine', *Le Parisien*, 10 July 2020, archive.ph/dSX9S.

52 A significant and recent exception is the US's indictment of five individuals accused of repressing or spying on dissidents in New York. US Attorney's Office 'Five individuals charged variously with stalking, harassing, and spying on US residents on behalf of the PRC secret police', US Department of Justice, 16 March 2022, archive.ph/Y7UwJ.